PUBLIC FINANCE AND PARLIAMENTARY CONSTITUTIONALISM

Public Finance and Parliamentary Constitutionalism analyses constitutionalism and public finance (tax, expenditure, audit, sovereign borrowing and monetary finance) in anglophone parliamentary systems of government.

The book surveys the history of public finance law in the UK, its export throughout the British Empire and its entrenchment in Commonwealth constitutions. It explains how modern constitutionalism was shaped by the financial impact of warfare, welfare state programmes and the growth of central banking. It then provides a case-study analysis of the impact of economic conditions on governments' financial behaviour, focusing on the UK's and Australia's responses to financial crises, and the judiciary's position vis-à-vis the state's financial powers.

Throughout, it questions orthodox accounts of financial constitutionalism (particularly the views of A. V. Dicey) and the democratic legitimacy of public finance. Currently ignored aspects of government behaviour are analysed in depth, particularly the constitutional position of central banks and sovereign debt markets.

WILL BATEMAN is Senior Lecturer in Law and the Deputy-Director of Research at the Law School of the Australian National University. He has worked at the apex of constitutional and financial law, including at the High Court of Australia and Herbert Smith Freehills.

PUBLIC FINANCE AND PARLIAMENTARY CONSTITUTIONALISM

WILL BATEMAN
Australian National University

CAMBRIDGE
UNIVERSITY PRESS

University Printing House, Cambridge CB2 8BS, United Kingdom

One Liberty Plaza, 20th Floor, New York, NY 10006, USA

477 Williamstown Road, Port Melbourne, VIC 3207, Australia

314-321, 3rd Floor, Plot 3, Splendor Forum, Jasola District Centre, New Delhi - 110025, India

103 Penang Road, #05-06/07, Visioncrest Commercial, Singapore 238467

Cambridge University Press is part of the University of Cambridge.

It furthers the University's mission by disseminating knowledge in the pursuit of education, learning and research at the highest international levels of excellence.

www.cambridge.org
Information on this title: www.cambridge.org/9781108746861
DOI: 10.1017/9781108784283

© Will Bateman 2020

This publication is in copyright. Subject to statutory exception and to the provisions of relevant collective licensing agreements, no reproduction of any part may take place without the written permission of Cambridge University Press.

First published 2020
First paperback edition 2022

A catalogue record for this publication is available from the British Library

ISBN 978-1-108-47811-3 Hardback
ISBN 978-1-108-74686-1 Paperback

Cambridge University Press has no responsibility for the persistence or accuracy of URLs for external or third-party internet websites referred to in this publication, and does not guarantee that any content on such websites is, or will remain, accurate or appropriate.

Dedicated to the Batemans.

CONTENTS

List of Figures   *page* x
Preface   xi
Acknowledgements   xiii
Notes on the Text   xvi
List of Abbreviations   xvii

1 Finance and Constitutionalism   1

   Dicey's System of Parliamentary Control   3

   Law and Public Finance in Parliamentary Government   11

   Argument, Method and Structure   17

   PART I **Historical Development of Parliamentary Public Finance**

2 History (I): Parliament and Executive   23

   Statutory Financial Authorisation   24

   Statutory National Debt   42

   Executive Financial Initiative   51

   Systematic Public Audit   56

   The Balance of Financial Authority   61

3 History (II): Judiciary   63

   Exchequer Litigation   63

   Suing the Treasury   67

vii

Bankers' Case   74

The Judicial Position in Public Finance   78

4 History (III): Exporting Parliamentary Public Finance   81

Congressional Divergence   81

Colonial Constitutions   83

Federal Constitutions   87

Commonwealth Constitutions   89

5 History (IV): Public Finance in the Modern State   95

Wars and Welfare   96

Money and Public Management   111

Public Finance in Modern Parliamentary Government   120

PART II **Parliamentary Public Finance in Operation**

6 Fiscal Authority   129

Delegated Fiscal Authority   131

Excess Expenditure   141

Executive Control of the Structure of Public Finances   145

7 Debt and Monetary Authority   151

Delegated Debt Finance Authority   157

Autonomous Monetary Finance   164

8 Judicial Power   171

Asymmetric Judicial Power   172

Expenditure and the Judiciary   179

Taxation and the Judiciary   188

PART III **Evaluating Parliamentary Public Finance**

9 Failure of Parliamentary Control   199
   Legal Control   204

   Effective Control   209

   Parliamentary Ratification   217

   Conclusion   225

10 Theory and Practice of Financial Self-Rule   227

   Virtues of Financial Self-Rule   227

   Law without Judges   230

   Public and Private Finance   232

   Bibliography   235
   Index   261

FIGURES

2.1 Public expenditure (1696–1800)   *page* 27
2.2 Public expenditure (1800–1900)   28
2.3 Retrospective appropriation (1867–1878)   37
5.1 UK expenditure and taxation (1900–1945)   96
5.2 UK sovereign borrowing (1900–1945)   97
5.3 Twentieth-century fiscal expansion   98
5.4 UK public expenditure by category (1900–1990)   99
5.5 Australia public expenditure by category (1900–1990)   100
II.1 UK GDP and public finance (2005–2016)   126
II.2 Australia GDP and public finance (2005–2016)   127
6.1 Australia balance of standing/annual appropriation (2005–2016)   138
6.2 UK balance of standing/annual appropriation (2005–2016)   139
7.1 Australia sovereign borrowing (2005–2016)   153
7.2 UK sovereign borrowing (2005–2016)   154

PREFACE

All constitutional systems grapple with a fundamental question: does ultimate power rest with the representative or governing institutions of state? This book addresses a subordinate enquiry: do parliaments or executive governments control public finance in the parliamentary tradition? Many jurists may find the answer given contentious: executives, not parliaments, hold the vast preponderance of constitutional authority over public finance.

This book was conceived in a period of financial panic and muted constitutional turbulence. In 2007, the North Atlantic financial system crashed as a result of widespread fraud in financial markets and a failure of bank regulation. As the financial tsunami raced from New York to London, Britain's executive government made a choice to rescue banks that had precipitated the crisis and followed an American project to pump liquidity into financial markets.

Constitutionally, the UK's response to the financial crisis was stunningly irregular.

Without any parliamentary or legislative consent, the UK Treasury spent almost £24 billion bailing out an insolvent commercial bank. That unlawful expenditure exceeded the Treasury's lawful budget by 119 per cent and amounted to 6 per cent of the entire UK central government's main estimates for fiscal year 2009. Parliament was never asked to authorise that expenditure because the Treasury made a strategic decision not to inform parliamentarians of its plans. Nor was Parliament asked, in 2009, before the Treasury agreed to indemnify the Bank of England's plans to give vast amounts of newly created money to financial institutions under the, euphoniously branded, 'quantitative easing' programme. When the Treasury and Bank of England agreed to subsidise Britain's sovereign debt issues, via the remittance of profits from quantitative easing, Parliament was never consulted, and no legislative framework authorised that debt monetisation programme. Perhaps Parliament would have done anything the Treasury asked, but perhaps not.

Conventional wisdom is that parliaments control public money. If that were true, those staples of the UK's response to the financial crisis were, in a non-marginal sense, unconstitutional. The research underpinning this book sought to understand why no constitutional eyebrows were raised. After several years of wading through a morass of financial legislation, public accounts and Hansard over several continents, it became clear that the financial structure of parliamentary government gives neither representative assemblies nor judiciaries any meaningful role in the state's financial fortunes. Executives hold the financial charge, parliaments ratify their plans and judiciaries intervene only sporadically in financial affairs, and not always in support of parliaments.

This book is devoted to explaining that distribution of constitutional power through an historical and contemporary analysis of the legal and financial behaviour of governments in the parliamentary tradition. In doing so, it confronts a conundrum: most jurists are repulsed by numbers, but public finance cannot be understood entirely non-quantitatively. Wherever possible, I have cast my treatment of finance, law and constitutionalism in terms which should be digestible for qualitative and quantitative scholars.

ACKNOWLEDGEMENTS

Many people helped bring this book to life, both by teaching its author how to think clearly and by providing the necessary support (financial, emotional and logistical) underpinning any major research project.

None of the research for this book could have been undertaken without the generous financial support of several research funding bodies: the Cambridge Trust, Cambridge Australia Scholarships and the Cambridge Australia Poynton Scholarship. I am extremely grateful for the extensive support provided by their donors, trustees and administrators.

Professor David Feldman supervised the doctoral research on which this book is based. Our meetings in his study between 2014 and 2017 were enriching and congenial discussions about constitutionalism, parliamentary government and the scholarly method. Together, we tried to overcome Hofstadter's law: 'it always takes longer than you expect, even when you take into account Hofstadter's law'.

During a doctoral intermission, the Hon. Justice Stephen Gageler impressed the importance of applying Occam's razor to legal and constitutional thought, while focusing on 'what matters'. His wisdom, patience and concision were inspirational. I hope he forgives me for the long-windedness of the following acknowledgements.

Back in Cambridge, I was lucky enough to spend time talking about constitutionalism with Professor Peter Cane, whose views had a major impact on my own thinking. I could not have understood constitutions as mechanisms for 'distributing' authority, save for Peter's introduction of that idea in a seminar in Lent term 2017.

Professors David Howarth and Tony Prosser provided very helpful comments on a dissertation-shaped version of this book. I consider myself extremely fortunate to have had the benefit of their accumulated professional and academic experience with all things financial, governmental and parliamentary.

In Cambridge, and latterly in Berlin, I was blessed to be part of a salon composed of Dr Jason Allen, Dr Ben Folit-Weinberg, Dr Jens van't

Klooster and Dr Justus Schollemeyer. Dr van't Klooster gifted me his deep knowledge of North Atlantic financial markets, the European philosophical canon and, most importantly, his friendship. Most of the good ideas in this book were gestated on or near Templehofer Feld in conversation with Jens. Without his steadfast support, this project would never have been completed.

Dr Jason Allen opened my mind to jural and monetary metaphysics. He also welcomed me, on more occasions than I deserved, into the domestic bliss he has built with Steffi and Poppy. Over unbelievably long conversations, Dr Ben Folit-Weinberg introduced me to the idea of the Parmenidean road, threw the best dinner parties and suffered through multiple retellings of my thoughts on finance, democracy and anglophone government. Dr Justus Schollemeyer kept me company in the low lights of the Staatsbibliotek zu Berlin and encouraged me to produce intellectual work of interest to people other than academics.

In Cambridge, Dr Anna Bachmann was a fount of wisdom, brunch and yogic inspiration; Dr Edward Cavanagh gifted me his historical perspective, raw intellectual firepower and camaraderie; Dr John Liddicoat provided quali-quant perspective; Dr Claire O'Callaghan kept me caffeinated; Dr Julia Powels ensured technology was on my radar; Dr Barry Solaiman's passion and integrity inspired me; and Dr Stefan Theil was a sympathetic and insightful friend whose predictive skills far surpassed my own. Major Mark Hammond DFC ensured that all intellectual heavy-lifting had a physical counterweight.

In London, Dr Cameron Miles has been a stalwart friend and intellectual supporter for the last decade, while Dr Jonathan Ketcheson gently encouraged perseverance when my patience with doctoral study was flagging. Dr Mike Grainger provided Singaporean succour. In Oslo, Lofoten and Brussels, Dr Johannes Meyer forced me to focus on data, not models, while Dr Felicitas Parapatis ensured that I remained, constructively, enraged.

In Canberra, Professors James Stellios and Leighton McDonald patiently taught me how to think and endured my garrulous learning style, while sharing their wisdom with me. Since I joined the Law School at the Australian National University, they have become cherished colleagues. Dr Lachlan McCalman and Ms Jacqualine Myint have been sources of mentally enlivening and spiritually nourishing friendship.

I extend deep thanks to the editorial team at Cambridge University Press, particularly Ms Finola O'Sullivan and Ms Marianne Nield, for their support for this book and fielding my neophyte queries with admirable patience. I am equally grateful to the anonymous reviewers of the draft manuscript whose suggestions and constructive criticisms enriched the final product. While this book was being prepared for production, I was lucky to have the editorial assistance of two talented law students, Ms Karen Chow and Mr Harry Fenton. Their capacity to think clearly under pressure bodes well for their professional futures.

In Sydney (and Tokyo) Mr George Blades provided unconditional friendship and shelter, while Mr Timothy Boyle and his long-suffering family, Lauren, Alfie and Piper, accommodated, belayed and supported me. Mr Mike Forster provided loyal friendship, surfing instruction and financial inspiration. Ms Georgia Huxley and Mr Nicholas Kelly both gifted me their valuable counsel and (more) shelter. Mr Mark Higgins provided many late-night Chinese dinners.

Ms Marion Poerio provided boundless love, logistical and typographical support, for which I am extremely grateful. Over two continents, she has kept me upright, sane, pried me away from dusty books and gifted me her energy, love and kindness. I am a very lucky man.

My final acknowledgement of gratitude must go to the Bateman family, whose members have patiently endured my professional and intellectual obsessions for the past three decades. My father and mother, Clara and Alan, built a family which cherished debate and learning above (almost) all else. Together, they robustly encouraged me to think for myself. My sister Eliza, herself a Doctor of Laws, supplied a much cherished moka pot, which powered me through my writing. My other sister Selena has been my closest friend and intellectual companion for as long as I can remember. Her influence on this book was foundational: by publishing an award-winning academic article on public finance and the Australian Constitution she inspired me to undertake doctoral research on public finance and constitutionalism.

NOTES ON THE TEXT

This book uses the following citation system.
Cases
First citation: Full case citation.
Subsequent citations: *Abbreviated case name* (Year), pinpoint.

Legislation
All citations: *Title and year* (Jurisdiction), section number.
UK legislation: Regnal years and chapter numbers appear until 1958.

Secondary Sources
First citation: Author (Year), *Title of book* or 'Title of article', pinpoint.
Subsequent citations: as above, omitting the title.

Government Documents
All citations: Institution, *Title* (Year), pinpoint.

ABBREVIATIONS

AGBP	Australian Government Budget Papers
ABS GFS	Australian Bureau of Statistics, *Government Finance Statistics*
ABS NA	Australian Bureau of Statistics, *Australian System of National Accounts*
BHS	Mitchel (1998), *British Historical Statistics*
ONS NA	Office of National Statistics, *National Accounts*
ONS PSF	Office of National Statistics, *Public Sector Finance Statistics*
PESA	HM Treasury, *Public Expenditure Statistical Analysis*

1

Finance and Constitutionalism

A paradox of parliamentary constitutionalism is that parliaments do not control public finance.

Despite enacting gargantuan tax and appropriation statutes, the financial powers of parliaments are ceremonial and passive, while executives' are practical and potent. Executive organs carry out all financial planning, possess a veto over all financial legislation, exercise broad delegated statutory power over public expenditure, determine when and how to issue sovereign debt, supervise the wider executive's use of economic resources and dictate the form and content of public accounts. Parliaments ratify the financial legislation developed by executives and exercise a weak form of ex post review of public spending. Judiciaries occupy no systemic position in public finance, lacking any meaningful jurisdiction over the legality of public spending, debt or monetary finance, while only intervening sporadically in taxation disputes and not invariably in support of parliaments. Central banks have stringent public financing powers which are exercised infrequently and, usually, via coordination with treasuries. Since the mid nineteenth century, that distribution of financial power has prevailed in the nation-states which grew from the British Empire, both republics and constitutional monarchies.

Much of the foregoing chafes against orthodoxy. Since the late Victorian era, mainstream jurists have assumed that executives are subordinate to parliaments, including where finance is concerned. That public money is governed by a 'system of parliamentary control'[1] has been assumed as mostly accurate, and no dedicated study has questioned parliaments' supposed constitutional superiority. Compared to the attention given to the clash of political and judicial authority in twentieth-century constitutional

---

[1] Dicey (1885), *Introduction to the Study of the Law of the Constitution*, 171–175 (references to Dicey are to the 1885 first edition, republished in: Allison (2013), *A.V. Dicey, The Law of the Constitution*).

affairs, the financial aspect of constitutionalism has been left to languish in obscurity.

This book brings public finance out from the constitutional shadows for examination. It argues that an historical and contemporary analysis of the legal practices governing public finance places the executive at the financial apex of the parliamentary tradition. That argument unfolds in the following structure.

Chapters 2–5 provide an historical account of the development of a model of parliamentary public finance which distributed the bulk of authority to executives, rather than parliaments or judiciaries, beginning in the UK, before widening to account for the imperial spread of parliamentary government. Chapters 6–8 provide a detailed case-study analysis of the contemporary operation of public finance law in varying economic circumstances: Australia and the UK between 2005 and 2016. Those case studies provide concrete examples of the complex interplay of legal authority, governmental behaviour and economic conditions, each of which contributes to the distribution of constitutional authority over public finance. Chapters 9 and 10 close the book by consolidating the ramifications of the foregoing historical and contemporary analyses for core doctrines of anglophone constitutional theory. Chapter 9 presents a detailed critique of the idea of 'parliamentary control of public finance' and explores alternative formulations of the balance of financial power between parliaments, executive and judiciaries. Chapter 10 moots a number of future avenues of intellectual enquiry on the topics of constitutionalism and public finance.

This introductory chapter surveys the intellectual and institutional background, clarifies critical ideas and summarises the book's central claims. It commences by explaining how public finance has been understood through the idea of 'parliamentary control'. Like many bedrock constitutional ideas, it traces to A. V. Dicey, and this book opens by reviewing Dicey's influence on prevailing thinking about finance and parliamentary government. After dealing with Dicey, the background literature and institutional practice necessary to appreciate this book's contribution are surveyed. Thereafter, the chapter introduces and explains the core concepts necessary to engage with public finance from a constitutional perspective, particularly the functions of fiscal, debt management and monetary activities. That explanation should be helpful for readers outside the financial *cognoscenti*. The chapter closes by summarising the book's central claims.

Dicey's System of Parliamentary Control

From the first edition of the *Law of the Constitution*, in his treatment of '[t]he Revenue',[2] Dicey wrote of the 'system of parliamentary control'[3] which governed 'the collection and expenditure of the revenue, and all things appertaining thereto'.[4]

Dicey's focus was novel. Other constitutional jurists had not allocated a totalising position of control to parliament over finance but had devoted their intellectual energies to explaining the constitutional functions of the Crown (Monarch and executive), while recognising, almost as subsidiary, the role played by parliament in the annual processes of supply and taxation.[5] Dicey swept aside the Crown's financial role and placed Parliament in a position of predominance in relation to tax, expenditure and audit.

On taxation, Dicey counselled 'putting the hereditary revenue out of our minds' and restyled the 'extraordinary' revenue as 'the Parliamentary revenue of the nation'.[6] He canvassed the distinction between annual and standing taxes to make the 'main point ... that all taxes are imposed by statute, and that no one can be forced to pay a single shilling ... which cannot be shown to the satisfaction of a judge to be due from him under Act of Parliament'.[7] On expenditure, he refuted the 'mediaeval notion' that money 'granted' by Parliament was 'the King's property', explaining that, 'at the present day', the 'whole of the public revenue is treated ... as public income'.[8] The 'details of the methods according to which supplies are annually voted and appropriated' were glossed over en route to Dicey's salient point that 'each item of expenditure' is 'directed and authorised' by 'some permanent Act' or 'by special Acts passed prior to the appropriation Act and enumerated therein'.[9]

---

[2] Ibid., 171.
[3] Ibid., 171–175.
[4] Ibid., 171.
[5] E.g., May (1851), *A Practical Treatise on the Law, Privileges, Procedures and Usage of Parliament*, chapter 21; Hearn (1886), *The Government of England*, chapters 8 and 9; Todd (1887), *Parliamentary Government in England*, volume 1, chapters 16 and 17; Todd (1889), volume 2, chapter 1; Palgrave and Bonham-Carter (1893), *Erskine May's Treatise on the Law, Privileges, Proceedings and Usage of Parliament*, chapter 22; Anson (1907), *The Law and Custom of the Constitution*, volume 1, 230–237; Anson (1907), volume 2, 284–335.
[6] Dicey (1885), 172.
[7] Ibid., 173. Chapter 3 examines some of the complications which attended that statement in 1885.
[8] Ibid., 173.
[9] Ibid., 174.

Dicey described the system of public audit and accounts as a *'security ... for the due appropriation of public revenue ... for its being expended in the exact manner which the law directs'*.[10] The *Exchequer and Audit Departments Act 1866* was singled out for special mention,[11] particularly those parts which conferred powers on the Comptroller and Auditor-General as 'comptroller' (to permit a withdrawal of money) and 'auditor' (to scrutinise the accounts of departments to ensure that expenditure occurred lawfully). Both powers, Dicey wrote, completed the system of providing 'parliament [with] complete control over the national expenditure'.[12]

Dicey included the judiciary in that system of parliamentary control, but trod cautiously. Full-throated approval was given to the judiciary's position as a protector of property rights, with Dicey stating that a public official trying to collect tax without statute would 'expose himself to actions or prosecutions'.[13] Far more circumspect language was used to describe the judiciary's positions vis-à-vis public expenditure: officials spending money without legislative approval 'would find it difficult to avoid breaches of definite laws which would expose them to appear before the Courts'.[14] That delicate language was surely intentional, as Dicey knew first-hand that the judiciary had no jurisdiction to enforce appropriation legislation against the Treasury, having successfully argued the point as counsel two years before publishing his lectures on constitutional law.[15]

Dicey's Legacies

Of course, Dicey did not design the UK's system of public finance, but his intellectual positioning of the constitutional principles concerning public finance left three intellectual legacies, which were passed down to later generations of constitutional jurists. The first was framing those principles within the language of 'parliamentary control' rather than available alternatives like: '[t]he Crown demands money, the Commons grant it

---

[10] Ibid., 171 (original emphasis).
[11] (29 & 30 Vict, c 39).
[12] Ibid., 174.
[13] Ibid., 200.
[14] Ibid.
[15] In *R v. Inland Revenue* (1884) 12 QBD 461 the Court of Appeal upheld Dicey's submission that earlier authority permitting the issue of mandamus against the Treasury for breach of an appropriation Act could not 'be maintained on any ground' and was 'wrong': at 476, 480. Chapter 3 explains the episode in greater detail.

and the Lords assent to the grant' or the 'executive's financial initiative'.[16] The language of 'parliamentary control' was not unknown before Dicey. It was tossed about in the House of Commons in relation to public expenditure from (at least) the 1840s and was invoked in relation to Gladstone's financial reforms of the 1860s.[17] Building on those artefacts of Victorian political culture, Dicey elevated the idea that parliament controlled public finance to a position of constitutional predominance.

Dicey's second legacy was to selectively rank the financial activities of government: taxation first, expenditure second, audit third, while sovereign borrowing and the Bank of England's public financing role were wholly ignored.[18]

Dicey's concentration on tax is understandable. Tax is constitutionally significant because it is the revenue-generating activity uniquely possessed by the state in virtue of its monopoly on lawful coercion. Everyone can *bargain* to raise funds; only the state can *command* people to fund it. But, even in Dicey's time, tax was neither the sole nor the most potent method of raising public money. In the decade before *The Law of the Constitution*, large sums were routinely advanced from the Bank of England to the Treasury. In 1877, the Bank advanced the Treasury £1 million, representing 1 per cent of total public receipts and 19 per cent of income tax receipts. In 1885, that number rose to £2.5 million (1 per cent total tax and 21 per cent of income tax receipts).[19] Between the 1850s and the 1880s, the annual average of outstanding Treasury debt stood at ~£18 million, representing ~22 per cent of total receipts and ~200 per cent of income tax receipts.[20] Both the advances from the Bank of England and the debt issued by the Treasury were authorised by legislation ignored by Dicey.

Dicey's attention to the constitutional practices surrounding public expenditure is equally understandable, particularly his focus on the annual process of parliamentary appropriation. Annual appropriation legislation has an obvious constitutional significance by tethering the

---

[16] May (1851), 411.
[17] HC Deb 11 August 1848, cc 93–100, and again following Gladstone's financial reforms of the 1860s (e.g., HC Deb 08 June 1875, cc 1522–60) about which more is said in Chapter 2.
[18] Inconsequential references to the charging of the 'National Debt' on the 'consolidated fund' and the location of public revenue 'in the Bank of England to the account of the Exchequer' exhaust Dicey's treatment of those aspects of public financial management: Dicey (1885), 175–176.
[19] Wormell (1999), *National Debt in England*, volume VI, 120; BHS, 582–583.
[20] BHS, 582–583, 602.

executive's budget to parliamentary will expressed through statute. Once again, however, the story is more complicated than depicted by Dicey.

When Dicey wrote, Britain's expenditure on debt-servicing costs was authorised under legislation which stood outside the annual parliamentary processes: *standing appropriation legislation*.[21] The amount of interest paid, and principal repaid, under that legislation was enormous. Between 1875 and 1885, public debt repayment averaged 35 per cent of total public spending, while non-debt military and civil expenditure averaged 32 per cent and 21 per cent respectively.[22] The proportion of public expenditure authorised by standing appropriation legislation would only increase as Dicey penned the latter editions of his tome. By the publication of his eighth edition in 1915, standing legislation had been enacted providing authority for early welfare state spending.[23] The large, and increasing, share of public expenditure authorised outside the annual appropriation process sat awkwardly with Dicey's ideas on parliamentary control of expenditure.

Dicey's third legacy was locating the idea of parliamentary control of public finance within the twin pillars of 'parliamentary sovereignty' and the 'rule of law'. His conclusion that public finance was 'governed by law, or, what is the same thing, may become dependent upon the decision of the judges upon the meaning of an Act of Parliament',[24] is exemplary of his broader project to model the English constitution within the confines of the rule of law and parliamentary sovereignty.[25] Thereby, Dicey framed the issue of the constitutionality of public money as one concerning parliament and the judiciary.

Notably underplayed was the executive's role, as well as the massive legal and administrative power held by the Treasury. Notwithstanding Dicey's famous antipathy to the growing British bureaucracy,[26] that is a curious omission. He acknowledged select parts of the *Exchequer and Audit Departments Act 1866* but omitted those which delegated vast financial authority to the Treasury: to determine how departmental

---

[21] Notably the *Act of 1787* (27 Geo III, c 33) which created the Consolidated Fund.
[22] BHS, 588, 602.
[23] *National Insurance Act 1911* (1 & 2 Geo, c 55).
[24] Dicey (1885), 178.
[25] Ibid., 180.
[26] Dicey attacked the 'administrative methods' of early welfare state legislation, such as the *National Insurance Act 1911* (1 & 2 Geo V, c 55), on the basis that they 'harmonise with the principle or the sentiment of collectivism', and called the combination of universal adult suffrage and old-aged pensions 'evil': Dicey (1917), *Law and Public Opinion in England During the Nineteenth Century*, xxxv, xxxix.

accounts would be prepared, to refuse a department's request for funds granted by parliament, to direct the Comptroller and Auditor-General to carry out audits and to determine the terms of public borrowing (from the Bank of England) to make up shortfalls in tax revenue.[27] When Dicey wrote, those provisions bolstered the Treasury's, rather than Parliament's, control over the administration of public expenditure. Unaltered in all material respects, they endure today.

Parliamentary Control of Public Finance

For constitutional jurists, the Diceyan idea of parliamentary control of finance became a basic unit of thought, even though interest in the legal and constitutional dimensions of public finance waned throughout the twentieth century.

Predictably, Wade and Phillips followed Dicey in framing their analysis of finance via 'parliamentary control of expenditure and taxation'.[28] Although they took fleeting notice of sovereign borrowing and observed the 'functions of the Treasury', they stayed within the Diceyan mainstream.[29] Jennings' engagement with public finance was characteristically focused on the legislative and administrative aspects of government,[30] but he still understood 'financial control exercised by the Commons' as a core constitutional principle.[31] His drift away from Dicey was, however, evident, including by recognising the importance of the Treasury and surveying the details of legislation concerning annual and standing appropriations. But public borrowing and banking were not prominent parts of Jennings' 'functionalist-style'[32] analysis of constitutions in the British tradition. Thereby, Jennings remained within the slipstream of Dicey's constitutional modelling of public finance.[33]

At the outset of the third millennium, parliamentary control is established at the intellectual core of the constitutional dimension of public

---

[27] *Exchequer and Audit Departments Act 1866* (29 & 30 Vict, c 34) ss. 12–14, 21–23.
[28] Wade and Phillips (1931), *Constitutional Law*, 191; (1946), *Constitutional Law*, 155.
[29] Wade and Phillips (1931), 106, 190; (1946), 156. That attitude aligns with Wade's remarks as editor of the ninth edition of Dicey (1939), *Introduction to the Study of the Law of the Constitution*.
[30] Rather than the judiciary: Loughlin (1992), *Public Law and Political Theory*, 168.
[31] Jennings (1939), *Parliament*, 282; (1957), *Cabinet Government*, 283.
[32] Loughlin (1992), 168.
[33] Specialist public finance texts, where they existed, also invoked 'parliamentary control' as the dominant constitutional principle concerning public money: see, e.g., Durrell (1917), *The Principles and Practices of Parliamentary Grants*, 3.

finance. McEldowney expressed 'Parliamentary control of the purse' as a 'basic principle of the [UK's] constitution',[34] and *Halsbury's Laws of England* states, as a 'basic' constitutional principle, that 'Parliamentary control is exercised in respect of (1) the raising of revenue; (2) its expenditure; and (3) the audit of public accounts'.[35]

Throughout the common law world, 'parliamentary control' also features prominently in constitutional actors' own explanations of the principles governing public money. In Dicey's home jurisdiction, the parliament spoke frequently in those terms. The UK's *National Audit Act 1983* (UK) bore the long title '[a]n Act to strengthen parliamentary control ... of public money'. Two decades later, the Commons would explain one of its 'core functions' as exercising 'effective control' over 'government expenditure'.[36] New Zealand's parliament adopted the same verbal formula in s. 22 of the *Constitution Act 1986* (NZ), entitled 'Parliamentary Control of Public Finance'. Executive agencies in Australia, Britain, Canada and New Zealand also frame their institutional relationship over finance through the idea of parliamentary control over 'government spending'.[37]

On the rare occasion that common law judiciaries have considered issues of public finance, they stayed close to the Diceyan shore. In 1912, a judge of the Chancery Division stated that '[b]y the ... Bill of Rights ... it was finally settled that there could be no taxation in this country except under authority of an Act of Parliament'.[38] In 1923, the Privy Council stated that '[a]ny payment out of the consolidated fund made without Parliamentary authority is simply illegal and ultra vires'.[39] The substance of those statements has since been adopted by the common law canon,[40]

---

[34] McEldowney (2015), 'Public Finance and the Control of Public Expenditure'; and the preceding four editions, (2011), 341; (2007), 364; (2004), 379; (2000), 190; McEldowney (2016), *Public Law*, 464.
[35] Blackburn (2014), 'Constitutional and Administrative Law', [470].
[36] Liaison Committee (2009), 'Financial Scrutiny: Parliamentary Control over Government Budgets'.
[37] HM Treasury, *Alignment (Clear Line of Sight) Project* (2009), 3. Treasury Board of Canada, *Guide on Grants, Contributions and Other Transfer Payments* (2002), 22; New Zealand Treasury, *A Guide to the Public Finance Act* (2005); Commonwealth of Australia Department of Finance, *Is Less More? Towards Better Commonwealth Performance* (2012), 13.
[38] *Bowles v. Bank of England* [1913] 1 Ch 57, 84.
[39] *Auckland Harbour Board v. The King* [1924] AC 318, 327.
[40] *In re McFarland* [2004] 1 WLR 1289, 1302; *Steele Ford & Newton Respondents v. Crown Prosecution Service (No 2)* [1994] 1 AC 22, 33; *Woolwich Equitable Building Society v. IRC*

while an adventurous Australian court has written Dicey's principle of parliamentary control directly into its constitutional jurisprudence.[41]

In the world of mainstream constitutional debates, the position of public finance, and parliamentary control, is less visible. As the 'concept of fundamental law in modern constitutional regimes' skewed towards 'the institution of judicial review',[42] scant attention has been paid to the constitutional dimension of finance. Debates about parliamentary sovereignty focus on the, supposed or real, friction between parliament's legislative sovereignty and the judiciary's law-speaking and law-finding functions.[43] Little ink has been spilt working out where the relationship, financial or otherwise, between parliament and executive fits in that debate. Contemporary rule-of-law debates are typified by a preoccupation with the common law judiciary's intellectual methodology,[44] particularly thick/substantive and thin/procedural/formal conceptions of the rule of law.[45] Similarly, analyses of the separation of powers (outside America) have tended to be conducted by reference to the judiciary's institutional independence from the non-judicial arms of government.[46]

As those debates are presently orientated, there is scarce room to think about the constitutional position of public finance,[47] which, taxation aside, operates almost entirely outside the purview of judges. No meaningful judicial time has been spent thinking about Auditors-General's legislative powers,[48] and annual appropriation legislation falls within the

---

[1993] AC 70, 177; *Attorney General v. Great Southern and Western Railway Company of Ireland* [1925] AC 754, 772; *Attorney-General v. Wilts United* (1922) 38 TLR 781.

[41] *Pape v. Commissioner of Taxation* (2009) 238 CLR 1, [294]; *Williams v. Commonwealth (No 1)* (2012) 248 CLR 156, [219]. A less unorthodox adoption appeared in Canada: *Confédération des Syndicats Nationaux v. Canada* [2008] 3 SCR 511, [21]; *Re Eurig Estate* [1998] 2 SCR 565, [32].

[42] Loughlin (2010), *Foundations of Public Law*, 288.

[43] The positions are collected in Knight (2009), 'Bi-Polar Sovereignty Restated'; Goldsworthy (2001), *The Sovereignty of Parliament*. Arguments for a more nuanced perspective on parliamentary sovereignty frame their preferred position in a similar way: see, e.g., Barber (2011), 'The Afterlife of Parliamentary Sovereignty'.

[44] A broader understanding of the rule of law, as constituted by 'the constant disposition to act fairly and lawfully' of the 'settled ethical character', has not featured in anglophone constitutional thought: Shklar (1987), *Political Theory and the Rule of Law*, 3, a position attributed to Dicey by Loughlin (1992), 151.

[45] Craig (1997), 'Formal and Substantive Conceptions of the Rule of Law'.

[46] Allison (2007), *The English Historical Constitution*, chapter 4.

[47] Being mentioned only en passant: e.g., Barber (2018), *Principles of Constitutionalism*, 80.

[48] The few existing cases have not been important enough to report: e.g., *Bakewell v. McPherson* (1992) BC9200236 (Supreme Court of South Australia).

core of subject matter which is not appropriate for judicial digestion: a fortiori legislation providing legal authority for sovereign borrowing and monetary financing.[49]

Given the low visibility of public finance in mainstream constitutional debates, public law scholars interested in public money have begun cultivating greener pastures.[50] Explicitly rejecting any debt to Dicey, Daintith and Page studied the constitutional dimension of finance using 'systems theory' and the idea of 'structural coupling' of parliament and executive.[51] Building on that heritage, Prosser analysed the position of finance within the 'economic constitution' with the assistance of 'the concept of regulation as both an academic discipline and a concern of practical politics', while assuming parliamentary control as a basic constitutional principle concerning 'getting and spending' public money.[52] Both works make significant contributions to scholarly understandings of the workings of public finance in the parliamentary tradition, but neither provides a root-and-branch rethink of the descriptive accuracy or normative power of Dicey's idea of parliamentary control of finance, nor do the few deeply sceptical accounts which follow Bagehot's view that parliamentary control of finance is more constitutional fiction than fact.[53]

---

[49] E.g., *National Loans Act 1968* (UK) ss. 12(1) and (7), 20A, Sch. 5(4); *Commonwealth Inscribed Stock Act 1911* (Cth), s. 3A; *Financial Administration Act 1985* (Can), s. 43; *Public Finance Act 1989* (NZ), s. 47. Exceptional cases exist at the supra-national level concerning the lawfulness of the European Central Bank's Outright Monetary Transactions Program (*Gauweiler v. Deutscher Bundestag* (c-62/14)) and Public Sector Asset Purchase Programme (*Weiss and others* (c-493/17)) under the prohibition on some forms of monetary finance contained in Art. 123 of the *Treaty on the Functioning of the European Union*.

[50] Scattered offerings in the Diceyan mould can be found, but only as piecemeal treatments of discrete cases or statutes, such as Jaconelli's analysis of *Bowles v. Bank of England* ((2010), 'The "Bowles Act" – Cornerstone of the Fiscal Constitution') and McEldowney's critique of the Contingencies Fund ((1998), 'Contingencies Fund and Parliamentary Scrutiny of Public Finance'); treatments available elsewhere in the common law world are deeply embedded in local constitutional and statutory regimes; Lawson (2008), 'Re-invigorating the Accountability and Transparency of the Australian Government's Expenditure' 879–921.

[51] Daintith and Page (1998) *The Executive in the Constitution*, 4–5 (but see 105) citing Teubner (1992), 'Social Order from Legislative Noise?'.

[52] Prosser (2014), *The Economic Constitution*, 17–18, 84, 111. An in-depth account of the 'regulatory enterprise' can be found in Prosser (2010), *The Regulatory Enterprise*.

[53] E.g., Harden (1993), 'Money and the Constitution: Financial Control, Reporting and Audit'.

Law and Public Finance in Parliamentary Government

This book steps back from the existing literature and looks directly at the way that authority over public finance is distributed between parliaments, executive governments and judiciaries by legal norms. It seeks to understand how financial authority is distributed in parliamentary systems of government, why that distribution of power arose and how it is affected by the economic/political/administrative context in which government carries out financial activities.

More pedantically stated, this book analyses the financial aspect of *parliamentary constitutionalism* through the prism of *public finance law*; being the legislative and judicial practices which concern the *financial activities* of *central governments*, being *fiscal, debt* and *monetary activities*. Each of those terms requires some introduction and explanation.

Fiscal, Debt Management and Monetary Activities

Governments finance their operations through a set of activities which are well understood in non-legal scholarly work and government practice,[54] but are likely to be highly obscure to most constitutional jurists and lawyers.

Fiscal activity describes the collection of public revenue from taxation, fees, fines, rent and royalties, and the expenditure of that revenue. That usage is reflected in the concept of a *fiscal deficit*: the gap between expected receipts and outlays before having recourse to debt markets.[55] *Debt finance* and *debt management activity* describes the sovereign borrowing undertaken by governments, which issue long-term debt (to fill fiscal deficits) and short-term debt (to plug holes in cash-flow from taxation and other fiscal receipts). The practical outworking of debt management activity cannot be isolated from fiscal activity because the extent of a government's debt exposure is assessed by reference to shortfalls in fiscal collection (described in some accounts as the *net cash requirement*). Similarly, a government's ability to service debt repayments is assessed by reference to its fiscal profile, reflected in, both, the

---

[54] See the general usage throughout Allen, Hemming and Potter (2013), *The International Handbook of Public Financial Management*.
[55] The precise metrics used to measure public debt and deficit are a matter of endless contest: Cf Irwin (2015), 'Defining the Government's Debt and Deficit' and Blejer and Cheasty (1999), *How to Measure the Fiscal Deficit*.

risk *premia* of its debt securities and sovereign risk rating.[56] Debt management activity also engages with central banks' operations, as sovereign debt securities are vital components of contemporary monetary policy operations.[57]

Monetary activities are the operations of public bodies which exercise *monetary authority*, being the power to issue money on behalf of the state.[58] In most modern economies, central banks exercise that power with the principal objective of achieving stable prices through *monetary policy*. Monetary policy operations have attempted to influence inflation (price stability)[59] by providing short-term loans, and emergency funding, to commercial banks.[60] A range of tools are used by central banks to carry out those operations. From, at least, the 1980s, 'conventional' monetary policy operations used short-term lending to private banks to influence interest rates in the wider economy.[61] More recent 'unconventional' operations of central banks have included the purchase of large amounts of government debt, described as 'quantitative easing'.

A central bank's monetary activities can directly or indirectly contribute to public finance through *monetary finance*.[62] In a broad sense, monetary financing occurs where the 'central bank expand[s] the money supply (which is a non-debt-creating alternative to domestic borrowing)' in a way that accrues a financial dividend to the central government.[63] That form of financing may be more or less direct. More

---

[56] For the theory, see Heinemann, Osterloh and Kalbb, (2014) 'Sovereign Risk Premia: The Link Between Fiscal Rules and Stability Culture'; for the practical impact of fiscal deficits on debt management in the UK, see DMO (2017), 'Debt Management Report 2017-18: Annex D', 'The Exchequer Cash Management Remit for 2017-18', 35.

[57] Whether used as collateral for short-term borrowing from central banks, assets for sale and re-purchase operations or purchased outright by central banks. For the complications which arise from the latter use of sovereign debt instruments, see Modern Bank of England and Debt Management Office, *Statement on Gilt Lending* (2009).

[58] Occasionally called 'monetary sovereignty' in other contexts: Proctor (2012), *Mann on the Legal Aspect of Money*, chapter 19.

[59] Central banks' other activities interlock, in varying degrees, with their monetary policy activities: *financial stability* activities (concerning prudential and disciplinary regulation of private banks), *issuing* or *currency* activities (concerning the issue of physical currency) and *settlement* activities (concerning the provision of inter-bank payments settlement facilities).

[60] See generally, Capie, Goodheart and Schnadt (1994), 'The Development of Central Banking'; Bindseil (2014), *Monetary Policy Operations and the Financial System*.

[61] Often called a central bank's 'open market operations': Lastra (2015), *International Financial and Monetary Law*, [2.129].

[62] Hemming (2013), 'The Macroeconomic Framework for Managing Public Finance', 21.

[63] Hemming (2013), 21; Turner (2015), 'The Case for Monetary Finance'.

direct monetary financing occurs when a central bank creates 'money for the government to spend as an alternative to incurring debt' by 'the central bank purchasing bonds directly from the government, extending it credit or printing currency to pay the government's bills'.[64] Less direct monetary financing occurs through the exercise of a central bank's monetary policy operations, which may result in a 'profit transfer' to the government.[65]

Fiscal, debt management and monetary activities are theoretically and operationally 'interdependent',[66] as the lively economic debates regarding the interaction of those activities illustrate. So it goes: too much tax can stifle economic production;[67] too little production can reduce tax receipts;[68] direct government spending can stimulate an increase in production;[69] but too much public expenditure can be inflationary,[70] requiring a central bank's intervention.[71] No final resolution to those economic debates should be expected, and none is attempted here. Parliamentary constitutionalism has endured through many different economic philosophies and should not be shackled to one which is currently voguish.

Central Government

Most parliamentary states contain several tiers of government that each carry out financial activities. Here, the focus is upon *central governments*. To be sure non-central governments, municipalities, states and provinces, engage in financial activities: raising taxes or rates, spending money and issuing debt. But, only central governments have final

---

[64] Hemming (2013), 22.
[65] Ibid.
[66] Wheeler (2004), *Sound Practice in Debt Management*, chapter 2; Fischer and Easterly (1990), 'The Economics of the Government Budget Constraint'. At a practical level, treasuries (and central banks) give immediate answers to those theoretical debates through macroeconomic models: Office of Budget Responsibility, *The Macroeconomic Model* (2013); Bank of England, *The Bank's Forecasting Platform* (2013); Bank of Canada, 'Analyzing and Forecasting the Canadian Economy through the LENS Model' (Technical Report 102, 2014); Reserve Bank of Australia, 'MARTIN Has Its Place: A Macroeconomic Model of the Australian Economy' (Research Discussion Paper, 2019–07).
[67] Hemming (2013), 18.
[68] Dornbusch and Draghi (1990), *Public Debt Management*, 3.
[69] Keynes (1936), *The General Theory of Employment, Interest and Money*.
[70] Gordon and Leeper (2002), 'The Price Level'.
[71] Lin and Chu (2013), 'Are Fiscal Deficits Inflationary?'; Phelps (1973), 'Inflation in the Theory of Public Finance'.

responsibility for coordinating the interrelated activities of financial management, monetary authority and practical access to sovereign debt markets. Responsibility for the national economy is thereby concentrated in central governments.

The concentration of economic responsibility in central governments is reflected in their relative financial impact.[72] Averaged over 2010–2016, central government spending accounted for 95 per cent of total public expenditure in New Zealand and 75 per cent in the UK. Central government tax was over 90 per cent of total tax in both jurisdictions, while central government borrowing was over 99 per cent of total public borrowing. Central governments in federations also occupy a dominant financial position. Over the same six-year period, Australian and Canadian central government spending and taxation stood at around 50–60 per cent of the total, and central government debt exceeded 95 per cent of the total.

Public Finance Law

This work's investigation of the distribution of financial authority concentrates on the design and operation of *public finance law*, an umbrella term which describes the collection of 'legal practices'[73] that govern the financial activities of central governments. Strictly speaking, common law systems recognise two types of law: statute and case law,[74] and this book reflects that strictness. The focus is on legislation and judicial decision-making concerning taxation, appropriation, sovereign borrowing and central banking.[75]

---

[72] All figures in this paragraph are drawn from the following data sets: ONS PSF, ABS GFS, Statistics Canada, *Canadian Government Finance Statistics* (data sets 385–0033 and 385–0042) and StatsNZ, *Government Finance Statistics (General Government): Year Ended June 2016* and *Local Authority Statistics: June 2017 Quarter*.

[73] The use of 'legal practices' is inspired by Hart (1994), *Concept of Law*, 240.

[74] Although customary laws constitute a third type in some jurisdictions: Matson (1993), 'The Common Law Abroad: English and Indigenous Laws in the British Commonwealth'; Paterson (2010), 'South Pacific Customary Law and Common Law: Their Interrelationship'.

[75] Legal rules concerning non-taxation revenue are excluded because of their negligible economic impact, while demands of space require passing over fiscal equalisation and sovereign investment: McLean and McMillan (2002), 'Fiscal Crisis of the United Kingdom'; Broadway and Watts (2004), 'Fiscal Federalism in Canada, the USA and Germany'; Blöchliger and Charbit (2008), 'Fiscal Equalisation'; Fenna (2008), 'Commonwealth Fiscal Power and Australian Federalism'; Bassan (2011), *The Law of Sovereign Wealth Funds*; Balding (2012), *Sovereign Wealth Funds*.

Many legal approaches to constitutional affairs prioritise case law, only turning to statue where the judges are silent. That approach is not adopted here. With the exception of judicially developed principles of tax law, public finance law lives almost exclusively in statutes, none of which are well known outside the *cognoscenti* who advise treasury and finance ministries on their legal rights and obligations. No textbook in Australia, Canada, New Zealand or the UK explains the form or function of the masses of annual and standing appropriation legislation in each jurisdiction,[76] or the statutes under which sovereign borrowing occurs, or the legislation governing the public finance activities of central banks.[77] Hidden within that intellectual void lies most of the law of public finance.

Law (as opposed to politics or economics) is selected as the focus of the constitutional analysis because law *qua* legislation has a foundational primacy in public finance: it provides a basic source for legitimate government behaviour and the structural framework within which financial activities are administered. There may be other ways to legitimate financial activity, including economic efficiency, political popularity or policy effectiveness, but law provides a uniquely authoritative type of legitimacy. Despite that foundational position, no existing work has analysed public finance from a pointedly legal perspective. Other scholarly and popular works have made different choices and broached financial aspects of parliamentary government from political, economic and administrative perspectives.[78]

Because law (mainly legislation) provide the authoritative basis for legitimate financial behaviour, this work takes legislation as the principal means for distributing authority to engage in financial activities between different public institutions. Throughout this book the expression

---

[76] Scatterings can be found in parliamentary practice manuals and solitary chapters in larger legal treatments: E.g., Jack (2011), *Erskine May's Treatise on the Law, Privileges, Proceedings and Usage of Parliament*, Part 5; Bosc and Gagnon (2017), *House of Commons Practice and Procedure*, chapter 18 (Canada); Wright and Fowler (2012), *House of Representatives Practice*, chapter 11 (Australia).

[77] Cf Lastra (1996), *Central Banking and Banking Regulation*; (2015), *International Financial and Monetary Law*, focusing on the legal frameworks governing central banks' monetary policy and prudential regulation, rather than public finance functions.

[78] Einzig (1959), *The Control of the Purse: Progress and Decline of Parliament's Financial Control*; Reid (1966), *The Politics of Financial Control*; White and Hollingsworth (1999), *Audit, Accountability and Government*; Wehner (2003), 'Principles and Patterns of Financial Scrutiny'; Wehner (2006), 'Assessing the Power of the Purse'; Wehner (2010), 'Cabinet Structure and Fiscal Policy Outcomes'; Dewar and Funell (2016), *A History of British National Audit*; Elliott and Thomas (2017), *Public Law*, 644–652.

financial authority refers to the authority to engage in financial activities provided by law and legal processes.

Parliamentary Constitutionalism

Public finance law varies widely between constitutional systems. The concern here is its operation in *parliamentary constitutional systems*. Abstractly, that term is a metonym for anglophone constitutional systems where the parliament: exercises supreme legislative authority, does not exercise direct governing authority and is the principal democratic institution to which governing authorities are accountable. Empirically, it describes the constitutional systems which devolved from the British Empire.

Congressional constitutional systems are the prime comparators.[79] In the English-speaking world, the only examples are found in the United States of America. As Chapter 3 explains, America's divergence from Britain left a very different set of public financial institutions and a different balance of constitutional authority over public finance.[80] The practical extent of that difference is illustrated by US legal publications concerning public expenditure. For almost forty years, the US Government Accountability Office has published the *Principles of Federal Appropriations Law* (informally, 'The Red Book'), currently spanning three volumes and containing over 3,000 pages of detailed legal analysis regarding the operation of federal appropriations law.[81] A database of legal advice relating to public money is also published which links to US federal court decisions involving public finance.[82]

No body of comparable legal materials exists in the parliamentary constitutional systems. The meek contenders are chapters in books on parliamentary procedure devoted to 'financial procedure', like *Erskine May's Parliamentary Practice*, Part 5 of which deals with financial procedure in around 90 pages.[83] One of this work's ancillary benefits is to

---

[79] Bradshaw and Pring (1973), *Parliament and Congress*; McKay and Johnson (2010), *Parliament and Congress*.
[80] Bradshaw and Pring, (1973), 305; McKay and Johnson (2010), chapter 6.
[81] The Government Accountability Office is a loose analogy to the UK National Audit Office.
[82] www.gao.gov/legal/appropriations-law-decisions/search.
[83] Jack (2011), 711–797. Excellent treatments of public finance law can, however, be found outside the Anglophone world, see De Bellescize (2019), *Le Système Budgétaire du Royaume-Uni*.

provide the foundation upon which a comparable literature could be built in the parliamentary tradition.

Collecting a wide diversity of constitutional systems under the banner of the 'parliamentary tradition' attempts no 'meta-Commonwealth' analysis. Parliamentary government as practised in Australia, Britain, India, Singapore and Papua New Guinea is neither uniform, nor static: it is inflected by the politics, culture and geography of its location. Striking uniformity does, however, exist in relation to the legal structure of the financial activities of central governments throughout the parliamentary world, as the analysis in Chapter 4 demonstrates. A desire to engage with the diversity and similarity of those jurisdictions has motivated this book's cosmopolitan attitude.

Argument, Method and Structure

Stated shortly, this book's argument is that a sober analysis of the design and operation of public finance law does not support a claim that parliaments control public money in parliamentary constitutional systems. A predominance of financial authority is distributed to executive governments, rather than parliaments.

Constitutions and the Distribution of Authority

By focusing on constitutionalism as a way of *distributing* authority, this work's method is slightly unusual in the anglophone constitutional tradition, which tends to focus on how constitutions *limit* or *confer* power on particular institutions. The temptation is always to declare a winner: parliament triumphing over executive and judiciary: judiciary triumphing over executive. That approach to constitutionalism mimics the win:lose calculus of common law litigation, but is an unsatisfying way to explain the institutional complexity of constitutional government.

Viewing the principal function of a constitution as distributing authority between institutions incorporates that complexity, albeit in a way which is less rhetorically effective than announcing a winner in a battle between parliament and executive. That approach is adopted here:[84]

> State power is not simply a function of state structure, it is also a function of state infrastructure. This complicates the picture, especially from a legal

[84] Loughlin (2010), *Foundations of Public Law*, 416.

perspective: in place of a clear, symmetrical, rule-based constitutional structure, we are obliged to examine a complex arrangement of government.

Applying that approach to an historical and contemporary examination of public finance in the parliamentary tradition produces three major claims.

Major Claims

This work's first major claim is that a distinct constitutional model of public finance exists in parliamentary systems of government, which locates executives, rather than parliaments, at the apex of public finance.

Chapters 2 and 3 narrate the growth of English, British and then the UK's legal institutions concerning public finance and the way they distributed authority between parliament, executive and judiciary. The narrative starts around the conclusion of the Civil War and stops at the turn of the twentieth century; including close examination of hitherto overlooked details of legislative, administrative and judicial history. Necessarily, that is a detail-intensive exercise. Sufficiently motivated readers will appreciate that the constitutional significance of the 'fiscal maze'[85] cannot be properly understood until the Baroque complexities of Britain's public finance law are explicated.

Chapter 4 surveys the export of the UK's model of parliamentary public finance: beginning in North America, moving to Australasia and then proliferating throughout the decolonised states which adopted written constitutions in the twentieth century. Throughout that export, the details of public finance law were adapted to local circumstances, but the basic model of parliamentary finance was not meaningfully altered. Chapter 5 explains how the parliamentary model of public finance continued to develop under the pressures of twentieth-century government. Parliaments lost even more authority to executive governments under the impact of the fiscal expansions of the World Wars, the adoption of the welfare state, the growth of central banking and paradigm shifts in public administration.

Those historical chapters are directed towards identifying continuity and change in the development of government institutions, rather than attempting to track an idea of 'parliamentary control' through different epochs. Methodologically, that use of history is designed to 'help liberate our legal thinking from the tyranny of the old' by explaining what is

---

[85] Brazier and Ram (2006), *The Fiscal Maze: Parliament, Government and Public Money*.

'contingent', rather than 'necessary' about the distribution of financial authority in parliamentary constitutional systems.[86] Expressed less grandly, the historical analysis reveals the pathway upon which the modern design of financial constitutionalism depends.

Economic Conditions and Constitutional Authority

This book's second claim, argued for in Chapters 6–8, is that the balance of financial authority between parliaments and executive governments can vary according to economic conditions, in a way largely unimpeded by judicial power. That claim is made by way of a case study of financial behaviour in Australia and the UK between 2005 and 2016.[87]

Chapter 6 focuses on the way that the design and operation of legislation governing fiscal activity (taxing and spending) influences the distribution of financial authority in radically different economic conditions. Chapter 7 undertakes the same inquiry for sovereign borrowing and monetary finance. Both chapters observe how the extent of financial authority delegated to executive governments can increase as economic output contracts and how economic emergencies can denude parliaments of all meaningful financial authority.

The claims made in those chapters are necessarily tentative. They are limited to the two parliamentary constitutions selected for analysis: Australia and the UK. They are also limited because the data set upon which the analyses proceed are based is limited in reach. Methodological caveats aside, clear evidence exists that financial authority moves away from parliaments during economic crises, and their aftermaths. Chapter 8 explains why the presence of judicial power does little to correct against that trend.

Impact on Constitutional Doctrines and Practice

The book's final claim, made in Chapter 9, is that the concept of parliamentary control of public finance fails to describe the distribution of authority in parliamentary constitutions. That claim is the culmination of the foregoing historical and contemporary analyses. It is dignified with an entire chapter on the basis that core constitutional ideas should not be lightly dismissed.

---

[86] Allison (2013), 'History to Understand, and History to Reform, English Public Law', 556.
[87] The rationale for using those two jurisdictions as case studies is given in the introduction to Part II.

Alert to both the strict legal form of public finance law, and the manner in which it operates, a wide 'deficit' of parliamentary control over finance is identified. Alternative conceptions are considered, 'interdependence' and 'executive control', and rejected as unsatisfying descriptions of the distribution of financial authority between parliaments, executives and judiciaries. A notion of 'parliamentary ratification' is proffered as an alternative conception, and its limitations are explained.

Rather than mooting different verbal formulations, the import of that claim is to illustrate the substantive loss of democratic legitimacy which flows from the model of parliamentary public finance.

The Future of Constitutionalism and Finance

The book's final chapter closes, not with additional claims, but with a recognition of the impact of its descriptive claims on future inquiries into constitutionalism and finance: How much financial power should be concentrated in representative assemblies? Does law govern the state if not enforced by the judiciary? Should an analytical wall be constructed between 'public' and 'private' finance in constitutional thinking? The difficult issues which may arise in future thinking about those questions are broached, but final answers must await another day.

PART I

Historical Development of Parliamentary Public Finance

A distinct constitutional model of public finance developed in Britain between 1700 and 1900.

Taxation, expenditure and public borrowing required statutory authorisation, yet Parliament's financial processes were subordinate to the executive government, which had unquestioned authority to formulate national budgets and could veto financial legislation. The Treasury enjoyed wide discretionary authority, delegated by statute, over sovereign borrowing, the supervision of public accounts and the economic control of the wider executive government. Parliamentary audit institutions provided a degree of post hoc financial accountability but were never wholly free of Treasury control. In that sense, the executive *qua* Treasury was the apex financial institution of British government, while Parliament's role was mainly passive and ceremonial.

Little about the allocation of institutional responsibilities between Treasury and Parliament was touched by judicial power. Judicial involvement in public finance stopped at resolving taxation disputes, wherein the judiciary adopted a set of principles which protected private property from taxation and explicitly endorsed tax evasion. Despite a brief flirtation in the mid-nineteenth century, British courts never established a tradition of resolving disputes about expenditure or sovereign borrowing.

Chapters 2 and 3 tell the tale of the development of that model of parliamentary public finance in Britain, starting shortly before the Civil War and ending around the turn of the twentieth century. Chapter 2 accounts for the development of the balance of financial authority between Parliament and executive. Chapter 3 explains the judiciary's position in public finance.

As Westminster-style government spread globally, the model of parliamentary public finance was exported throughout the British Empire. Adopted first by colonial, then dominion constitutions, it was eventually embedded in the constitutional traditions of the independent Commonwealth states which adopted parliamentary constitutions. Chapter 4 accounts for that process of export, and shows the durability of the distribution of financial power to executive governments, rather than parliaments, and the ambivalent financial position of judiciaries.

Aspects of parliamentary public finance continued to develop in the twentieth century, to accommodate the fiscal needs of total war and welfare state policies, as well as the institutional demands of independent monetary authorities and fiscal discipline regimes. Continuing the trajectory set in the nineteenth century, ever-greater shares of authority were allocated to executive governments, particularly over sovereign borrowing, monetary finance and public expenditure. Chapter 5 covers those developments.

2

History (I): Parliament and Executive

Traditionally,[1] historical accounts of public finance and British constitutionalism tend to sweep through the growing demands, from the thirteenth century, for representative consent to taxation, stopping at the enactment of Article 4 of the *Bill of Rights 1688*:[2]

> *That levying Money for or to the Use of the Crowne by pretence of Prerogative without Grant of Parlyament for longer time or in other manner then the same is or shall be granted is Illegall.*

Both before and after 1688, the story is more complicated.[3] Telling it properly requires attention to the political and economic drivers of Britain's fiscal expansion from the end of the Civil War, and the details of legislation concerning tax, expenditure, sovereign borrowing and public audit. Constitutional attentions must focus primarily on the financial balance of authority between Parliament and the executive (*qua* Treasury, mostly), as the interaction of those two institutions sets the basic structure of parliamentary public finance. For the purposes of this work, the critical developments occur between the end of the seventeenth and nineteenth centuries.

The chapter begins by explaining the development of statutory authorisation of taxation and public expenditure, before moving to survey the growth of statutory public borrowing and the appointment of the Treasury at the financial apex of Westminster government. The chapter

---

[1] E.g., Anson (1907), volume 1, 234–235, 265; Hearn (1886), chapter XIII.
[2] (1 & 2 Wm & M, c 2).
[3] Demands of space require skirting-over numerous matters of great interest and undoubted importance, including: the history of the Civil List (Reitan (1966), 'The Civil List in Eighteenth-Century British Politics'), the sudden disappearance of the Commissioners for the Reduction of the National Debt (created by the *National Debt Reduction Act 1786* (26 Geo III, c 31), who last met in October 1860), the battles between the Exchequer and the Treasury (Dewar and Funnell (2016), *A History of British National Audit*, chapters 2–4), and the growth of the professional civil service (Chester (1981), *The English Administrative System*, 123–166, 282–311).

closes by surveying the development of the system of public audit which grew towards the end of the nineteenth century. The judiciary is absent throughout but will receive due attention in the following chapter.

Statutory Financial Authorisation

Prior to the seventeenth century, there was no settled practice of statutory authorisation of taxation and expenditure.

The law concerning the Monarch's income and expenditure flowed from a mixture of custom, prerogative and statute.[4] The economically dominant sources of revenue flowed from remnants of feudal dues, later described as the 'ordinary', 'hereditary' or 'prerogative' revenues. Where that revenue fell short of expenditure, the Monarch would claim rights to tax revenue (later called 'extraordinary' revenue) through Parliament. Those extractive claims would ignite many constitutional confrontations.

Early frictions resulted in various assertions of limitations on the Monarch's rights to demand revenue, some of which survived in prominent documents, like *Magna Carta*.[5] Despite the significance of those documents, the limitations they asserted were not observed with any regularity and established no settled practice that all taxation would be the subject of parliamentary legislation.[6] To that extent, there is no unbroken line between *Magna Carta* and an invariable constitutional requirement that no extractive dues would be levied without parliamentary consent.

Several factors underpinned the failure to establish such a practice prior to the Civil War, most prominently Parliament's institutional weakness relative to the Monarchy.[7] Although Parliament's institutional character became fixed from the fourteenth century,[8] its independence from the Crown remained tenuous,[9] and it had little practical control

---

[4] The old learning on those matters is complex: Maitland (1908), *The Constitutional History of England*, 93–96; Anson (1907), volume 2(2), chapter VII 124–134; Dowell (1884), *A History of Taxation and Taxes in England*, volume 2.

[5] And later, less prominent, documents; Anson (1907), volume 2(2), 126–127; Maitland (1908), 179–181.

[6] Baker (2017), *The Reinvention of Magna Carta*, 184–187.

[7] The Crown in its dual personality: Loughlin (2010), *Foundations of Public Law*, 41–45; Kantorowicz (1997), *The King's Two Bodies*, chapter 4; Maitland (1901), 'The Crown as Corporation'.

[8] Lyon (1980), *A Constitutional and Legal History of Medieval England*, 408–430, 535–536, 595–611; Loughlin (2010), 243–252.

[9] Despite intermittent moments of greater influence: Maitland (1908), 177–179.

over the management of the Monarch's money, which was held in the royal custody of the Exchequer.[10] Parliament, of course, had a role in taxation and expenditure prior to the Civil War and increasingly sought to regulate the Monarch's demands for revenue.[11] Attempts to impose some form of legislative constraint on the Monarch's spending prior to the Civil War are identifiable,[12] but English Monarchs continued to enjoy broad rights to spend without legislation.[13]

The final settlement of the financial disputes between Crown and Parliament occurred during the Civil War. Lawyers' accounts of that settlement tend to start by focusing on several pre-war *causes célèbres*,[14] particularly the lawsuit which grew from Charles I's notorious decision (despite his assent to *The Petition of Right 1628*)[15] to impose a tax, in the form of 'ship money' payable by inhabitants of non-coastal areas in peacetime.[16] The legality of ship money was tested and affirmed in *Hampden's Case*.[17] The popular opposition to the case caused the enactment of the *Ship Money Act 1640*, which voided the judgment and declared the imposition of ship money 'contrary to and against the Laws and Statutes of this Realm the right of property the libertie of the Subjects'.[18] That enactment hastened the drive to Civil War and, upon the cessation of hostilities, the denial of the Monarch's power to tax in the absence of legislation was a central plank in the political settlement of the Glorious Revolution which culminated in the *Bill of Rights 1688*.

Country Ideology and Parliamentary Government

Albeit momentous, the enactment of the *Bill of Rights* provides only a partial explanation for the growth of statutory financial authorisation. Certainly, it provides evidence of the political thinking underlying statutory tax and appropriation: a privileging of parliamentary self-

---

[10] Anson (1907), volume 2(1), 173–175.
[11] Via the Commons committees of 'Ways and Means' and 'Supply' established during the 1640s (Thomas (1971), *House of Commons in 18th Century*, 23–24), the post-Civil War functions of which are explained in greater detail below.
[12] Maitland (1908), 94.
[13] Ibid., 184.
[14] Also *Bate's Case* (1606) 2 ST 371 and the *Five Knights Case* (1627) 3 How ST 1, see Poole (2015), *Reason of State*, 26–35.
[15] Particularly, Articles 1, 2 and 10.
[16] Mendel (1989), 'The Ship Money Case'.
[17] (1637) 3 ST 826; Kier (1936), 'The Case of Ship Money'.
[18] It was also during this period that the view of direct taxation as trifurcated into 'estates' ceased with the surrender of the clergy's right to tax its estate to the laity: Anson (1897), *The Law and Custom of the Constitution*, 47–48.

government and a reduction in the power left to the Monarchy following the Stuarts' abuses.

Some historians have described that thinking as 'country ideology ... persuasion ... or interest':[19]

> a political sensibility with a long and stout pedigree which jealously guarded rights and privileges – whether local, individual or parliamentary – was suspicious of executive power and committed to the notion of responsible government.

Country ideology's 'favourite measures' included:[20]

> the encouragement of parliamentary scrutiny of the executive, the enactment of legislation to secure regular and frequent parliaments, the passage of bills to reduce the number of placemen and the size of the standing army, and the implementation of social and moral reform. All of these proposals spoke to the fear that more government would produce worse government.

That political thinking explains the continual growth of statutory authorisation of expenditure in the form of annual appropriation legislation throughout the first decades of the eighteenth century. Appropriation legislation was an intimate part of bringing the Monarchy (and its ministers) to parliamentary heel, particularly visible in the exchange of the Monarch's hereditary revenues for a statutorily confined budget in the form of a 'civil list'.[21]

The *Bill of Rights* and the political thinking underpinning it cannot, however, explain why statutory taxation became the dominant form of public revenue. Article 4 of the *Bill of Rights* forbids the levying of money under 'pretense' of prerogative, a form of drafting which left extant the Crown's non-statutory revenue sources. In that sense, the growth of statutory taxation did not prevent the Monarchy (or its ministers) from having resort to non-statutory sources of revenue. Financial realities, rather than political principles, best explain that matter. Brewer explains that non-statutory forms of revenue-raising were 'recognized either as economically undesirable or as politically unfeasible after the Glorious Revolution'.[22] A large part of the economic undesirability of the ancient

---

[19] Brewer (1989), *Sinews of Power*, 126; Brooks (1984), 'The Country Persuasion and Political Responsibility'; Hayton (1984), 'The "Country" Interest and the Party System, 1689-c. 1720'.
[20] Brewer (1989), 126.
[21] Maitland (1908), 433–434.
[22] Brewer (1989), 73.

forms of revenue-raising was the massive increase in eighteenth-century public expenditure.[23]

Britain's Fiscal Expansion

As the seventeenth century closed, the spending needs of the English, then British, state spiked as a result of expensive military endeavours. Although the precise figures are contested,[24] it is clear that Britain's public expenditure increased significantly in absolute terms throughout the eighteenth century: as a percentage of gross national income, net expenditure increased by roughly fourfold between 1692 and 1782.[25] The respective shares of that expenditure yo-yoed through peace and wartime.[26]

As Figures 2.1 and 2.2 vividly illustrate, throughout the eighteenth and nineteenth centuries British public money was mostly spent on two activities, paying for war (and military costs of imperial expansion) and servicing war-debt. Despite its later significance, civil government was an insignificant spending item before the twentieth

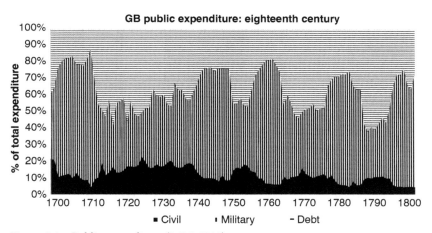

Figure 2.1 Public expenditure (1696–1800)

---

[23] Braddick (2000), *State Formation in Early Modern England*, 246.
[24] UK historical economic data is a topic of constant academic revision: e.g., Allen (2016), 'Revisiting England's Social Tables Once Again'.
[25] Net public expenditure stood at 7.1 per cent of gross national income in 1692; by 1722, that figure had increased to 10.2 per cent; it was 24.7 per cent by 1782. See Clark (2009), 'The Macroeconomic Aggregates for England 1209–2008'.
[26] Data for this and the following figure were collected from *BHS*, chapter XI.

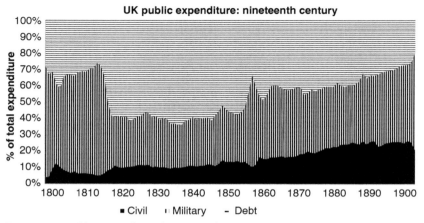

Figure 2.2 Public expenditure (1800–1900)

century. It never rose above 25 per cent of total government expenditure, recording an annual median of 10 per cent of total expenditure in the eighteenth century and 12 per cent in the nineteenth century.

The sharp peaks of expenditure necessitated a sharp rise in revenue, which was met through a combination of increased taxation and debt issues secured against that taxation. British tax receipts doubled between 1678 and 1697, during the Nine Years War. They had doubled again by the 1740s, during the War of Austrian Succession, and had grown 'sixfold' at the *terminus* of the War of American Independence.[27] Throughout those escalations, the types of tax relied on (the *tax mix*) remained relatively limited, with '90 per cent of the state's revenue in the century after the Glorious Revolution' being raised by three taxes: customs, excise and land tax.[28] The land tax started the eighteenth century contributing ~50 per cent to total receipts, and finished the century contributing ~20 per cent.[29] Excises started the eighteenth century at ~20 per cent of total receipts and finished at ~40 per cent, while customs receipts hovered at ~20–30 per cent.[30] The UK's taxation profile remained generally stable throughout the nineteenth century. Indirect tax, custom and excise duties, contributed the overwhelming

[27] Brewer (1989), 74.
[28] Ibid., 78.
[29] Ibid., 79.
[30] Ibid., 80. Excises were charged on domestic commodities, including 'beer, spirits, wine, cider, malt, hops, salt, leather, soap, candles, wire, paper, silk and starch': Ibid., 82.

majority of fiscal receipts. Income tax spiked during wartime, but only contributed an average of ~12 per cent of total fiscal receipts prior to 1900.

Where tax fell short, sovereign borrowing grew in scale and complexity throughout the eighteenth century, particularly during wartime.[31] Average annual borrowing between 1739 and 1748 (the War of Austrian Succession) increased total public debt by over 62 per cent, leaving a debt corpus representing 118 per cent of wartime tax receipts, and 87 per cent of expenditure. Between 1756 and 1763 (the Seven Years War), borrowing increased total debt by 174 per cent, with similar relative impacts on tax revenue and of expenditure. During the War of American Independence (1775–1784), borrowing levels were astronomical, leaving a total debt liability standing at roughly 220 per cent of wartime tax receipts, and 130 per cent of expenditure. Nineteenth-century sovereign borrowing was extensive, although absolute numbers were lower than the eighteenth century.[32]

One constitutional consequence of those financial developments was that the non-statutory sources of revenue remaining at the end of the seventeenth century[33] were robbed of any economic significance.[34] More significantly, the growth of Britain's 'fiscal-military state'[35] coincided with the development of a system of parliamentary finance which accommodated the executive's enormously increased demand for expenditure.

Parliamentary Financing

The priority given to Britain's expenditure needs was reflected in parliamentary financial processes. Sitting as the Committee of Supply, the Commons deliberated and voted on estimates of expenditure. Reconstituted as the Committee of Ways and Means, the Commons then deliberated and voted on the method of raising revenue necessary to fund that expenditure: tax and borrowing.[36] Financial legislation then issued from Ways and Means and passed through the remaining stages of the legislative process.

---

[31] The following relativities were calculated using the raw figures in Brewer (1989), 23–24.
[32] *BHS*, chapter IX.
[33] Maitland (1908), 430–436.
[34] From the latter eighteenth century, they began to be stamped out by legislation: Anson (1907), 120–121; Chitty (1820), *A Treatise on the Law of the Prerogatives of the Crown*, 200–202; Binney (1958), *British Public Finance and Administration 1774-92*, 116–121. The messy residuum was financially insignificant: Chitty (1820), 147–148, 151–152.
[35] Brewer (1989), 130, or the 'fiscal-naval state': O'Brien (2005), 'Fiscal and Financial Preconditions for the Rise of British Naval Hegemony 1485–1815'.
[36] May (1851), 419.

That system of financial committees had a number of interesting features. From the perspective of financial administration, it produced a crude form of fiscal discipline. Procedural rules prevented the Commons from voting 'ways and means in excess of the expenditure voted by the committee of [S]upply':[37] thus, total public expenditure formed a limit on total taxation and borrowing. That form of fiscal discipline prioritised national expenditure requirements over minimising tax burden. It was not focused on deficit control, which would have required an inversion of the process: public expenditure being limited by tax yield.

From the perspective of practical politics, the committee system reflected the concentration of financial power in the Commons. Financial affairs were, however, subject to intra mural skirmishes. Between 1670 and 1680, the Commons resolved that it would originate, and that the Lords would have no power to amend, all taxation measures.[38] The Lords acquiesced in, but never positively approved the Commons' assertion and an ambitious exercise of the Commons' powers over money bills led to the Lords' assertion of their own right to reject financial bills to which other contentious matter had been 'tacked'.[39]

Most relevant to jurists is the legislation produced by the British system of parliamentary finance. Three distinct types of financial legislation issued from Ways and Means: *Supply Acts* and *Appropriation Acts* (each authorising expenditure and public borrowing), and taxation (later *Finance) Acts*. The devilish detail of those statutes reflected the complex distribution of financial power between Parliament and the executive government.

Expenditure Legislation

The first type of expenditure legislation to emerge from the annual parliamentary financial processes were *Supply Acts*.[40]

---

[37] Ibid., 415; Palgrave and Bonham-Carter (1893), *Erskine May's Treatise on the Law, Privileges, Proceedings and Usage of Parliament*, 559.

[38] The relevant resolutions are extracted in May (1844), 407 and Maitland (1908), 310.

[39] Anson (1897), 266–268; May (1844), 410; Maitland (1908), 310; Einzig (1959), 194–199. That resolution did not quash all intracameral disputes, and a final resolution regarding the rights of Commons and Lords in respect of money bills was not reached until the enactment of the *Parliament Act 1911* (1 & 2 Geo V, c 13).

[40] Maitland (1908), 441; Redlich and Ilbert (1903), *The Procedure of the House of Commons*, 163–164.

A *Supply Act* had two main functions: authorising spending and conferring authority on the Treasury to borrow to finance expenditure. *Supply Acts* authorised the payment of a lump sum of money, which represented an aggregate of the estimates voted in the Committee of Supply. Unlike *Appropriation Acts*, the release of funds authorised by *Supply Acts* occurred in aggregate, rather than line items limited by quantum and subject matter:[41]

> there shall and may be issued and applied for or towards making good the Supply granted to Her Majesty for the Service of [1838] ... the sum of [£8 million] out of the Consolidated Fund.

From the turn of the nineteenth century, *Supply Acts* would also be known as *Consolidated Fund Acts*. That shift in nomenclature marked the creation of the 'Consolidated Fund'[42] as the pool into which most tax receipts would flow, from which appropriation legislation would authorise withdrawals of money, and against which sovereign debt repayments were secured.

In addition to authorising lump-sum expenditure, *Supply Acts* also conferred statutory authority for the Treasury to borrow and issue securities up to the limit of the lump sum of supply. As explained below,[43] *Supply Acts* thereby imposed a legal limitation on sovereign borrowing by reference to the amount of annually approved expenditure. Thereby, they linked the annual expenditure cycle to the Treasury's sovereign borrowing activities.

The second type of annual expenditure legislation was the *Appropriation Act*, passed towards the conclusion of the parliamentary session. Like a *Supply Act*, an *Appropriation Act* authorised a lump sum release of funds (for the relevantly approved estimates), but took the further step of providing legal authorisation for the totality of supply granted throughout the parliamentary session:

> [a]ll sums granted by this Act and the other [Supply Acts of the session] out of the ... Consolidated Fund towards making good the supply granted to Her Majesty amounting ... in the aggregate to [£46.9 million] are appropriated and shall be deemed to have been appropriated as from the date of the passing of the first [Supply Act of the session] for the purposes and services expressed in [the schedule].

---

[41] *Consolidated Fund Act 1838* (1 Vict, c 21), s 1.
[42] *Act of 1787* (27 Geo III, c 13), ss 52–53.
[43] See text accompanying footnote 108.

While the discrete content of *Appropriation Acts* varied throughout the eighteenth and nineteenth centuries, their basic structure remained constant.

Unlike *Supply Acts*, that authorisation, or 'appropriation', enumerated the total expenditure by line items contained in a schedule.[44] A very early example is provided by an *Appropriation Act of 1729*, which contained line items of public services and public offices:[45]

£ 986,025 for Half Pay to Sea Officers and other Naval Services
£ 100,000 For Greenwich Hospital
£ 90,249 For the Ordinance for Land service
£ 1,352,138 For Land Forces, that is to say
    £ 784,983 For 22,955 Men, including Commission and Non-Commission Officers and Invalids for Guards, garrisons, and six Independent Companies for Service for the Highlands and other Land Forces relating to Forces for 1729
    £ 160,357 For Forces and Garrisons in the Plantations, Minorca and Gibraltar and for Provisions for Garrisons at Annapolis Royal, Placentia and Gibraltar for 1729
    £ 12,800 For Out Pensions of Chelsea Hospital for 1729

That list was followed by the 'appropriation': a statutory command that:[46]

> The said Aids and Supplies provided ... shall not be issued or applied to any Use, Intent or Purpose whatsoever, other than the Uses and Purposes before mentioned.

That appropriation imposed several forms of legal limitation on the use of money: one concerned the quantum to be spent (only £100,000, not £200,000, for Greenwich Hospital), the other concerned the activity or subject matter upon which the funds would be spent (£784,983 for 22,955 soldiers, not 25,000 soldiers).

From their earliest iterations, *Appropriation Acts* imposed legal limitations on spending at a greater level of generality than the detail that appeared in the estimates voted in Supply.[47] For example, the line item

---

[44] *Consolidated Fund (Appropriation) Act 1874* (37 & 38 Vict, c 56), s 3.
[45] *Act of 1729* (2 Geo II, c 18), s 6. That Act was an example of 'hypothecated' taxation and appropriation, earmarking receipts derived from alcohol duties, a loan from the Bank of England and a temporary land tax (*Acts of 1728* (2 Geo II, cc 1, 3 and 4)) to the enumerated public service.
[46] *Act of 1729* (2 Geo II, c 18), s 14.
[47] Chester (1981), 196.

appropriated by the *Act of 1729* (above) to '*£12,800 For Out Pensions of Chelsea Hospital for 1729*' was expressed in far greater detail in the estimates presented to the Commons via the Committee of Supply:[48]

[Estimate detail]	Per Diem (l. s, d)	For 365 Days (l. s, d)
3,003 Out-pensions, standing at present upon the Books of the Hospital, at 5d per Diem each	£62.11,3	£22,835.6,3
100 Letter Men, at 12d per Diem each	£5.00	£1,825.00
50 Serjeants, at 9d per Diem each	£1.17,6	£684.7,6
[Sub-total]	£69.8,9	£25,344.13,9
From which deduct		
The Sum of [£12,500], which, by Estimation, may be applicable towards defraying this Expense, out of the Poundage of the Forces for the Year 1729	£12,500.00	
[Total]		
Remains to be granted, upon account, for the Out-Pensions of Chelsea Hospital, for the Year 1729	£12,844.13,9	

The legal limitation on expenditure imposed by the *Appropriation Act* applied only to the basic quantum and subject matter expressed in the legislated line item ('*£12,800 For Out Pensions of Chelsea Hospital for 1729*'), rather than the four line items appearing in the estimate.[49] As will be explained shortly, the Treasury was only legally bound by the more-general limitations in the *Appropriation Act*, and had freedom to adjust the amounts between the more detailed line items in the estimate.

[48] Commons Journal, 27 January 1728, 197.
[49] Chester (1981), 196.

As the administration of public finances developed in the mid-nineteenth century, the legal limits of an *Appropriation Act* would be described as 'heads' (or 'votes') of an estimate and the detailed line items would be referred to as 'sub-heads' of the estimate.[50] Despite changes in the design of expenditure legislation, that basic division between detailed accounting material in the estimates and very general legislated limits in *Appropriation Acts* endured.

The system of expenditure authorisation provided by *Supply* and *Appropriation Acts* had two signal features: it left an enormous degree of flexibility to the executive, mainly the Treasury, and was predominately retrospective.

Virement

The flexibility conferred on the Treasury by annual expenditure legislation is most visible in 'the practice of virement, i.e. the transfer of funds allotted for one purpose or service to another'.[51] Within the virement genus, two distinct species developed. The first was virement between the legal limits set by the *Appropriation Act*: 'virement between votes'. The second was virement within an *Appropriation Act's* legal limits, but between the line items contained in an estimate: 'virement within votes'.

Virement between votes most often applied to military expenditure and thereby, the majority of expenditure throughout the eighteenth and nineteenth centuries. By the mid-nineteenth century, it was expressly authorised by appropriation legislation:[52]

> if the Exigencies of the Public assigned to any of the separate Services comprised in the aggregate Sum granted by this Act for [naval, army, or ordnance services], the Department in which such Necessity shall have arisen shall represent the Circumstances which may have led to it in Writing to the [Treasury] and it shall be lawful for such Department, [with the Treasury's written permission], to apply in aid of the deficient Grant, a further limited Sum out of any Surplus ... under other Heads of Service in the Same Department; Provided always, that the aggregate Sum [for naval, army, or ordnance services] shall not be exceeded.

By the enactment of that provision, Parliament authorised breathtaking freedom of financial action. It transformed the separate legislative appropriations for the army, navy and ordnance, into a single undifferentiated

---

[50] Ibid., 197.
[51] Chester (1981), 192.
[52] *Appropriation Act 1846* (9 & 10 Vict, c 116), s 24.

pool of funds for military expenditure.[53] Although military expenditure stood at 28 per cent of total expenditure in 1846, within ten years it rose to 50 per cent and would remain around 35 per cent for most of the nineteenth century. In that sense, virement between votes operated to loosen, with Treasury approval, an *Appropriation Act*'s legal limits for a very significant proportion of total government expenditure.[54]

'Virement within votes' existed in relation to both military and civil expenditure from at least the mid-nineteenth century and never received explicit statutory approval. Instead, it operated as a grey area between the 'great detail' contained in the estimates and the 'only legal limitation on the Treasury ... that it should not exceed the sum stated' in the *Appropriation Act*.[55] Administrative details of virement practice fluctuated throughout the nineteenth century, but it was confidently stated by the Chief Paymaster to the War Office in 1917 that:[56]

> The power of deviation between sub-heads has never been explicitly given by Parliament ... the accepted practice, which has never been seriously disputed is to regard the department as not being bound by the totals of the sub-heads of votes, subject to treasury approval.

In that sense, the Treasury's freedom 'to vire' represented the extent of the legal limits imposed by an *Appropriation Act*.

Civil Contingencies

Appropriation for civil contingencies spending also illustrated the flexibility afforded to the executive by annual expenditure legislation: replacing the dual limitations of quantum and subject matter, with a simple quantitative limit on unusual or unanticipated spending. The practice dates clearly from the opening of the nineteenth century. For example, the *Appropriation Act 1815* authorised spending of £200,000 for 'such Expenses of a Civil Nature as do not form part of the Ordinary Charges of the Civil List'.[57] Over the next five decades, that general slush fund regularised into an express grant for 'contingencies' in the annual *Appropriation Acts*.[58] The civil estimates for

---

[53] Chester (1981), 192–193.
[54] Civil contingency spending (dealt with below) could also be understood as a form of virement between votes, because it permitted spending within an aggregate limit, and with Treasury approval, on any civil department or programme.
[55] Chester (1981), 196.
[56] Durell (1917), 297.
[57] *Appropriation Act 1815* (55 Geo III, c 187); Durell (1917), 77.
[58] Chester (1981), 193.

1833–1834 included an estimate 'that a sum not exceeding [£140,000] be granted to his Majesty for making good the charge for civil contingencies'[59] and the *Appropriation Act 1833* authorised 'any Sum or Sums of Money not exceeding [£140,000], to make good the Sum required to defray the Charge for Civil Contingencies'.[60] That amount represented ~3 per cent of total civil expenditure (£4.7 million) in 1833.[61]

From 1862, *Appropriation Acts* began authorising expenditure 'to defray the Charge which will come in course of Payment during [that financial year], for certain expenses which have heretofore been charged upon the Vote for Civil Contingencies'.[62] That unusual shift in wording reflected the fact that the Treasury had begun maintaining a 'Civil Contingencies Fund', with limited working capital for urgent expenditure during the year.[63] However legally structured, appropriation of contingency expenditure imposed no legal limit on the quantum or subject matter of significant amounts of public expenditure.

Retrospective Appropriation Legislation

Perhaps surprisingly to the contemporary legal mind, annual appropriation legislation operated in a predominately retrospective manner. Because *Supply Acts* were enacted months (sometimes years) before *Appropriation Acts*, money which was subject to the legal limitations in the *Appropriation Act* had often already been spent under the aggregate authority provided by a *Supply Act*. In that important sense, legal limitations on the quantum and subject matter of spending imposed by *Appropriation Acts* operated retrospectively by reference to spending programmes which had already occurred.[64]

The other retrospective feature of appropriation legislation was its authorisation of previous year overspends. Technical jargon described the retrospective authorisation of prior-year overspends as 'excess votes'.[65] From 1866, excess votes appeared in almost every *Appropriation Act*. For example, a *Supply Act* enacted on 29 March 1901 authorised the issue of £5.2 million

---

[59] HC Deb, 7 August 1833, c 427.
[60] *Appropriation Act 1833* (3 & 4 Will IV, c 96) s 17.
[61] *BHS*, chapter XI.
[62] *Appropriation Act 1862* (25 & 26 Vict, c 71), s 25.
[63] Chester (1981), 193.
[64] The latter distinctions between votes 'on account', and 'main' and 'supplementary estimates' did little to undo the retrospective operation of appropriation legislation: Durell (1917), 32–35, 47–53. Votes on account were a stop-gap vote authorising expenditure before the main estimates were presented.
[65] By reference to the language in s 26 of the *Exchequer and Audit Departments Act 1866*.

HISTORY (I): PARLIAMENT AND EXECUTIVE

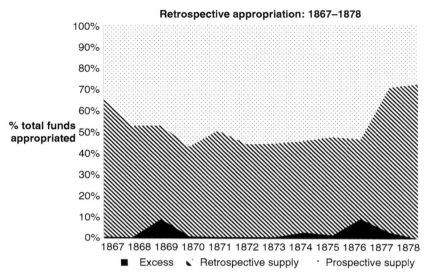

Figure 2.3 Retrospective appropriation (1867–1878)

for the services of two previous fiscal years (1899 and 1900).[66] The *Appropriation Act 1901* appropriated that sum along with the other supplies granted for 1901 and 1902, totalling £86.7 million.[67] The result was that almost 6 per cent of the amount appropriated by the annual *Appropriation Act* had been spent two years before its enactment.

Excess votes were the most significant example of retrospective appropriation legislation because they represented the (known) amount of the executive's spending in violation of the legal limits set by an *Appropriation Act*. As explained below,[68] excess votes only became a systematic part of *Appropriation Acts* from 1866 onwards.

The total extent of retrospective appropriation is only revealed when the retrospective supply granted by *Supply Acts* is added to excesses, and then compared with the portion of supply prospectively appropriated by *Appropriation Acts*.[69] Figure 2.3 visualises that effect for the decade 1867–1878.

There was no particular magic to the decade selected, and the balance between retrospective and prospective appropriation maintained the same general profile throughout the latter nineteenth century.

[66] *Consolidated Fund Act (No 1) 1901* (1 Edw VII, c 1), s 1.
[67] *Appropriation Act 1901* (1 Edw VII, c 21), s 3 and sch A.
[68] See text following footnote 193.
[69] The data for Figure 2.2 was collected from the UK's *Supply* and *Appropriation Acts* 1867–1878.

Standing Appropriation Legislation

Alongside annual appropriation legislation, there grew another kind of legislation authorising public expenditure which was disconnected from the annual process of Treasury estimates and the voting of supply: *standing appropriation legislation*.

The original standing appropriation legislation concerned the expenses of the Monarch and select officials via the civil list. Because the Monarch was responsible for paying the salaries and emoluments of senior government officials, legal authorisation for those costs fell within the civil list grant. A clear example is provided by an *Act of 1760*, which granted a civil list to George III as well as 'the salaries of the Lord Chancellor, the judges and of the Civil Service'.[70] As the professionalised public service grew and separated from the Royal Household in the eighteenth and nineteenth centuries,[71] charges relating to the operation of government were removed from the civil list and transferred to the Consolidated Fund.[72] That type of standing appropriation was institutionally, but not economically, significant. Removing the funding streams for senior official salaries from the annual parliamentary process ensured the institutional independence of those office-holders from other parts of the executive, although the amounts spent were not significant.

A second form of standing appropriation appeared on the statute book as Britain's public debt ballooned throughout the eighteenth century: appropriation for the payment of interest and repayment of principal on public debt. From 1692, legislation authorising sovereign borrowing customarily contained a statutory guarantee of the payment of interest and, if relevant, principal from the proceeds of particular hypothecated taxes. After the creation of the Consolidated Fund in 1787, that central pool of government revenue was subject to a standing appropriation to service the costs of sovereign debt.[73]

Removing the legal basis of sovereign debt servicing from the annual parliamentary process was both economically and institutionally significant. Its economic significance lay in the volume of expenditure it authorised. As already observed, debt servicing expenditure imposed an enormous financial burden throughout the eighteenth and nineteenth centuries. The use of standing appropriation legislation to authorise that

---

[70] *Act of 1760* (11 Geo III, c 1) s 7; Anson (1907), 163–166.
[71] Chester (1981), 182–191.
[72] E.g., *Public Revenues and Consolidated Fund Act 1854* (17 & 18 Vict, c 94).
[73] *Act of 1787* (27 Geo III, c 13), s 53.

expenditure insulated that large portion of financial activity from annual parliamentary scrutiny. The institutional significance of debt servicing standing appropriation lay in its role in providing 'parliamentary security'[74] for public borrowing, thereby promoting the British government's access to long- and short-term debt markets.[75]

Despite its distance from the annual parliamentary process, standing appropriation legislation did not authorise payments in a manner entirely severed from parliamentary approval. Salary payments under standing appropriations were tightly connected to legislative conditions, because they were limited by the statutorily prescribed amount of salary.[76] As will be explained in greater detail later,[77] debt-servicing standing appropriations were also connected to legislative conditions on payment set by *Supply Acts* and other legislation authorising sovereign borrowing, although, by the nineteenth century most meaningful decisions regarding sovereign debt were made by the Treasury, rather than Parliament. Accordingly, the existence of standing appropriations did not necessarily deprive Parliament of involvement in the administration of public expenditure authorisation.

Taxation Legislation

A greater level of parliamentary involvement occurred in relation to taxation legislation, although, again the matter is not entirely straightforward.

The popular hostility to tax throughout the eighteenth and nineteenth centuries built a particular type of legal framework around tax: time-limited statutory tax liability. The critical importance accorded to time-limited taxation was reflected in the terms of Article 4 of the *Bill of Rights*, which declared the exaction of money 'without Grant of Parlyament *for longer time* or in other manner then the same is or shall be granted is Illegall'.[78] Legislative sun-setting of a tax statute served two purposes: to ensure that Parliament met again to impose the tax when it ceased and to limit the imposition of state demands on private capital. A political tract from 1753 captures the mood: 'as a general maxim, ... a revenue for

---

[74] Dickson (1967), *The Financial Revolution in England*, 45.
[75] See text accompanying footnote 97 below.
[76] The salaries of senior public officers last appeared in the *Civil List Act 1837* (1 & 2 Vict, c 2).
[77] See text following footnote 106 below.
[78] Emphasis added.

a certain and short term, was the best security that the nation could have for frequent parliaments'.[79]

Not all taxes were, however, time-limited. Many indirect taxes, such as customs and excises, were 'perpetual',[80] in the sense that they did not cease at a pre-set time. In 1893, 'customs duty upon tea' was the only 'annual' indirect tax, while duties on malt (1822), tobacco (1826), offices and pensions (1836) and sugar (1846) were all made perpetual in the indicated year.[81] The direct taxes, mainly on property, were, however, usually very tightly time-limited and required annual parliamentary approval before being collected. Although lower-yield through the eighteenth century, time-limited taxes increased in economic and political significance throughout the nineteenth century. Annual parliamentary approval was required to raise the land tax,[82] although relatively small receipts would flow into consolidated revenue: 16 per cent of total fiscal receipts in 1800 and only 8 per cent in 1850.[83]

Of more enduring importance was the growth of a time-limited income tax. 'Pitt's' embryonic income tax was imposed from 1797 to 1802.[84] Thereafter, income tax was subject to a significant revision in the *Income Tax Act 1803*: charged 'during the present [Napoleonic] War, and until [6 May] next after the Ratification of a Definitive Treaty of Peace and no longer'.[85] Peace ensued, and the tax ceased. Income tax was next imposed by the *Income Tax Act 1842*, and was 'charged until [6 April 1845] and no longer'.[86] At the sunset date, Parliament enacted an *Act of 1845*, which imposed income tax for three years.[87] An *Act of 1848* continued the tax for the same period, and *Acts of 1851* and *1852* charged the tax for a single year only, while a seven year charge to tax was imposed by an *Act of 1853*.[88] It was not until 1860 that annual charging of income tax became the norm, when an *Act of 1860* provided that income tax 'shall be charged, collected and paid for One Year commencing on [6 April 1860]'.[89] The next

---

[79] Burnet (1753), *Bishop Burnet's History of his Own Time*, 549.
[80] Palgrave and Bonham-Carter (1893), 556.
[81] Ibid.
[82] Brewer (1989), 81.
[83] BHS, 581–582.
[84] Harris (2006), *Income Tax in Common Law Jurisdictions*, chapter 5.
[85] *Income Tax Act 1803* (41 Geo III, c 122), s 231.
[86] *Income Tax Act 1842* (5 & 6 Vict, c 35) s 193.
[87] *Act of 1845* (8 & 9 Vict, c 4).
[88] *Act of 1848* (11 & 12 Vict, c 8); *Act of 1851* (14 & 15 Vict, c 12); *Act of 1852* (15 & 16 Vict, c 20); *Act of 1853* (16 & 17 Vict, c 34).
[89] *Act of 1860* (23 Vict, c 14), s 1.

financial year saw a cognate *Act of 1861*, charging income tax for a single year only and consolidating all annual legislative amendments of direct and indirect taxes:[90] marking the birth of the annual *Finance Act*.

Insofar as tax administration was concerned, the eighteenth and nineteenth centuries saw many innovations, moving from a predominately privatised collection system of 'tax farming' to a professionalised system of public revenue officials.[91] Common to both systems was the absence of Parliament, which never acted as a tax administration body.

Constitutional Significance of Statutory Public Finance

Throughout the eighteenth and nineteenth centuries, the basic legislative principles concerning tax and expenditure became concrete: all lawful public expenditure and economically important taxation had to be authorised by Parliament through statute. Understood at that level of generality, those principles seem to tether the executive's economic freedom of action to Parliament's will expressed through legislation. That was certainly how Dicey understood them, as Chapter 1 explained.

A detailed appraisal of the legislation governing tax and expenditure reveals a more complicated set of practices. Annual appropriation legislation was extremely flexible and predominately retrospective. Standing appropriation legislation permitted the expenditure of vast sums with no annual parliamentary oversight. Taxation legislation was never wholly annual and relied on the executive to interpret and enforce its terms.

Collectively, those features reveal that Parliament retained only limited primary authority over public finance, delegating significant financial authority to the executive through appropriation and taxation legislation.

The only primary authority maintained by annual *Appropriation Acts* was over the very general legislated line items. To the executive (*qua* Treasury) financial authority was delegated to spend within those general limits, as recognised through virement and civil contingencies spending. Parliament also delegated formal legal authority to the executive by permitting the use of aggregate sums in *Supply Acts* which would only later be the subject of retrospective legal limitations in *Appropriation Acts*. Given Parliament's absence from any meaningful role in tax collection, an important limit on the executive's delegated authority was

---

[90] *Act of 1861* (24 Vict, c 20).
[91] Brewer (1989), 76–78; Pearce (2009), 'The Role of Central Government in Determining Liability to Income Tax in England and Wales'.

temporal: authority to collect tax was partially delegated, but only to a particular point in time and only for select taxes. The relevant constitutional conclusion is that the legislation through which Parliament sanctioned the most basic public financial activities (spending and taxing) gave significant authority to the executive government.

Despite that conclusion, Parliament did retain a meaningful share of primary authority, perhaps counter-intuitively, through standing appropriation legislation. Standing appropriations for executive salaries did not signal a delegation of financial authority to the executive, because they secured payment under conditions set by Parliament. As will shortly be explained, Parliament also retained a relatively large degree of primary authority over sovereign debt issues: the creation of a standing appropriation for debt servicing expenditure did not delegate significant financial authority to the executive. Viewed in that way, early standing appropriation legislation represented a strong example of Parliament's primary authority over public expenditure.

The legislative practices of appropriation and taxation are undoubtedly significant, but a blinkered focus on them leaves large blank spaces regarding the development of public finance law. Between the 1690s and the 1860s, other seminal financial institutions grew from the British state's combined commitment to parliamentary government, the fiscal demands of imperial expansion and a desire for economy in public finances. Parliamentary legislation came to underpin all significant public borrowing and the initiative in all financial legislation was gifted to the executive government. Both developments sought to accommodate the military and imperial ambitions of the British state in the eighteenth century. In the mid-nineteenth century, legislation created a streamlined system of public audit to cure the inefficient complexities of the financial system which had developed in the previous century.

Each of those developments resulted in the delegation of vast authority to the executive government *qua* Treasury; scarce financial authority was retained by Parliament.

Statutory National Debt

From the turn of the eighteenth century, it became settled practice to rely on parliamentary legislation to borrow money to fund the British state. Alike statutory taxation and appropriation, that development was driven by the financial demands of Britain's military and imperial expansion.[92] Several milestones of sovereign borrowing law had particularly potent constitutional consequences. From 1692, long- and short-term public borrowings were pushed onto the statute book. Throughout the eighteenth century, the Bank of England was established by statute as a vital financier of the British state. At the turn of the nineteenth century, British sovereign debt and national tax revenue were linked through the standing appropriation for debt service on the Consolidated Fund.

Legislative Borrowing Authority

The late seventeenth century witnessed the establishment by statutory authority of the corpus of debt liabilities which would later be given the title 'the National Debt'.[93] Before that period, debt incurred by English Monarchs did not necessarily have a legislative basis: despite examples of Parliament pledging specific tax revenue as security for borrowings, the Monarchs remained free to obtain large amounts of debt-finance without parliamentary approval.[94]

Public borrowing without parliamentary authorisation did not endure, and the legal authority to issue both long- and short-term public debt would come to have a settled legislative basis. That push onto the statute book occurred for two reasons. The first was a need for revenue which far outstripped fiscal receipts, causing large-scale recourse to debt financing.[95] The second, and critical, reason was the parlous state of the Monarch's personal credit. Charles II's decision to force a discount on his creditors in the debt restructuring episode known as the 'Stop of the Exchequer' in 1672 was 'undoubtedly a severe blow to the English Monarch's financial prestige'.[96] The lesson learned by disappointed financiers was that, 'had loans been "on parliamentary security", instead of being backed only by the Crown's promises, they would not have been repudiated'.[97]

---

[92] Brewer (1989), 130; O'Brien (2005), 'Fiscal and Financial Preconditions for the Rise of British Naval Hegemony 1485–1815'.
[93] Maitland (1908), 438–439.
[94] Ashton (1957), 'Deficit Finance in the Reign of James I' and (1960), *Crown and Money Market*.
[95] Dickson (1967), *The Financial Revolution in England*, 46–47.
[96] Ibid., 43, 44–45. As Dickson explains, the 'stop' was only a 'partial repudiation of part of the Crown's debts', eventually resolved by paying only 'ten shillings in the pound with interest' and 'other sectors of credit [administered by the Exchequer] – loans in anticipation of customs, excise and direct taxes – continued to function smoothly'.
[97] Ibid., 45; Kier (1955), *The Constitutional History of Britain*, 275.

Obtaining parliamentary security required asking Parliament to enact legislation which authorised the issue of debt and linked debt repayments to particular streams of revenue. The ground-breaking example of such a parliamentary secured debt issue occurred by the passage of an *Act of 1692*,[98] which authorised the raising of funds by way of a tontine or annuities:[99]

> A sum of £1 m was to be lent to the government at an interest of 10% until midsummer 1700 and 7% thereafter. That interest was secured on new excise duties settled for ninety-nine years from 25 January 1693 ... The interest was to be paid to each contributor pro rata and tax-free during his own life or the life of ... his nominee ... until only seven nominees were left. It would then abate as each remaining nominee died ... The Act provided that if the £1 m wanted had not been lent on a tontine basis by 1 May 1693, the rest could be taken up by the sale of 14% single-life annuities ... tax-free. A contributor's interest in both the tontine and the life annuities could be assigned to a third party.

From that Act, 'it is usual to date the foundation of a national debt, a debt contracted upon the security of act of parliament'.[100] Taking the commercial structure of tontines and annuities, that debt was long term.

Where short-term debt was concerned, prior to the 1690s England obtained short-term finance from diverse sources, only some of which had parliamentary backing. The main sources of short-term debt (Exchequer 'tallies' and 'bills') were not comprehensively regulated by legislation.[101] The basic design of both forms of short-term debt was to pledge receipts from a particular tax to the holder of a tally or bill. As issues of short-term debt exceeded tax receipts in the 1690s, it was restructured and secured by parliamentary legislation. For tallies,[102] the critical enactment was an *Act of 1697*, which provided a consolidation of various Exchequer receipts into a general pool to satisfy outstanding tallies:[103] the 'First General Mortgage'.[104] For Exchequer bills, the *Land Bank Act 1696* provided 'authority to make out' bills up to '£1,500,000 ...

---

[98] (4 W & M, c 3).
[99] Dickson (1967), 53.
[100] 100 Maitland (1908), 439.
[101] Other forms of very short-term credit (such as that provided by the City of London) were 'authorised by Parliament and charged on specific direct taxes', but were economically marginal: Dickson (1967), 343.
[102] There was some evidence of parliamentary involvement in Exchequer tallies from 1665: *Act of 1665* (7 Ch II, c 1); Ibid., 351.
[103] (8 & 9 Will III, c 20).
[104] (7 & 8 Wm III, c 31) as explained by Dickson (1967), 353–355.

carrying 3d% a day interest (4% p.a.)'.[105] The needs of the War of Spanish Succession quickly exhausted the mandate provided by that Act and later enactments were required, authorising 'new and much larger amounts' including '£5.6 m' for 'supply in 1707, 1709 and 1713'.[106]

Parliament's involvement with the details of public borrowing only intensified throughout the nineteenth century. Discrete legislation continued to be passed authorising specific long- and short-term debt issues, often with very detailed provisions relating to interest rate and maturity. An example of long-term debt to finance the Crimean War appeared in an *Act of 1854*:[107]

> *It shall be lawful for the Commissions of Her Majesty's Treasury to issue Exchequer Bonds, bearing Interest from [8 May 1854] ... at Three Pounds Ten Shillings per Centum per Annum, to be paid off at Par on [8 May 1858].*

In addition to legislation for stand-alone debt issues, sovereign debt was also authorised by annual expenditure legislation. Nineteenth-century *Supply Acts* conferred authority on the Treasury to borrow, and contained detailed provisions regarding interest and maturity:[108]

> *The Commissioners of the Treasury may borrow from time to time on the credit of the said sum of [£6million] any sum ... of equal or less amount ... and shall repay the moneys so borrowed with interest not exceeding [5 per cent pa] out of the growing produce of the Consolidated Fund at any period not later than the next succeeding quarter to that in which the said sums were borrowed.*

Short-term statutory debt was dealt with on that piecemeal basis until the milestone enactment of the *Treasury Bills Act 1877*.[109] That Act applied where 'the Treasury have authority under any Act of Parliament (passed either before or after the passing of this Act) to raise money by the issue of Exchequer bills or of Treasury bills'.[110] Within that confine, the Act conferred standing power on the Treasury to issue and determine the rate of interest on all Treasury Bills, while payment of interest and principal was charged on the Consolidated Fund.[111] The *Treasury Bills Act 1877* also provided

---

[105] Ibid.
[106] Ibid., 373.
[107] (17 Vict, c 23).
[108] E.g., *Consolidated Fund Act 1872* (35 Vict, c 1), s 2.
[109] (40 & 41 Vict, c 2).
[110] Section 3.
[111] Sections 3–5.

a standing authority to re-finance any short-term debt issued within the financial year,[112] and permitted debt issues in any denomination and in any currency.[113]

Despite the prominence afforded the Treasury by most legislation concerning sovereign borrowing, much important debt finance work was done by the Bank of England.

Bank of England

The Bank was itself 'instituted' as part of a major long-term debt financing of the 'war with France':[114] after the tontine *Act of 1692*, establishing the Bank was Parliament's next major financing venture. Its founding *Act of 1694*[115] authorised the Treasury to borrow £1.2 million at 10 per cent per annum secured against various taxes on imports and beverages, with any shortfall falling on 'so much of any Treasure or Revenue' held by the Crown.[116] In exchange for the provision of credit to a government whose financial fortunes were flagging, the subscribers were given stock and significant banking privileges as a corporation.[117] Express power was conferred on the Bank of England to deal in:[118]

> *Bills of Exchange, or in buying or selling Bullion, Gold or Silver, or in selling any Goods, Wares or Merchandize whatsoever, which shall really and bona fide by left or deposited with the said Corporation for Money lent and advanced thereon.*

Combined with a permission to issue assignable bills of exchange,[119] that provision gave the subscribers significant powers to act as financers in London.

A since forgotten feature of the *Bank of England Act 1694* was its regulation of the terms under which the Bank could lend money to the Crown. Section 29 prohibited the Bank from lending money to the Crown without parliamentary permission:

> *if the Governor ... or other Members of the [Bank] ... shall upon the account of the said [Bank] ... advance or lend to their[e] Majesties ... any*

---

[112] Section 6.
[113] Wormell (1999), volume VI, 96–98.
[114] McLeod (1875), *Theory and Practice of Banking*, 415.
[115] (5 & 6 W & M, c 20) initially called the *Tunneage Act*, but later known as the *Bank of England Act*.
[116] Sections 16, 33.
[117] Sections 24–27.
[118] Section 27.
[119] Section 28.

su[m]me or su[m]mes of money by way of Loan ... fonds of the Revenues now granted ... other than ... such fond ... of the said Revenues only on which a credit[t] of Loan is or shall be granted by Parliament that then the said Governor ... or other Members of the said [Bank] ... being thereof lawfully convicted shall for every such offence forfeit[e] treble the value of every such sum[me] ... of money so[e] lent ...

Viewed in its original context, the requirement for parliamentary consent before lending to the executive was an extension of the general constitutional requirement for 'parliamentary security' for public borrowing.

Throughout the eighteenth century, the Bank served as one of the Crown's lenders of last resort; trading cheap credit to the government for the grant of statutory banking privileges.[120] In 1697, the Bank lent £1 million in exchange for: monopoly banking status in London, an extension of its incorporation, tax-exempt status for its stock and exemption from foreign attachment.[121] In 1709, the Bank's stockholders advanced £400,000 at 6 per cent to the Crown and permission to double their capital stock, in exchange for a 4 per cent haircut on the interest of their original stock.[122] In 1713, the Bank advanced the Crown £100,000 secured on 3 per cent Exchequer Bills in exchange for an extension of its Charter to 1742.[123] In 1716, the Bank forgave around £256,000 of Crown debt in exchange for exemption from usury laws and the indefinite prolongation of its existence as a corporation.[124] In 1742, 20 years after absorbing some of the ruined loan portfolio of the South Seas Company in 1720,[125] the Bank lent £1.6 million interest free to the Crown in exchange for a monopoly on bank notes payable on demand or within six months of issue.[126] In 1746, the Bank traded a cancellation of £986,000 Exchequer Bills in exchange for a 4 per cent annuity.[127] In 1746, the Bank swapped an 'absolute gift of £100,000 to the nation, and a loan of £1 million on Exchequer bills for two years at 3% interest' for a renewal of its charter for around twenty years.[128] A subsequent charter renewal in 1781 was exchanged for an advance to the Crown of £2 million at 3 per cent for three years.[129]

---

[120] McLeod (1875), 406-446.
[121] *Act of 1697* (8 & 9 Will III, c 20).
[122] *Act of 1709* (8 Ann, c 1).
[123] *Act of 1713* (12 Ann, c11).
[124] *Act of 1716* (3 Geo I, c 8).
[125] Detailed in McLeod (1875), 424-428.
[126] *Act of 1742* (16 Geo II, c 13).
[127] McLeod (1875), 431.
[128] Ibid., 433.
[129] Ibid., 434.

A milestone was reached in 1793, when (under Pitt's direction) legislation was passed which released the Bank from the statutory prohibition on advancing money to the Crown without parliamentary approval.[130] Thereafter followed a period of high-volume (and essentially forced) lending by the Bank to the Crown, the diminution of the Bank's gold reserves and a currency crisis in England.[131] By 1819, the statutory restriction on the Bank lending to government without parliamentary approval was restored,[132] but customarily displaced by annual finance legislation which permitted the Bank to absorb and re-sell a proportion of short-term Treasury debt to be issued under *Supply* and *Appropriation Acts*.[133] In that way, the Bank's financing activities were linked to annual parliamentary processes.

Greater latitude was eventually given to the Bank to provide short-term finance to the Treasury. The *Audit Act 1866* and the *Treasury Bills Act 1877* gave the Bank standing authority to finance cash deficits. The latter Act cemented the Bank's position as the agent for short-term public stock, requiring that Treasury Bills 'shall be issued by the Bank of England', granting the Bank an 'allowance' for 'the management of Treasury bills' and providing standing authority for the Bank to 'lend to Her Majesty, upon the credit of Treasury bills, any sum or sums not exceeding in the whole the principal sums named in such bills'.[134]

The *Treasury Bills Act* illustrated the Bank's preeminent status as the intermediary between the Treasury and the sovereign debt market: authorising the Bank to be the chief agent for the Treasury's debt issues by the mid-nineteenth century. Parliament actively facilitated that position by enacting legislation which authorised the Bank to 'take, accept and receive' debt instruments issued by the Treasury and 'to advance or lend to Her Majesty' up to a certain credit limit.[135]

---

[130] *Act of 1793* (33 Geo III, c 32).
[131] McLeod (1875), 446.
[132] *Bank of England Act 1819* (59 Geo III, c 76), s 1.
[133] E.g., *Exchequer Bills Act 1838* (11 Vict, c 12) s 7; *Consolidated Fund Act 1848* (11 Vict, c 3).
[134] Section 8, 11, 13. Section 12 of the *Exchequer and Audit Departments Act 1866* (29 & 30 Vict, c 39) gave standing authority for the Bank of England (and Ireland) to make advances on application by the Treasury to fill shortfalls between the revenue and charges on the Consolidated Fund.
[135] *Consolidated Fund Act 1838* (11 Vict, c 21) s 5. Words to a similar effect can be found throughout the nineteenth-century statute books.

An enduring feature of that statutory practice was the growth of the Bank's 'Ways and Means Advances' to Treasury. Those advances were described by a nineteenth-century internal Bank memorandum as being a power:[136]

> given to the Treasury ... to borrow temporarily ... by statute ... [i]n order to prevent a stoppage of the public services, which may arise by reason of insufficiency of revenue or other distributing emergency.

Ways and Means Advances were not interest free, but were repayable 'without notice, whenever the state of the Exchequer balance admits of an issue'.[137] Ways and Means Advances were not insignificant during the late nineteenth century; they increased exponentially during the World Wars and would later occupy a critical monetary financing role in the first major financial crisis of the twenty-first century, discussed in Chapter 7.

Linking Taxation and Sovereign Debt Liability

A curious set of events led to the charging of all debt servicing expenditure on Britain's collected tax revenue via the Consolidated Fund. Although that charge had profound ramifications for Britain's sovereign debt profile, it appears to have stemmed from discontent, with a poorly managed system of public accounts, rather than a desire to bolster the efficiency of Britain's debt management.

From the early eighteenth century, sovereign borrowing legislation linked the repayment of debt to receipts from particular streams of tax revenue,[138] creating an elaborate system of 'hypothecated [secured] taxes', wherein holders of public debt had an interest in 'this or that mode of taxation'.[139] That system had the benefit of confining the creditor's rights against the British government to a limited stream of revenue but concurrently damaged the health of Britain's financial administration, particularly in the opportunities for graft and waste which arose from the tangle of different public accounts marking each tax receipt to each debt repayment. So much was explained by the voluminous *13th Report of the Commissioners appointed to Examine,*

---

[136] Wormell (1999), volume VI, 118.
[137] Ibid., 120.
[138] As in the tontine *Act of 1692* (4 W & M, c 3) and the *Bank of England Act 1694* (5 & 6 W & M, c 20).
[139] Maitland (1908), 441; Redlich and Ilbert (1903), *The Procedure of the House of Commons*, 163–164.

Take, and State the Public Accounts of the Kingdom, published in 1785.[140]

Earlier attempts had been made to consolidate fiscal receipts into a single fund in order to provide a consolidated source from which to pay down the national debt. In 1714 and 1716, various funds were created with the intention of pooling tax receipts to retire the national debt.[141] Those experiments failed, as successive governments raided the funds such that they were 'no longer a means of debt reduction but an instrument in the management of the very funds [they] had been established to abolish'.[142]

The solution proposed in the *Audit Report of 1785* was simple: bring the overwhelming majority of tax receipts into a single fund and secure all public debt against that fund. The consolidation would ensure that the 'one great Fund of Revenue, composed of the Annual Income of the State will be the ample Security to every Public Creditor for the Payment of his Annuity; and the collateral Security to that Fund, the Property of the Nation'.[143] An *Act of 1787* met that report's ambition, establishing the 'Consolidated Fund' as the source of all major past and present tax receipts, and then charging those pooled funds with all major past and future debt liabilities.[144]

The charging of debt issues on the Consolidated Fund provided a legal basis (additional to the requirement for legislative authorisation of public borrowing) for the 'parliamentary security' enjoyed by public-creditors: the creation of the Consolidated Fund had the effect of linking Britain's aggregate tax revenue to its aggregate debt liability.

By the mid-nineteenth century, that link between the UK's national debt liability and national tax revenue was complete, as the repayment of both long- and short-term debt was customarily charged on the Consolidated Fund.[145]

---

[140] *Audit Report of 1785*, 55.
[141] See, e.g., *Act of 1714* (1 Geo I, c 12) (aggregate fund'); *Act of 1717* (3 Geo I, c 9) ('sinking fund'); Dowell (1884), volume 2, 458.
[142] Brewer (1989), 99.
[143] *Audit Report of 1785*, 64.
[144] (27 Geo III, c 13), ss 52–53.
[145] E.g., *Act of 1854* (17 Vict, c 23), s 4 (concerning a discrete issue of long-term debt) and *Consolidated Fund Act 1872* (35 Vict, c 11), s 3 (concerning short-term debt authorised by annual appropriation legislation).

Constitutional Dimension of Sovereign Debt

As matters stood by the end of the nineteenth century, Parliament had delegated only some of its financial authority over sovereign borrowing to the executive government.

The detailed legislative treatment of the commercial structure of long-term debt issues left a relatively large measure of primary authority with Parliament, as did the maintenance of a link between annual parliamentary processes and authority to acquire short-term debt. Similarly, Parliament maintained high levels of legal authority over the Bank of England's public borrowing powers, by requiring advance statutory consent before finance could be extended to the Crown. However, significant authority was given to the Treasury to determine the commercial structure of short-term debt, and standing authority was eventually given to the Bank of England to finance cash deficits.

In that sense, debt finance authority was shared between Parliament and the executive government. A far less cooperative arrangement existed in relation to the 'financial initiative', which Parliament entirely delegated to the executive.

Executive Financial Initiative

From the eighteenth century's outset, the executive was allocated the exclusive power to formulate, originate and amend most public financial legislation: the financial initiative. Thereafter, the Treasury would obtain practical responsibility for the preparation of the 'Budget' and legal responsibility for the oversight of financial activity by the rest of the executive: treasury control. Those developments had a heavy impact on Parliament's capacity to govern public finances. Parliament's prerogatives to authorise financial activity through legislation remained formally intact, but were stripped of much practical substance as the political value of parliamentary self-government was traded off against the need for efficient and effective public finances.

Rule by Financial Assembly

It was clear from the conclusion of the seventeenth century that all economically effective taxation and public expenditure would require parliamentary legislation. Still unsettled, however, was whether that constitutional practice necessitated a form of *financial rule by assembly*.

Precisely how unsettled was revealed in an episode of the 1705–1706 parliamentary session which saw the presentation of petitions to the Commons for specific grants 'either claiming an arrear of pay as officers, or making some other demand upon the public'.[146] Those petitions mainly concerned claims for funds for military expenses:[147]

> promoted by Members who were friends to the parties, and carrying with them the appearance of justice or of charity, induced the rest of the House to wish well to, or at most to be indifferent to their success; and by this means large sums were granted to private persons improvidently, and sometimes without sufficient grounds.

The Commons responded to that opportunism by resolving that:

> this House will receive no Petitions for any Sum of Money, relating to publick Service, but what is recommended from the Crown.[148]

A mere resolution (without effect beyond a single session) did not stymie the practice of petitioning Parliament for funds, which gradually resumed. The final straw settled in 1713, when the 1706 resolution was enacted as a standing order, the substance of which endured.[149] On that account, the financial initiative was given to the executive in order to prevent pork-barrelling.

Brewer explains that allocating the legislative initiative to the 'Treasury front bench' was part of a broader move to allocate public financial responsibility to the growing executive: 'if, under William, government fiscal policy was constantly thwarted, after 1702 it was almost never checked by parliamentary opposition'.[150] The parliamentary practices which grew thereafter 'gave the Treasury a monopoly over fiscal legislation',[151] which has been identified as the primary constitutional element supporting the Treasury's 'preeminence' in the 'national financial arrangements'.[152] The resulting constitutional position prevented the introduction of any financial legislation without Crown permission.

---

[146] Hatsell (1818), *Precedents of Proceedings of the House of Commons*, 241–242.
[147] As disclosed in the Commons Journal, funding was sought for: 'Army debentures' (21/11/1705 at 33), 'Irish army arrears' (22/11/1705 at 33), clothing for a 'Marine regiment' (26/11/1705 at 39), 'Irish arrears' (7/12/1705 at 56), (16/1/1706 at 90), 'Army arrears' (18/12/1705 at 69), (14/1/1706 at 86), (22/1/1706 at 103), (24/1/1706 at 107), 'Army debts' (15/1/1706 at 88), (17/1/1706 at 91), 'Debentures on Irish forfeitures' (23/1/1706 at 106).
[148] Hatsell (1818), 241.
[149] Ibid., 242.
[150] Brewer (1989), 121.
[151] Thomas (1971) 69, 72.
[152] Chester (1981), 205.

At the level of parliamentary procedure, a labyrinthine maze of standing orders and parliamentary custom immunised the Treasury's expenditure (Supply) and taxation (Ways and Means) proposals from scrutiny and amendment by the greater body of parliamentarians. Standing orders required that 'no amendment' could 'be proposed' to (nor 'a condition or an expression of opinion to a grant' or alteration of the 'destination' of) an estimate without withdrawing 'the original estimate' or presenting 'a revised estimate'.[153] A proposed reduction to an estimate would only be permitted if 'of a substantial and not of a trifling amount'.[154]

Those standing orders, coupled with the parliamentary sequence of annual finance legislation (first a *Supply Act*, then an *Appropriation Act*) reduced, almost to nothing, the opportunity to amend financial legislation. Because the *Appropriation Act* was passed after aggregate sums of 'supply' had already been legislatively granted by *Supply Acts*, amendments to change the quantum or subject matter were ruled irrelevant and out of order.[155]

Taxation bills stood in a slightly different position. Unlike the strict prohibition on legislative alteration of supply and appropriation legislation, the Commons could vote to reduce or refuse tax measures in Ways and Means and procedural protections abounded for the right of parliamentarians to 'propose ... to reduce a burthen upon the people'.[156] Originating and increasing a tax remained, however, the exclusive purview of the executive: '[n]o augmentation of a tax or duty asked by the Crown ... can be proposed to [Ways and Means], nor tax imposed, save upon the motion of a minister of the Crown'.[157]

The total impact of those parliamentary procedures was profound. Control over the content and presentation of the estimates and the power over the origination of expenditure, tax and borrowing legislation lay exclusively with the Treasury. The constitutional effect was explained in 1893 by the Clerk of the Commons:[158]

> *The constitutional principle which vests in the Crown the sole responsibility over national expenditure, and which forbids the Commons to increase the*

---

[153] Ibid., 580.
[154] Ibid., 583.
[155] Ibid., 562.
[156] Palgrave and Bonham-Carter (1893), 567.
[157] Ibid., 589.
[158] Ibid., 580.

> sums demanded by the Crown for the service of the state is strictly enforced in the committees of supply and ways and means.

Nothing about that allocation of power to the executive government was qualified by the growth of the annual 'Budget'.

A considered study of the Commons in the eighteenth century observes that only conjecture supports the identification of an annual Budget prior to the 1750s.[159] While the precise parliamentary outworkings of the Budget evolved considerably throughout the eighteenth century, by the 1770s it had consolidated into a presentation by the Chancellor of the Exchequer to Ways and Means of 'the state of finances during the session, the ways and means he proposes of raising the supply, the certain and probable expenses of the year, the new taxes, and in general the revenue and sources of the empire'.[160]

Despite its political grandeur, the Budget did not necessarily indicate the commencement of legislation giving effect to the government's financial proposals. 'Many of the taxes would already have been voted by delivery of the budget speech' and the government's expenses had already 'been voted in the Committee of Supply'.[161] In that sense, the annual Budget was more about political programmes, than financial authorisation.

The prominence accorded to the executive *qua* Chancellor of the Exchequer in the Budget process did, however, illustrate the Treasury's unchallenged authority over the broader executive's use of public money.

Treasury Control

As the eighteenth century progressed, the Treasury's authority over the formulation of financial proposals would be fused with a monopoly on legal authority to control the broader executive's use of public money. That monopoly would later be labelled 'Treasury control',[162] which had two aspects: legal and economic control over the central government departments.[163] Treasury's *legal control* involved ensuring spending occurred within the legal limits set by an *Appropriation Act*. Its *economic control* required the exercise of economic judgment to ensure the most efficient spending options were pursued by the broader executive.

---

[159] Thomas (1971), 78–79.
[160] Ibid., 79.
[161] Ibid.
[162] Roseveare (1969), *The Treasury*; (1973) *The Treasury 1660–1870*.
[163] Chester (1981), 204–205.

Although existing de facto from the beginning of the eighteenth century,[164] from the 1770s, Treasury's control received statutory backing.[165] The early legal framework was provided by three Acts passed between 1783 and 1785; it gave the Treasury power to fix salaries of senior officers of the civil government, provide compensation for the former holders of abolished venal-offices and control the recently created audit officers.[166] So significant was the extent of parliamentary support for the Treasury's control functions, that the 'Treasury was the first department to cease to exist purely or largely on prerogative powers'.[167]

Treasury's legal control made it the predominant authority to ensure that the wider executive complied with appropriation legislation, while its economic control gave it authority over the administration of executive departments, extending to 'establishment, pay and conditions' of the civil departments. The same degree of control was not enjoyed over military departments, although military estimates were required to be submitted to Treasury before being presented to Supply, and Treasury approval was required before the War Office could vire between votes.[168]

That concentration of legal and economic control in the Treasury conferred on it a special position within the executive. By 1810, senior Treasury officials explained the Treasury's position as discrete from the wider executive: 'a superintending and directing, not an executive department'.[169] By 1855, it was confidently stated that the Treasury was:[170]

> the chief office of the Government ... two-thirds of the Civil Establishment are directly subordinate to it, and the expenditure of the remaining third is under its superintendence. No estimate can be laid before Parliament, no new appointment can be created, and no alteration can be made in any Civil or Military allowances, without its sanction. The whole Public Service is, therefore, either directly or indirectly subjected to the influence of this Office.

The only serious constraint on the Treasury's economic control was the high-level policy decisions of Cabinet, which the Treasury was (by ministerial hierarchy) bound to follow,[171] but the position of the

---

[164] Brewer (1989), 76.
[165] Chester (1981), 193–207.
[166] *Act of 1782* (23 Geo III, c 82); *Act of 1783* (23 Geo III, c 82); *Act of 1785* (25 Geo III, c 52).
[167] Chester (1981), 199.
[168] Ibid., 206.
[169] Ibid., 204 (quoting Assistant Secretary to HM Treasury, George Harrison).
[170] Ibid., 208 (quoting Assistant Secretary to HM Treasury, Charles Trevelyan).
[171] Ibid., 208.

Chancellor of the Exchequer in Cabinet reduced the likelihood of conflict between Treasury and Cabinet.

Constitutional Impact of the Executive's Financial Initiative

Conferring the financial initiative on the executive and the growth of treasury control had a profound impact on the distribution of constitutional authority. By allocating the financial initiative to the executive, Parliament abnegated its authority to formulate financial proposals and to originate appropriation, taxation and borrowing legislation. No less momentous ramifications flowed from the statutory conferral of treasury control, whereby Parliament delegated to Treasury supervisory authority over the receipt and outlay of public funds by the broader executive government. By the exercise of that authority, Treasury assumed absolute superintendence over the broader executive's use of money.

Once it is appreciated that the Treasury was the executive institution with authority to exercise the financial initiative and superintend the broader executive's use of money, it emerges as a distinct entity within the executive: formulating the economic content of Parliament's financial legislation and directing the wider executive's use of public money. As Chapter 4 records, the diffusion of UK styles of thinking about public finance throughout the British Empire embedded treasuries at the financial apex of parliamentary constitutional systems beyond the North Atlantic.

The parliamentary rules concerning the financial initiative also provided the formal basis upon which a vote on supply could become a de facto confidence motion in the government. Because a supply vote could only be originated with the executive government's consent, a rejection of supply in the Commons had the effect of depriving a government of all legitimate financial resources: once a supply vote had been rejected, a government could neither choose the basis upon which to finance its activities, nor could any other parliamentary coalition impose a budget on the government. The only constitutionally proper option would be to form a government which could exercise the financial initiative in a way which would garner the approval of a majority in the Commons.

Systematic Public Audit

The final significant aspect to the model of parliamentary public finance was an institution with systematic responsibility for public accounts and audit. That institution's development breaks into two timeframes: before and after 1866.

Before 1866

From 1700 to 1866, the legislative patchwork of enactments concerning expenditure provided no system of audit which was independent of the Treasury. That patchwork was widely blamed for waste and graft in public finances.

Addressing those concerns, Parliament appointed Commissioners of Audit in the 1780s, whose statutory mandate charged them with recommending a 'System of strict Economy in the Administration of the Public Revenue'.[172] The Commissioners' activities uncovered extreme maladministration of the public accounts. For example, they 'discovered that the Pay Offices of the Navy and Army had been £75 million in arrears for more than twenty-four years'[173] and that in 1780 'the expenses of Exchequer operations met from public funds was £8,000, but the fees and poundage collected from government departments and the public amounted to more than £82,000. This left £74,000 to be shared out amongst the aristocratic sinecurists.'[174]

In addition to recommending the establishment of the Consolidated Fund,[175] the Commissioners also recommended audit reforms designed to create an institutional buffer between the Treasury and Parliament. The Board of Audit was created in 1785, significantly expanded in 1806 and eventually assumed control over all audit functions in 1835. By 1856, it was combined with the Exchequer to create a 'fused comptrolling and auditing body',[176] but its chief weakness remained its practical 'domination' by the Treasury.[177] Its institutional position was so weak that it could not report to Parliament, without first obtaining the Treasury's permission.[178]

A large gap was left between the hope for, and reality of, efficient public finances. Gladstone drove the *Audit Act 1866* through that breach.

After 1866

Gladstone's role in systematising British financial administration has been given deep scholarly attention,[179] and a recent review of the field concluded that he 'set a standard in government finance that

---

[172] Dewar and Funnell (2016), 61.
[173] Ibid., 62.
[174] Ibid., 65.
[175] See text preceding footnote 143 above.
[176] Ibid., 100.
[177] Ibid., 70.
[178] Ibid., 68–72.
[179] The sources are collected in Campbell (2004), 'Sound Finance', 14–19.

overshadowed all contemporary and subsequent Chancellors of the Exchequer'.[180] That standard was set by reference to an 'ideology' of 'sound finance', which imposed the 'simple but strict' stipulates of 'balanced budgets, imposition of taxation to make up a deficit, reduction of existing debt, accurate and transparent annual budget statements, and responsible Parliamentary control of expenditure'.[181] Gladstone's commitment to sound finance was so totalizing that the resulting institutions have been described as a 'fiscal constitution'.[182]

Gladstone's fiscal constitution was not guided by perfecting representative democracy, but optimising financial efficiency. His reform project:[183]

> was not primarily motivated by abstract or constitutional concepts about accountability to Parliament. Rather, the driving force... was his obsession with economy in public spending. He saw better information on departmental spending and an effective audit, preferably under Treasury direction, as key factors in controlling expenditure and eliminating extravagance and waste.

Political and economic conditions made that project attractive, 'particularly the increase in public expenditure on the Crimean War in the 1850s, as public expenditure grew by 58 per cent in absolute terms: making demands for financial restraint in government even more popular'.[184]

The *Audit Act 1866* was Gladstone's legislative centrepiece and the 'pinnacle of nineteenth-century developments in public financial accountability and audit'.[185]

It had three critical features.

The first was the creation of the office of 'Comptroller and Auditor-General': an officer appointed by the Crown, prevented from holding any other Crown office and dismissible only on address of Commons and Lords, with a salary paid from the Consolidated Fund.[186] Thereby, the Comptroller and Auditor-General enjoyed a degree of institutional separation from the Treasury and the rest of the executive. The *Audit Act 1866* did not, however, completely insulate the Comptroller and Auditor-General from the Treasury. Prominently, the Treasury retained

---

[180] Ibid., 9.
[181] Ibid.
[182] Daunton (2007), *Trusting Leviathan*, 104.
[183] Dewar and Funnell (2016), 97.
[184] Ibid.
[185] Ibid., 80.
[186] Sections 3 and 4.

the power to staff the 'Department of the Comptroller and Auditor-General' and to veto 'orders and rules for the conduct of internal business' within that Department.[187]

The second critical feature was the conferral of 'comptroller' functions on the Comptroller and Auditor-General, which were tethered to the Treasury's economic control. Comptroller functions involved scrutinising Treasury requests for money under both annual ('supply') and 'standing' appropriation legislation.[188] Essentially, the Comptroller and Auditor-General checked whether Treasury's requests were in conformity with legal limits set by appropriation legislation, leaving the Treasury's authority to vire and its economic control of the broader executive untouched.

The third critical feature concerned the Comptroller and Auditor-General's audit functions, which involved examining whether expenditure had occurred in accordance with the legal limits of annual and standing appropriation legislation. Accounts of standing appropriations were prepared by Treasury, examined by the Comptroller and Auditor-General and reported to Parliament.[189] More detailed provision was made for preparation and audit of the 'appropriation accounts . . . of the several supply grants contained in the Appropriation Act of each year'.[190] The Comptroller and Auditor-General was to examine those annual appropriation accounts and report to Parliament on any legally unauthorised expenditure.

In common with its treatment of comptroller functions, the *Audit Act 1866* left the Treasury wide authority in relation to the Comptroller and Auditor-General's audit functions. It imposed no freestanding obligation on executive departments to prepare 'appropriation accounts', rather the Treasury was given power to determine 'by what departments such accounts shall be prepared and rendered to the [Comptroller and Auditor-General]'.[191] The *Audit Act 1866* also left 'plan of account books and accounts . . . under the superintendence of the Treasury'.[192] The method of 'examination' by

---

[187] Sections 8 and 9. The audit functions of the CAG were interlinked with the 'Public Accounts Committee', first appointed on Gladestone's urging in 1861: Dewar and Funnell (2016), 104.

[188] Sections 13 and 14.

[189] Section 21, which was only repealed in 1968 by the *National Loans Act 1968* (UK), c 13, s 24.

[190] Section 22 which was eventually repealed by the *Government Resources and Accounts Act 2000* (UK), c 20, s 29.

[191] Section 22.

[192] Section 23. The modern position of departmental Accounting Officers arose from the deceptively simple provision in s 22 of the 1866 Act that the duty placed on departments to prepare and submit appropriation accounts 'shall be construed as including any public

the Comptroller and Auditor-General expressly permitted the Treasury retrospectively to vire if the Comptroller and Auditor-General discovered expenditure had been made without 'the authority of the Treasury'.[193]

The audit provisions of the *Audit Act 1866* had a profound impact on financial administration of annual *Appropriation Acts*, particularly excess votes. Section 26 provided:

> Every appropriation account when rendered to the [Comptroller and Auditor-General] ... shall ... contain an explanatory statement of any excess of expenditure over the grant or grants included in such account.

The effectiveness of s 26 is illustrated in the subsequent reckoning of excess expenditure. Retrospective appropriation of excesses in 1869 stood at +10 per cent of total annual appropriations and the estimates for 1870 include excesses going back to 1864.[194]

The *Audit Act 1866* also affected matters beyond accounting and audit, most prominently in the standing statutory authority it provided for the Bank of England to advance money to the Treasury to fund cash shortfalls. Standing authority was conferred on the Bank of England to advance short-term finance to the Consolidated Fund, upon a request of the Comptroller and Auditor-General and Treasury 'to an amount not exceeding in the aggregate of' any 'deficiency in the income of the Consolidated Fund'.[195] That provision wrapped up the Comptroller and Auditor-General in the process of parliamentary approval of sovereign borrowing (to fund cash-deficits) for the purposes of the legislative regulation of the Bank's lending to the Crown.[196]

Quasi-independent Audit Authority

The creation of the Comptroller and Auditor-General and appropriation accounts and the establishment of a systematic process of financial scrutiny imposed meaningful limitations on the Treasury's financial authority. The effectiveness of those limitations can be seen in the regular appearance of excess votes from 1866: revealing the difficulty of concealing financial maladministration or profligacy within spending departments or the Treasury.

---

officer or officers to whom that duty may be assigned by the Treasury': Dewar and Funnell (2016), 113.
[193] Section 27.
[194] Commons Journal, 14 March 1870 cc 1954–1958.
[195] Section 12.
[196] Wormell (1999), volume VI, 121. It was repealed (without comment) by the *Finance Act 1954* (2 & 3 Eliz II, c 44).

Other aspects of the *Audit Act 1866*, however, did little to fill existing deficits in Parliament's financial authority. Importantly, the *Audit Act 1866* did not abolish the Treasury's legal control over the form of accounts used by departments or its economic control over departmental spending. Additionally, the cash-deficit borrowing authority in the *Audit Act 1866* delegated short-term debt financing authority to the Treasury. Critically, it maintained the Treasury as the superintendent of government accounts; reinforcing its position of financial dominance within the broader executive.

Perhaps most importantly, the prominence accorded to the Comptroller and Auditor-General and Treasury left no obvious role for the judiciary in enforcing the legal limitation on the executive's financial behaviour. The next chapter provides an account of the judiciary's absence from most aspects of the public financial system.

The Balance of Financial Authority

The major conclusion of this chapter's analysis of the historical development of public financial institutions of the UK's central government is to identify the manner in which legal institutions developed to distribute authority over public finance between Parliament and executive government. Although Parliament had ultimate responsibility for the legal authorisation of taxation and public expenditure its financial powers were heavily qualified by its gift of the financial initiative to the executive government *qua* Treasury.

The Treasury exercised all significant financial planning authority, leaving Parliament to rubber-stamp expenditure legislation and impotent to create tax laws. The annual appropriation process permitted extraordinary levels of flexibility in the use of public funds, including permitting the Treasury to adjust the subject matter and quantum limitations contained in estimates approved by the Commons. *Supply* and *Appropriation Acts* authorised most public expenditure retrospectively and all appropriation legislation required the Treasury's permission before being enacted.

Expenditure of economically significant sums of public money was authorised outside the annual parliamentary process through standing appropriations for debt-servicing expenditure. Because Parliament gave the Treasury power to determine the commercial structure of short- and long-term debt securities, the ultimate amounts paid in servicing that debt were never subject to parliamentary consideration or approval. Only a small portion of tax was imposed annually, with most significant tax receipts being authorised through 'perpetual' legislation.

Parliament also delegated vast supervisory powers to the Treasury, which operated as a financial executive, standing apart from the wider executive where financial management was concerned. Legislation appointed the Treasury as the sole institution with effective authority to supervise the wider executive's compliance with expenditure legislation, and to impose its understanding of economic efficiency on the use of money granted by Parliament. Parliament's independent auditing institution, the Comptroller and Auditor-General, was subordinate to the Treasury in important respects. Even after the *Audit Act 1866*, the Comptroller and Auditor-General's functions were legally and practically dependant on the Treasury's legal and economic control over the wider executive's accounts and use of resources. Thereby, the Treasury had significant legal authority to direct the Comptroller and Auditor-General in its administrative and audit functions.

Understood in that way, the development of British government created a legal model of public finance which conferred the predominant share of authority to the executive government, rather than the Parliament. Armed with that conclusion, it now falls to consider the impact of the judiciary on the distribution of financial authority.

3

History (II): Judiciary

Throughout the eighteenth and nineteenth centuries, the judiciary engaged with various aspects of Britain's public finances, but left large aspects of the government's financial activities uncontrolled by judges.

Tax litigation represented the high point of judicial involvement, but the judges' hostility to fiscal legislation did little to bolster Parliament's revenue-raising interests. Mid-nineteenth-century explorations with judicial review of appropriation legislation failed to develop into a settled practice of judicial review of public expenditure and no discernible judicial practices developed regarding the legal limits of public borrowing (by the Treasury) or lending (by the Bank of England). By the conclusion of the nineteenth century, it was clear that the common law judiciary would not have a prominent role in the model of parliamentary public finance which was exported throughout the common law world.

Exchequer Litigation

The growth of statutory taxation, explored in Chapter 2, did little to change the judiciary's established role as the constitutional guardian of claims to the legality of taxation. From the nineteenth century, the judiciary pursued a general pro-taxpayer policy, which fitted the prevailing constitutional thought regarding the protection of property rights and presented significant obstacles to the effectiveness of statutory taxation.

Continuity in Judicial Review of Tax

The position of the common law judiciary as superintendents of the legality of Crown demands for revenue was not materially affected by the settling of constitutional practices concerning statutory taxation through the eighteenth century.

Long before the Civil War, the Exchequer, in its judicial mode,[1] had exercised jurisdiction in cases between Crown and subject concerning the legality of public revenue. A 'court of crown revenue',[2] the Exchequer was established 'principally to order the revenues of the Crown, and to recover the King's debts and duties'.[3] Those duties required the Exchequer to decide 'what thing belongs to the King, which brings revenue to him, and what not, and what is the law touching the same'.[4] Prior to the seventeenth century, those answers did not predominately concern parliamentary enactments, but claims regarding the scope of common law and custom. As the legal basis of taxation was pushed onto the statute book, there 'arose the immense fabric of the present code of revenue statute law' and a concomitant downgrading of the relative importance of questions concerning the Monarch's prerogative and hereditary legal entitlements.[5] However, '[t]he writs and processes which had been framed for the getting in of the old revenue were applied, with certain necessary alterations, to the recovery of the new'.[6]

Thereby, the adjudicative processes and culture developed by the common law judiciary before the Civil War were applied in the world of statutory taxation which rose to dominate public fiscal demands.

'The Principle of all Fiscal Legislation'

As the role of the judiciary in resolving disputes between state and subject regarding taxation travelled into the realm of statutory taxation it developed a taxpayer- (or private-property-)protecting approach to the interpretation of tax legislation.

The principle underlying that approach was neatly expressed in *Partington* v. *Attorney General*,[7] a 1869 case concerning the narrow question whether probate duty was payable on an estate which was creatively structured across England and the USA. Although finding in

---

[1] '[T]he Revenue Side of the Exchequer', described as distinct from the 'Plea Side of the Exchequer' as 'a general Court of Common Law for the adjudication of Civil Pleas': Price (1830), *A Treatise on the Law of the Exchequer*, 50, 51.
[2] Subtitle of Price (1830).
[3] Ibid., 2, quoting Blackstone.
[4] Ibid., 3, quoting Plowden quoting *The Case of Mines* (1568) 1 Plowden 310 [75 ER 472].
[5] Ibid., 26.
[6] Ibid., 29.
[7] (1869–1870) LR 4 (HL) 100.

favour of the revenue, Lord Cairns isolated the core taxpayer-protecting principle:[8]

> As I understand the principle of all fiscal legislation it is this: If the person sought to be taxed comes within the letter of the law he must be taxed, however great the hardship may appear to the judicial mind to be. On the other hand, if the Crown, seeking to recover the tax, cannot bring the subject within the letter of the law, the subject is free, however apparently within the spirit of the law the case might otherwise appear to be.

That principle translated into a rule that taxation statutes must be interpreted in a 'strict' manner.[9]

An 1875 text on statutory interpretation illustrated the link between that rule of 'strictness' and the judiciary's taxpayer-protecting approach to tax legislation:[10]

> The subject is not to be taxed unless the language by which the tax is imposed is perfectly clear and free from doubt. In a case of doubt the construction most beneficial to the subject is to be adopted.

That same text exposes a viable alternative approach to the interpretation of tax statutes, orientated towards protecting parliamentary claims to revenue:[11]

> [i]n America ... revenue laws are not ... construed with great strictness in favour of the defendant. They are regarded rather in their remedial character; as intended to prevent fraud, suppress public wrong; and promote the public good; and are so construed as to most effectually accomplish those objects.

That attitude never migrated across the Atlantic, and by the nineteenth century's conclusion, the taxpayer-protecting approach of the common law judiciary became ever more potent.

Its acme was reached in an early twentieth-century case:[12]

> Every man is entitled if he can to order his affairs so as that the tax attaching under the appropriate Acts is less than it otherwise would be. If he succeeds in ordering them so as to secure this result, then, however unappreciative the Commissioners of Inland Revenue or his fellow taxpayers may be of his ingenuity, he cannot be compelled to pay an increased tax.

---

[8] Ibid., 122.
[9] *Pryce* v. *The Directors and Company of the Monmouthshire Canal and Rail Way Companies* (1879) 4 App Cas 197, 206.
[10] Maxwell (1875), *On the Interpretation of Statutes*, 259.
[11] Ibid., 261.
[12] *Commissioners of Inland Revenue* v. *Duke of Westminster* [1936] AC 1, 19.

While the taxpayer-protecting approach did not invariably lead to success for the revenue,[13] it was the defining feature of the common law judiciary's attitude towards tax legislation from the mid-nineteenth century.[14]

The impact of the taxpayer-protecting principle is the best way to understand the *cause célèbre*: *Bowles* v. *Bank of England*.[15] Decided in 1913, *Bowles* concerned an attempt to prevent the Bank of England from withholding income tax on dividends paid on Mr Bowles' government shares. The essential question was whether the income tax on the dividend payments had been lawfully imposed.

Mr Bowles contended that the well-established practice of collecting tax on the basis of a Ways and Means resolution in advance of a *Finance Act* was prohibited by the *Bill of Rights 1688*. That argument was upheld by a single judge in Chancery:[16]

> By the statute ... usually known as the Bill of Rights, it was finally settled that there could be no taxation in this country except under authority of an Act of Parliament. The Bill of Rights still remains unrepealed, and no practice or custom, however prolonged, or however acquiesced in on the part of the subject, can be relied on by the Crown as justifying any infringement of its provisions. It follows that, with regard to the powers of the Crown to levy taxation, no resolution, either of the Committee for Ways and Means or of the House itself, has any legal effect whatever.

The reasoning in *Bowles* has been properly criticised on the basis that the critical articles of the *Bill of Rights* do not speak in terms of 'Acts', but 'Grant[s]' of Parliament,[17] and Ways and Means resolutions authorising the imposition of a tax was a form of parliamentary 'grant'.[18]

When, however, *Bowles* is understood in light of the taxpayer-protecting approach, its position in the common law canon becomes clearer: the judiciary approved of a tenuous, but legally plausible, technical avenue to protect a taxpayer from paying income tax. Understood in that way, *Bowles* also displays the difficulty of viewing the judiciary as

---

[13] Cf *Inland Revenue Commissioners* v. *Sheffield and South Yorkshire Navigation Company* [1916] 1 KB 882.
[14] It also fitted neatly within prevailing social and political attitudes to taxation: Stebbings (2009), 'Consent and Constitutionality in Nineteenth-Century Taxation'.
[15] [1913] 1 Ch 57.
[16] Ibid., 84.
[17] Jaconelli (2010), 'The "Bowles Act" – Cornerstone of the Fiscal Constitution', 585.
[18] It also clashed with almost half a century of uninterrupted parliamentary support for the process of administering the tax collection system on the basis of Ways and Means resolutions, rather than legislation: *Bowles* (1913), 71–72, 74–75.

an institutional mechanism for protecting parliamentary claims to revenue through taxation. The judiciary's constitutional position was orientated towards reducing, rather than maximising, the efficacy of taxation legislation.

Suing the Treasury

Viewed next to the judiciary's well-embedded position regarding statutory taxation, the historical record of judicial review of appropriation legislation is sparse. For a moment, in the mid-nineteenth century, the judiciary intervened to police the public purse, but withdrew after the enactment of the *Audit Act 1866*.

Treasury as 'Trustees for an Individual'

In 1835, the King's Bench ordered mandamus to force the Treasury to pay money out under an *Appropriation Act*: *The King* v. *Lords Commissioners of the Treasury; in re Smyth*.[19]

An *Act of 1822* authorised the Treasury to grant public officials a 'Superannuation Allowance' upon proof of 'Infirmity of Mind or Body', to be paid for out of annually granted supply.[20] Mr Smyth was the former Paymaster of Exchequer Bills, who, upon falling ill, was promised a superannuation allowance by a Treasury official who undertook that 'my Lords will submit a vote to Parliament for granting to you a retired allowance'.[21] Mr Smyth's pension was mentioned in the Treasury's Supply estimates, but did not appear in the annual *Appropriation Acts*, which simply granted money generally 'to defray the Charge of Retired Allowances and Superannuations to Persons formerly employed in the Public Offices or Departments of the Public Services'.[22]

Mr Smyth never received his pension and sought a mandamus against the Treasury to force payment.

Opposing payment, the Treasury's core argument was that '[i]t is against principle that the Court should order a mandamus in the name of the King, directing the King to pay money'.[23] Chief Justice Denman forthrightly rejected that argument:[24]

---

[19] (1835) 4 Ad & E 286 [11 ER 794].
[20] (3 Geo IV, c 113) ss 2, 3.
[21] *Smyth's Case* (1835), 287.
[22] *Appropriation Act of 1846* (9 & 10 Vict, c 116), s 17.
[23] *Smyth's Case* (1835), 290–291.
[24] Ibid., 294–295.

> *Lords of the Treasury ... have the money, and have the control over it: but they seek to annex conditions to its payment, which they have no right to do ... They are officers under the Crown, but the Crown has no more to do with them, for this purpose, than with any other officers. They are merely parties who have received a sum of money as trustees for an individual, under the provision of an Act of Parliament.*

The other judges agreed, and Mr Smyth got his mandamus.[25]

From *Smyth's Case* emerged the principle that the Treasury held appropriated funds as trustees for the people or entities referenced in Supply estimates approved by Parliament. That principle's potential was profound: it appeared to open the way to judicial review of the Treasury's public expenditure functions, as a treatise on the prerogative writs published in 1853 recognised:[26]

> *if public officers, as the lords of the treasury, have the custody of money for a specific purpose, as for the payment of a pension, &c., and do not fulfill that purpose, a mandamus will be granted, commanding them so to do.*

Between 1835 and 1872, the Treasury fought hard against that principle, but failed to kill *Smyth's Case* as a precedent, despite winning on factual findings,[27] or distinguishable legal bases.[28] As a matter of strict doctrine, *Smyth's Case* appeared secure. The principle that the judiciary would enforce the boundaries of appropriation legislation was, however, threatened by the other developments of public finance law, most consequentially the enactment of the *Exchequer and Audit Departments Act 1866*. After that momentous enactment,[29] it became clear that the judiciary was not positioned as the default institution for superintending the executive's public expenditure.

Treasury as 'Servants of the Crown'

Smyth's Case received its quietus in the 1872 decision *The Queen v. The Lords Commissioners of the Treasury*,[30] a case in which mandamus was

---

[25] But not his pension because the Treasury's revocation of Mr Smyth's superannuation allowance was subsequently ruled lawful: *R v. Lords Commissioners of the Treasury* (1836) 4 Ad & E 976 [111 ER 1050].
[26] Tapping (1853), *The Law and Practice of the High Prerogative Writ of Mandamus*, 265.
[27] *The King v. Lords Commissioners of the Treasury; in re Hand* (1836) 4 Ad & E 984 [111 ER 1053], 989–990.
[28] *Re Baron de Bode* (1845) 8 QB 208 [115 ER 854], 792.
[29] See further, Chapter 2.
[30] (1872) 7 QB 387.

sought to compel the payment of money to defray the costs of criminal prosecutions.

An *Act of 1826* provided a crude form of funding for public prosecutions, by empowering a court, hearing a felony charge, to order payment of 'such Sums of Money as to the Court shall seem reasonable and sufficient to reimburse such Prosecutor and Witnesses for the Expences that shall have severally incurred ... in ... carrying on the Prosecution'.[31] Payment was to be made from the resources available to the county in which the prosecution occurred.

In 1836, the Commons resolved that half the costs ordered under the *1826 Act* should be paid from the Consolidated Fund. From 1847 to 1870, the Committee of Supply voted sums 'for prosecutions at assizes and quarter sessions, in England, formerly paid out of county rates'.[32] In 1870, the Treasury 'disallowed or reduced in amount fifty-one of the items in the bills returned'. Mandamus was sought by out-of-pocket prosecutors to compel the payment of those amounts.

Opposing mandamus, the government's counsel again attacked *Smyth's Case*, repeating the argument that:[33]

> there is no obligation on the Treasury to pay any sums; but they may pay them. These sums are given to the Crown, and there is no legal obligation on the Crown which this Court can enforce.

Supporting that familiar argument was 'the meaning of the word "appropriated"' as 'appropriated as between the Crown and the House of Commons', so the:

> effect of the annual Appropriation Act is not to give any third person a right to the money; but it is to prevent the Crown from appropriating money given for one purpose to another.

Despite the general lack of support for that argument over four decades, by 1872, the *Audit Act 1866* had materially changed the public finance landscape. That Act built a comprehensive system of public accounts and audit presided over by the Comptroller and Auditor-General. As part of that reform package, the *Audit Act 1866* contained an omnibus repeal, which included a repeal of the 1822 Act upon which Mr Smyth's superannuation had been granted.[34] Those developments were critical to the

---

[31] (7 Geo IV, c 64) s 22.
[32] *1872 Treasury Case* (1872), 387.
[33] Ibid., 390.
[34] Section 46 and Schedule C.

resolution of the *1872 Treasury Case*, where mandamus was refused and *Smyth's Case* disavowed as a 'very doubtful authority'.[35]

At the level of formal principle, the Court finally accepted the Treasury's argument that money paid under an *Appropriation Act*:[36]

> is paid to the Lords of the Treasury, as servants of the Crown; and ... I cannot say that there is any duty, which makes it incumbent upon them to do what I cannot hesitate to say they ought to have done, except as servants of the Crown: because in that character they have received this money, and in no other.

From that statement of principle, the Court derived the conclusion that it had no jurisdiction to make an order against the Treasury because the duties imposed by an *Appropriation Act* were not:[37]

> dut[ies] at law which by any legal proceeding or by the exercise of the prerogative jurisdiction of this Court we can enforce.

The total effect of the reasoning in the *1872 Treasury Case* was that the prerogative writs would not issue against the Treasury in respect of their use of funds under an *Appropriation Act*, because they held money granted by appropriation legislation as 'servants of the Crown', and the prerogative writs would not issue against the Crown or its servants.

Curiously, all judges held that the Treasury had made a grave error in refusing to make the payments under the *Appropriation Act*. Cockburn CJ described the Treasury's actions as 'monstrous', resting on a 'very great mistake' and of a 'most unsatisfactory character'.[38] Mellor J held that the Treasury had:[39]

> disregarded the operation of the Appropriation Act. The clause provides for expenses of prosecutions at assizes; it is not as the Solicitor General suggested, that they 'may' pay, it is that they are to pay a sum not exceeding the given sum.

Lush J described the Treasury's action as being in 'violation of the terms of the Appropriation Act'.[40] Those holdings reveal the Court's commitment to shield the Treasury from judicial review, despite also finding that

---

[35] *1872 Treasury Case* (1872), 395.
[36] Ibid., 395. See also, 398, 400, 402.
[37] Ibid., 395.
[38] Ibid., 393, 395.
[39] Ibid., 401.
[40] Ibid., 402.

the Treasury's refusal to make the payments under the *Appropriation Act* was illegal.[41]

The fate of the mid-nineteenth-century experiment with judicial review of appropriation legislation was sealed in a tax decision of 1883, in which Dicey appeared for the revenue. There, the Court of Appeal condemned *Smyth's Case* as unable to 'be maintained on any ground' and 'wrong'.[42] Thereafter, the judiciary would have no settled role in policing the legality of the Treasury's actions in paying money (or not) under an *Appropriation Act*.

The rise and fall of judicial review of expenditure decisions under appropriation legislation in the mid-nineteenth century was surely influenced by developments inside and outside the courts.

Inside the courts, the experiment in *Smyth's Case* coincided with the flowering of ideas of public 'trusteeship', and the doctrinal growth of the 'crown' as the legal personality of central government.[43] The death of *Smyth's Case* coincided with statutory developments which made it far easier to sue public officials in private law actions rather than seek prerogative relief to secure the release of money. The lodestar was the *Petitions of Right Act 1860*,[44] which provided a concrete avenue to sue the Crown for restitution of money or damages for breach of contract.[45] That Act operated *within*, rather than *adding to,* the legislative practices of annual appropriation. It expressly provided that the satisfaction of judgment debts or costs by the Crown were to be paid by the Treasury 'out of any moneys ... voted by parliament for that purpose';[46] requiring that payment of judgment debts be conditioned on the existence of annual appropriation legislation.

Looming over the chicanery of common law litigation were the changes wrought to the structure of British government in the 1860s,

---

[41] Shocking though they may be to the contemporary legal mind, that holding fits within a stream of nineteenth-century doctrine which recognised that some legal wrongs could want for *vinculum juris* and be binding as a matter of conscience only: *Gibson v. East India Company* (1839) 5 Bing (NC) 262 [132 ER 1105]; *Ex parte Napier* (1852) 18 QB 692 [118 ER 261].

[42] *R v. Inland Revenue* (1884) 12 QBD 461, 476, 480; see also *The Queen v. Secretary of State for War* (1891) 2 QBD 326, 338.

[43] Maitland (1901); McLean (2012), *Searching for the State in British Legal Thought*, chapter 5.

[44] (23 & 24 Vict, c 34).

[45] Clode (1887), *The Law and Practice of Petitions of Right*, chapters 9 and 10.

[46] *Petitions of Right Act 1860* (23 & 24 Vict, c 34), s 14. The same essential structure appears in the modern *Crown Proceedings Act 1947* (10 & 11 Geo VI, c 44), s 37. See generally, Hogg (2000), *Liability of the Crown*.

which included replacement of venal 'offices' with a professional public service.[47] Additionally, the *Audit Act 1866* surely impacted the judiciary's attitude to review of appropriation legislation, including its provision of an independent enforcement mechanism for the legality of public expenditure (the Comptroller and Auditor-General), and the conferral on the Treasury of economic and legal control of public finance, both explained in Chapter 2. Precisely how the judiciary would superimpose common law strictures on central government expenditure, under those circumstances, was not clear and was never addressed.

Judicial Disinterest in Appropriation Legislation

By the commencement of the twentieth century the extent of the judiciary's lack of interest in appropriation legislation was illustrated by the Privy Council's 1924 decision in *Auckland Harbour Board v. The King*.[48]

Auckland Harbour involved a private law claim of the New Zealand central government against a statutory authority, the Auckland Harbour Board, for money paid by the government without legal authority. That claim was raised as a defence to the Harbour Board's petition of right seeking payment of money against the central government.

The central government's payment of money had been authorised by a statutory standing appropriation on the condition that a separate liability had arisen under an agreement between the central government and the Harbour Board. As events transpired, the separate liability never arose, but the central government still paid the money under authority of an annual appropriation Act; a payment approved by New Zealand's Auditor-General. The central government later reversed its position, attempting to claw-back the money on the basis that the liability which would trigger the standing legislation had never crystallised. The Harbour Board responded that the money was properly paid under annual appropriation legislation and approved by the Auditor-General. In that sense, the heart of the case concerned the relationship of standing and annual appropriation legislation.

The Privy Council held in favour of the central government. Putting the annual appropriation legislation entirely aside, it resolved the case by reference to the non-existence of the separate liability:[49]

---

[47] Chester (1981), 122–136.
[48] [1924] AC 318.
[49] *Auckland Harbour* (1924), 326.

It was said, and it appears to have been the fact, that the Controller and Auditor-General subsequently passed the sum handed over as having been payable out of public moneys appropriated in general terms for railway services by the New Zealand Parliament in 1914. But this is not a sufficient answer to the contention that the payment was not authorized.

[the standing appropriation legislation] provide[d] that the sum ... was to be payable to the appellants only on a condition ... The provision which Parliament thus made was to be in itself a sufficient appropriation, but only operative if the condition was actually satisfied. Their Lordships have not been referred to any appropriation or other Act which altered these terms. If, as must therefore be taken to be the case, it remained operative, the authority given by Parliament is merely the conditional appropriation provided in [the standing appropriation legislation] ... for a condition which was not fulfilled.

Placing the annual appropriation Act aside, the Council then expounded its famous passage of obiter:[50]

The payment was accordingly an illegal one, which no merely executive ratification, even with the concurrence of the Controller and Auditor-General, could divest of its illegal character. For it has been a principle of the British Constitution now for more than two centuries, a principle which their Lordships understand to have been inherited in the Constitution of New Zealand with the same stringency, that no money can be taken out of the Consolidated Fund into which the revenues of the State have been paid, excepting under a distinct authorization from Parliament itself. The days are long gone by in which the Crown, or its servants, apart from Parliament, could give such an authorization or ratify an improper payment. Any payment out of the Consolidated Fund made without Parliamentary authority is simply illegal and ultra vires, and may be recovered by the Government if it can, as here, be traced.

Although that statement has become notorious,[51] it studiously avoided engaging with the detailed interplay of standing and annual appropriation legislation in New Zealand, which mirrored the British model in all relevant respects.

In the court below, the Chief Justice of New Zealand engaged with that legislation and found *against the central government* on the basis that the money had been lawfully paid under the annual appropriation legislation, not the standing legislation, and so no question of an illegal

---

[50] Ibid., 326–327.
[51] *Woolwich Equitable Building Society* v. *Inland Revenue Commissioners* [1993] AC 70, 177; Lewis (2014), *Judicial Remedies in Public Law*, [15–127]; Mitchell (2010), 'Recovery of Ultra Vires Payments by Public Bodies', 756–764; Prosser (2014), 111.

payment arose.⁵² Viewed in that way, *Auckland Harbour* falls within the judiciary's general approach (post-*1872 Treasury Case*) of avoiding imposing judicial oversight of the legality of annual appropriation legislation.

Thereby, the British judiciary largely removed itself, and each court within the common law hierarchy, as an enforcer of parliamentary appropriation legislation, which meant that no bespoke jurisprudence developed akin to the taxpayer-protecting approach in tax litigation. The constitutional effect was that disputes regarding the expenditure side of the relationship between Parliament and executive would be untouched by judicial power, leaving compliance with appropriation legislation to the Treasury, with post hoc oversight provided by the Comptroller and Auditor-General.

Bankers' Case

Even compared to the paucity of litigation concerning appropriation, the judicial record concerning sovereign borrowing is spartan. It breaks into two phases, before and after the *Bankers' Case*.

Bankers' Case

The *Bankers' Case* arose from the English sovereign default in 1672: the 'Stop of the Exchequer'.

The legal details of the *Bankers' Case* are very complicated,⁵³ but the litigation essentially concerned recovery of unpaid interest owed to holders of public debt.⁵⁴ Critically, that debt had no parliamentary backing, simply being issued on the Monarch's personal security.⁵⁵ After initial set-backs,⁵⁶ the creditor plaintiffs obtained an order that the outstanding amounts be paid. The debt was not, however, satisfied, and they were left to petition Parliament, which eventually appropriated funds to pay part, but 'curtailed' ~44 per cent, of the debt.⁵⁷

Until recently, the *Bankers' Case* had been lightly touched by legal scholars: Maitland and Dicey glanced only briefly at it and most legally-orientated

---

⁵² *Auckland Harbour Board v. The King* [1919] *Gazette Law Reports* (NZ) 352, 356–357.
⁵³ Horsefield (1982), 'The "Stop of the Exchequer" Revisited', 518–521.
⁵⁴ Desan (2015), *Making Money: Coin, Currency, and the Coming of Capitalism*, 281–287.
⁵⁵ Dickson (1967), 44–45; Horsefield (1982), 513–518.
⁵⁶ Winning at first instance in the Exchequer (1691), losing on appeal in the Exchequer Chamber (1693) and wining in the Lords (1700).
⁵⁷ Horsefield (1982), 522–523.

constitutional histories wholly ignore it.[58] The case has, however, received important attention in Desan's recent constitutional history of money. There, it is argued that the case changed 'the legal design of public debt' by promoting the position that 'the courts could, and indeed should, protect [creditors'] interests ... shifting the relevant positions of the sovereign, the courts and the creditors'.[59] That interpretation places the common law judiciary in the position of an enforcer of sovereign debts: '[t]he bankers could sue for their money; indeed, they had sued and won'.[60]

Curiously underplayed in Desan's account are the Treasury and Parliament,[61] but the respective constitutional position of those institutions provides critical context to the *Bankers' Case* in two respects.

First, the conclusion of the *Bankers' Case* (1700) post-dated the adoption of the practice of parliamentary security for public borrowing (1962–1964).[62] In that sense, whatever judicial doctrine the litigation may have spawned, a secure market in public debt securities was created by legislative rather than judicial action. Secondly, the judiciary accepted that the only remedial option for the creditors lay in parliamentary appropriation, not judicial order and not monarchical (prerogative) expenditure.[63] The fact that the amount eventually appropriated by Parliament was significantly discounted[64] further indicates Parliament's (not the judiciary's) final say in controlling the terms of debt repayment. Shortly after the conclusion of the *Bankers' Case*, Parliament lost the right to initiate financial legislation to the executive (*qua* Treasury) and any debt-servicing payments approved by Parliament required prior-approval by the executive government.[65]

Taking account of those two contextual matters, the *Bankers' Case* emerges as providing support for viewing Parliament and Treasury (not the judiciary) as the predominant constitutional institutions providing the legal foundation of the eighteenth-century sovereign debt market. That conclusion is supported by the fact that, after the *Bankers' Case*, judicial consideration of the legal limitations on the power to issue

---

[58] E.g., Maitland (1908), 438–439 and Dicey (1885), 24.
[59] Desan (2015), 287.
[60] Ibid.
[61] Desan does, however, acknowledge that the *Bankers' Case* is 'cryptic in the larger context': Desan (2015), 287.
[62] Explored in Chapter 2.
[63] *Act of 1701* (12 & 13 Will III, c 12).
[64] Horsefield (1982), 523.
[65] As explained above.

England's public debt runs dry and the abundance of legislation authorising the Treasury to issue long- and short-term debt was never the subject of serious judicial consideration.

Judging the Bank of England

The eighteenth and nineteenth centuries did, however, witness a modest body of litigation concerning the Bank of England, all of which treated the Bank as a 'trading corporation' which did not act 'for public purposes' or perform 'public duties'[66] and stunted the growth of a discrete jurisprudence concerning the Bank's public financing functions.

To be sure, the courts did engage with the legal character of the Bank's promissory notes, including the circumstances in which the Bank should pay on presentation of a note which had been: stolen before presentation,[67] cancelled in the morning and cashed in the afternoon,[68] and not indorsed by the drawer.[69] Similarly the courts dealt with controversies concerning stock sold by, or registered in, the Bank, including, whether the Bank: had to pay out stock transferred under a forged power of attorney,[70] was liable in damages for failing to sell stock when directed,[71] and could refuse an executor's request to transfer public stock specifically bequeathed.[72]

Those cases treated the Bank as any other financial corporation,[73] hinting at the judiciary's perception of it as a private financial intermediary, rather than an independent public financial institution,

---

[66] *The King* v. *The Governor and Company of the Bank of England* (1819) 2 Barnewall and Alderson 620 [106 ER 492].

[67] *De la Chaumette* v. *The Bank of England* (1831) 2 Barnewall and Adolphus 385 [109 ER 1186].

[68] *Haward* v. *the Bank of England* (1722) 1 Strange 550 [93 ER 693].

[69] *Governor and Company of the Bank of England* v. *Newman* (1703) 12 Modern 241 [88 ER 1290].

[70] *Davis* v. *The Governor and Company of the Bank of England* (1824) 2 Bingham 393 [130 ER 357].

[71] *Sutton, Bart* v. *The Governor and Company of the Bank of England* (1824) Ryan & Moody 52 [171 ER 940].

[72] *Franklin* v. *The Bank of England* (1826) 1 Russell 575 [38 ER 221].

[73] Including in relation to proving debts in the administration of bankrupt estates (*Ex parte The Bank of England, in the Matter of Richard Stephens, a Bankrupt* (1818) 1 Swanston 10 [36 ER 277]) and pecuniary liability for a failure to pay dividends (*Foster* v. *The Governor and Company of the Bank of England* (1846) 8 Queen's Bench Reports 689 [115 ER 1032]; *Partridge* v. *The Governor and Company of the Bank of England* (1846) 9 Queen's Bench Reports 396 [115 ER 1324]).

bearing obligations separate to the government on whose behalf it transacted.[74]

That hint is confirmed by two cases (of 1780 and 1819) where mandamus was unsuccessfully sought against the Bank.

The 1780 case concerned mandamus to compel the Bank to transfer public stock in circumstances where the administration of the deceased estate was complicated by a claim that the testator was a bastard whose stock reverted to the Crown upon death.[75] Refusing mandamus, Lord Mansfield held that '[t]he bank is ... in the nature of a stake-holder only. The real question is between the Crown ... and the executors'.[76] Implicit in that holding was that the Bank exercised no special public role in regard to public debt instruments.

In the 1819 action, a stockholder in the Bank sought mandamus against the Bank's officers 'to compel them to produce their accounts, for the purpose of declaring a dividend of the profits'.[77] The application was peremptorily refused, with the King's Bench deciding that the Bank was a 'trading corporation' which did not act 'for public purposes' or perform 'public duties'.[78] The judiciary's attitude towards the public character of the Bank was pithily captured by Best J, whose entire reason for refusing relief was that, '[i]f we were to grant this rule, we should make ourselves auditors to all the trading corporations in England'.[79]

Treating the Bank as a private institution followed naturally from the judicial perception of the Bank as a private financer *of government*, rather than *itself being a part of* the apparatus of public finance. An 1840 House of Lords appeal illustrates that attitude in the context of judicial enforcement of the Bank's statutory monopoly on carrying on a banking business of more than six persons within 65 miles of London:[80] *Booth v. Governor and Company of the Bank of England*.[81]

---

[74] Cf *Governor and Company of the Bank of England* v. *Davis* (1826) 5 Barnewall and Cresswell 185 [108 ER 69]. The judiciary would, of course, recognise legislative obligations placed especially on the Bank: *Sloman* v. *Bank of England* (1845) 1 Holt Equity Reports 1, 9 [71 ER 649].
[75] *The King, on the Prosecution of Parbury and Another, Executors of Dawes* v. *The Governor and Company of the Bank of England* (1780) 2 Douglas 524 [99 ER 334].
[76] Ibid., 526.
[77] *The King* v. *The Governor and Company of the Bank of England* (1819) 2 Barnewall and Alderson 620 [106 ER 492].
[78] Ibid., 622–623.
[79] Ibid., 623.
[80] *Act of 1833* (3 & 4 Will IV, c 98).
[81] *Booth* v. *Governor and Company of the Bank of England* (1840) VII Clark & Finnelly 509 [7 ER 1163].

Booth arose from an action by the Bank to injunct the London Joint Stock Bank from issuing bills drawn by a 'manager' not a 'partner', in contrived breach of the Bank's statutory monopoly. Upholding the Bank's entitlement to an injunction, the Lords stated that:[82]

> The exclusive privileges conferred on the Bank of England by Parliament are founded on a contract between that Body and the Public. For the original grant, and also for the renewal and confirmation of such privileges, the Bank of England has from time to time paid very large sums of money to the Public; and no member of that Public can justify either doing, or procuring to be done, any act which, for the protection of such rights and privileges, has been forbidden by law.

That view of the Bank, as a bargaining party with the UK government, positively affected its entitlement to an injunction:[83]

> The privilege granted to the Bank of England by Parliament is a positive right conferred upon that body for a valuable consideration, which the law will no more permit to be infringed by third persons without a responsibility.

Rather than being a public institution, the Bank was understood as an arm's-length negotiator with the Parliament and its 'contracts' (which were actually 'statutes') would ground relief in equity's auxiliary jurisdiction.

Judicial consideration of the Bank of England's legal powers left it largely untouched by the slowly developing system of judicial review. The judiciary treated the Bank as a private trading corporation, rather than a public institution with constitutional responsibilities regarding public debt. Despite litigation on peripheral issues, the judiciary never became involved in enforcing the legislation conferring debt finance authority on the Treasury and Bank of England. While the *Bankers' Case* evidences strong judicial support for parliamentary security of sovereign borrowing, the eighteenth- and nineteenth-century reports never really returned to the topic. Sovereign borrowing joined public expenditure as non-juridicalised parts of public financial administration.

The Judicial Position in Public Finance

Throughout the eighteenth and nineteenth centuries, the British judiciary adopted an asymmetric position vis-à-vis public finances: intense

---

[82] Ibid., 540.
[83] Ibid., 544.

review of the decisions under taxation legislation, but no meaningful oversight of appropriation or sovereign borrowing statutes.[84]

The judges' ancient interest in guarding against expropriation of private property continued in their forthright review of the decisions of tax officials, but their explicit endorsement of tax evasion did little to bolster Parliament's fiscal authority. Early Victorian flirtations with review of expenditure legislation aside, the judiciary never adopted a similarly assertive position towards the legality of public expenditure. After the *Bankers' Case*, sovereign debt, including that held by the Bank of England, never assumed a position of any prominence in the judiciary.

The absence of the judiciary from a systemic financial position is the final piece in the model of British parliamentary finance. The Treasury reigned supreme as the apex institution: originating all financial plans and exercising a veto right over financial legislation. Legal and economic supervision of the executive's use of public money fell principally to the Treasury, notwithstanding the Comptroller and Auditor-General's quasi-independent oversight role and the post hoc review of Parliament's Public Accounts Committee. Legislation gave the Treasury exceptionally broad authority to acquire debt finance and procure the issue of monetary finance from the Bank of England, and standing appropriations for debt servicing costs removed much of the Treasury's debt management activities from the annual parliamentary process.

Compared to the breadth of the Treasury's authority, Parliament's financial position was almost entirely passive. Despite the centrality of financial processes to its annual calendar, Parliament's authority was limited to approving or rejecting, rather than modifying, the Treasury's expenditure and taxation proposals. Such was the consequence of Parliament's surrender of the financial initiative to the executive. By the conclusion of the nineteenth century, Parliament had delegated most authority over debt and monetary finance to the Treasury. Establishing the Comptroller and Auditor-General augured a potentially greater role for parliamentary oversight of the Treasury, but the dependence of that parliamentary agent on the Treasury's legal and economic power brought no major realignment of authority towards Parliament. Judicial power made no meaningful contribution to the protection of parliamentary financial authority.

---

[84] Of course, the Comptroller and Auditor-General provided a form of non-judicial *ex post* scrutiny of public expenditure which was (in important respects) contingent on the executive *qua* Treasury's own 'control' of the broader executive.

One consequence of that conclusion is that Dicey's glowing endorsement of parliamentary control of public finance, observed in Chapter 1, becomes very difficult to maintain. Parliament had given away a large share of its financial authority to the executive government and the judiciary had also declared that it would not sit in judgment over the executive's administration of appropriation legislation. Constitutionally, public finance appeared not to be supported by either pillar of parliamentary sovereignty or the rule of law.

Recognising the limits of Dicey's vision has the added benefit of dispelling any suggestion that the heterogeneous organisation of nineteenth-century British public finance should be dismissed as either contrary to constitutional expectations or an imperfect, adolescent attempt to build a constitutional order with Parliament in full control of public finance. None of the legal practices of public finance breached any constitutional convention or principle, and certainly not one which required Parliament to 'control' public finance. Quite to the contrary, they were understood to be conformable with the growth of parliamentary government, which was in the process of being exported throughout the British Empire.

4

History (III): Exporting Parliamentary Public Finance

As the British Empire expanded and then dissolved, the distinct model of parliamentary public finance developed in the UK was exported to the colonies, dominions and independent states which adopted parliamentary governments. The exported model contained all the main features explained in Chapters 2 and 3. Treasuries (and, where separated, finance ministries) held the bulk of financial authority: originating all financial plans, holding a veto right over any financial legislation and possessing largely untrammelled statutory authority to acquire debt. Parliaments had a largely passive institutional position, limited to approving or rejecting the executive's expenditure and taxation proposals, with no substantial authority over debt and a limited capacity to supervise the executive's financial activities. Common law judiciaries maintained their asymmetric position in the resolution of financial disputes. Taxation remained a staple of the common law diet, while sovereign borrowing had no meaningful judicial profile.

Explaining the export of parliamentary public finance requires travelling quickly across a wide geographic span: beginning in North America in the late-eighteenth and mid-nineteenth centuries, moving to the Australasian colonies in the latter nineteenth century and then expanding to the proliferation of constitutions which accompanied the rapid decolonisation of the British Empire in the twentieth century. By the conclusion of that constitutional itinerary, the distribution of financial authority between Parliament and the executive government in nineteenth-century Britain became the norm prevailing in the parliamentary constitutional world.

Congressional Divergence

As the British Empire expanded, constitutional disputes of a financial character persisted, particularly in the North American colonies, which would eventually adopt a very different distribution of financial authority in the constitutions of post-Revolutionary America.[1] Certainly, the *United States Constitution* followed British financial practice in important respects. Legislative power over taxation, public expenditure, public borrowing and debt repayment was constitutionally conferred to the Congress; thereby, ultimate power to authorise financial behaviour would be statutory.[2] An express prohibition on removing 'money from the treasury, but in consequence of appropriations made by law' entrenched the constitutional assumption underpinning British appropriation legislation.[3]

Those commonalities aside, the *US Constitution*'s treatment of public finance sharply diverged from late-eighteenth-century British practice. Most significantly, the financial initiative was withheld from the President and Executive Branch, leaving the Congress free to originate appropriation legislation and formulate the expenditure proposals underlying that legislation. That adjustment of financial power between the Executive branch and Congress was deliberate: 'if it were otherwise, the executive would possess an unbounded power over the public purse of the nation; and might apply all its monied resources at his pleasure'.[4] Other divergences stemmed from federalism and elected bicameralism: both houses of Congress were permitted to originate appropriation legislation. That gave the Senate, representing the States, a significant share of the financial initiative regarding public expenditure.[5] Conferring co-extensive authority over public expenditure on the second parliamentary chamber was a sharp divergence from the established position in the UK, where all expenditure legislation originated in the Commons.[6]

Despite the sharp constitutional break between the USA and Britain, the treatment of public money in the *US Constitution* remains significant as an alternative written constitutional model, devoid of the executive's

---

[1] Keith (1930), *Constitutional History of the First British Empire*, 344–346, 350–358, 360–366, 383–385. For the early colonial legal thinking on parliamentary public finance see 'Pratt-Yorke Opinion' (1757) in Chalmers (1814), *Opinions of Eminent Lawyers*, 230–231; Campbell v. Hall (1774), 212–214; Keith (1928), *Responsible Government in the Dominions*, 92–93, Todd (1883), *Parliamentary Government in the British Colonies*, 169–176.

[2] *USA Constitution*, Article I §8.

[3] *USA Constitution*, Article I §9.

[4] Story (1833), *Commentaries on the Constitution of the United States*, volume 3, 214.

[5] An historical review can be found in Fisher (1979), 'The Authorisation–Appropriation Process in Congress'.

[6] The Senate's co-extensive power over expenditure was not replicated in relation to taxation, as the House of Representatives was given exclusive power to originate taxation bills (Article I §7(1)).

financial initiative, and without any exclusive power in the more representative parliamentary house to originate expenditure legislation.[7] As events transpired, the colonies in the British Empire, and the independent nations which they later became, followed British, rather than American, practices of public finance: replicating, mostly unaltered, the constitutional distribution of financial authority developed in Britain.

Colonial Constitutions

Responsible government in the Australasian and North American colonies brought a model of public finance law, prominent parts of which were secured in written constitutions. The development of those constitutions followed a discernible trajectory: commencing with the Canadian *Act of Union 1840*, passing through the *New South Wales Constitution Act 1855* and then being broadly adopted throughout the British Empire.[8]

Canadian Union

The first major colonial enactment concerning public finance occurred in the *Act of Union 1840*: an early written constitution for the British colonies in Canada and an influential template for later constitutional treatments of public money. The *Act of Union 1840* was a response to protests for greater self-rule, or responsible government, in the Canadian colonies.[9] The UK government's response to those protests was published in a report of Lord Durham, a special Governor-General sent to Canada to investigate. That report provided a blueprint for the export of British-style parliamentary public finance.[10]

Durham's report attributed the tensions in British North America to two sources: 'an ill-contrived constitutional system'[11] and conflict between English and French inhabitants of Canada. Both ills were to be cured by uniting Upper (majority-Anglophone) and Lower (majority-Francophone) Canada under 'English laws and language ... to trust its government to none but a decidedly English legislature ... formed by

---

[7] For the institutional complexity of that arrangement, see Fenno (1966), *The Power of the Purse*.
[8] *Act of Union 1840* (3 & 4 Vict, c 35); *New South Wales Constitution Act 1855* (18 & 19 Vict, c 54).
[9] Amongst other issues, including racial and class conflict: Kennedy (1922), *The Constitution of Canada*, chapter XI.
[10] Durham, *Report on the Affairs of British North America* (1839).
[11] Ibid., 260.

a legislative union'.[12] The legislative union would conform to 'the principles of the British constitution',[13] wherein all aspects of government, including finance, would be modelled on 'cabinet government in the British constitutional sense'.[14]

Durham only faintly sketched the legislative details, but singled out the executive's financial initiative for special attention. '[T]hat no money vote should be proposed without the previous consent of the Crown'[15] was considered critical to protecting against the 'scramble for local appropriations, which chiefly serves to give an undue influence to particular individuals or parties'.[16] Thereby, no rule by financial assembly, along US lines, would be established in Canada.

Durhams' commitment to a UK, rather than US, model of public finance was reflected in the *Act of Union 1840*,[17] which gave the power to originate tax or appropriation Bills to the legislative assembly, but prohibited the enactment of 'any Vote, Resolution, or Bill for the Appropriation of any Part ... of the ... Consolidated Revenue Fund, or of any ... Tax' which had not 'been first recommended by a Message of the Governor to the said Legislative Assembly'.[18] Importantly, a consolidated fund (in line with the 1787 British model) was created, which was charged with 'the annual Interest of the Public Debt', thereby ensuring 'parliamentary security' for Canadian public borrowing.[19] Reflecting the unfinished state of business in Britain, the character of Canadian audit institutions was left to be 'directed by any Act' of the legislative assembly.[20]

Australasia

The *Act of Union 1840*'s model of financial provisions was transported to the Australian colonies at the *terminus* of their own push for 'responsible

---

[12] Ibid., 288–289, 307.
[13] Ibid., 278.
[14] Kennedy (1922), 175.
[15] Durham (1839), 328.
[16] Ibid., 287.
[17] Kennedy (1922), 198.
[18] Section 57.
[19] Sections 50 and 56. The remaining finance provisions of the *Act of Union 1840* provided for a complex brokerage of financial power between the British colonial administration, the local population, and various religious bodies, including standing appropriations for the costs of revenue collection and salaries of senior public officials: Sections 51, 52–54.
[20] Section 51.

government'.[21] From the turn of the nineteenth century, disputes had smouldered between the white-settler population of the Australian colonies and the Home government regarding the power to tax and appropriate.[22] Between 1850 and 1852, colonial temperatures boiled over and the New South Wales Legislative Council sent a *Declaration and Remonstration* to the Commons: demanding responsible government, complete control over domestic revenues and financial control of the government, accompanied by an allusive threat of rebellion.[23] The Home government eventually conceded and enacted the *New South Wales Constitution 1855*,[24] a document drafted in the colony, containing financial provisions largely replicating those in the *Act of Union 1840*.

A 'Consolidated Revenue Fund' was established, into which flowed all 'Taxes, Imposts, Rates, and Duties, and all territorial, casual, and other Revenues of the Crown (including Royalties) from whatever Source arising within this Colony'.[25] The fund was permanently charged by standing appropriation with the costs of its 'collection, management and receipt', and the salaries of senior officials.[26] The legislative assembly was given exclusive power to originate money bills, which was limited by the executive's financial initiative, in line with established UK constitutional practice.[27] Parliamentary security for public borrowing was recognised in the proviso that consolidation of revenue 'shall not affect the Payment of the annual Interest, or Principal Sums [of] any outstanding Debentures'.[28] Alike the *Act of Union*, the *1855 Constitution* did not provide a complete codification of the rules of public money,[29] but its

---

[21] Melbourne (1963), *Early Constitutional Development in Australia*; Sweetman (1925), *Australian Constitutional Development*. The *New Zealand Constitution Act 1852* (15 & 16 Vict, c 72) contained a similar treatment of financial matters (ss 25, 54, 65–66).

[22] Financial autonomy had been withheld from the colony's domestic political institutions by four constitutional documents enacted by the Home Parliament for the Australian colonies between 1823 and 1850: *New South Wales Act 1823* (4 Geo IV, c 96); *Australian Courts Act 1828* (9 Geo IV, c 83); *New South Wales Constitution Act 1842* (5 & 6 Vict, c 76); *Australian Constitutions Act 1850* (13 & 14 Vict, c 59).

[23] *Votes and Proceedings of the Legislative Council of New South Wales*, 01/05/1851 and 10/08/1852: Twomey (2004), *The Constitution of New South Wales*, 7–11; Sweetman (1925), 256–270.

[24] (18 & 19 Vict, c 54).

[25] Section 47.

[26] Sections 49–50.

[27] Sections 1, 54.

[28] Section 53.

[29] Also omitting any meaningful treatment of audit: s 48.

financial provisions provided the template for most of the remaining Australian colonial constitutions.[30]

Colonial Financial Legislation

Where colonial constitutional documents were silent on public finance, colonial legislatures spoke loudly. Parliamentary expenditure practice followed British traditions, colonial legislatures voted on estimates prepared by treasury departments and enacted annual expenditure legislation.[31] Importantly, Australian, Canadian and New Zealand *Appropriation Acts* maintained the flexibility of their British parents, appropriating at a higher level of generality than voted estimates and retrospectively appropriating excesses from previous years. A particularly striking example of the latter practice appeared in nineteenth-century New Zealand annual appropriation legislation, which dealt with excesses by enacting a provision identifying the precise amount 'issued ... in excess or without appropriation by parliament' and declaring that the 'application and discharge of the said sums are hereby sanctioned'.[32]

Colonial taxation practice followed English legislative precedents, although the precise tax mix varied.[33] Treasury control was also established in Australasia and Canada by legislation conferring authority on treasuries to determine the manner of keeping accounts and establishing Auditors-General, styled on the British Comptroller and Auditor-General.[34] Legislation also provided the legal foundation for public borrowing, debt security issues and standing appropriations for debt servicing. Treasuries were given broad authority to borrow by annual Acts, which sometimes indicated the purposes for which money was to be borrowed and the total amount to be borrowed.[35] Framework legislation

---

[30] Except the *South Australian Constitution 1856* (SA); *Tasmanian Constitution Act 1855* (Tas).

[31] The fine detail of nineteenth century *Supply* and *Appropriation Acts* differed. For example, New Zealand began enacting *Supply* (separate to *Appropriation*) Acts in the 1870s, while, by the 1880s, no such separate Acts were passed by the Canadian Parliament.

[32] *Appropriation Act 1895* (NZ), s 13 and Sch 1.

[33] The Australasian and Canadian colonies relied heavily on indirect taxes (customs and excises) and land tax: Di Matteo (2017), *A Federal Fiscal History*, 28; Dick (2014), 'Taxation in Australia up until 1914'; Littlewood (2016), 'In the Beginning: Taxation in Early Colonial New Zealand'.

[34] E.g., *Audit Act 1870* (NSW); *Audit Act 1858* (NZ); *Audit Act 1878* (Can) c 7.

[35] E.g., *New Zealand Loans Act 1904* (NZ); *Loan Act 1888* (Can); *Public Works Loan Act 1884* (NSW).

provided the more granular provisions for public debt, and sometimes included standing authority to borrow to fill shortfalls in public receipts.[36]

Finally, the UK judiciary's position vis-à-vis financial activities was largely replicated throughout Britain's settler colonial empire. Colonial judiciaries were occasionally drawn into financial disputes,[37] but no established practice of policing the boundaries of appropriation or public borrowing grew. Colonial cognates of the British *Petitions of Right Act 1860* were enacted which provided a statutory framework within which public officials could be sued for monetary amounts in private law and required parliaments to appropriate funds for the payment of a judgment debt against the government.[38]

Federal Constitutions

As the British colonies in Australasia and Canada evolved into Dominions, written federal constitutions were enacted which contained 'Finance' chapters for the newly created polities: the *British North America Act 1867* and the *Commonwealth of Australia Constitution Act 1901*.[39] The development of each federal constitution had distinctly different trajectories,[40] but both finished products contained foundational similarities to late-nineteenth-century British and colonial financial practices: no money could be drawn from consolidated revenue unless appropriated by legislation; only the executive could introduce appropriation and taxation bills, and such bills had to originate in the more representative lower house of parliament.[41]

Australian and Canadian federal constitutions did, however, provide two opportunities for divergence from the existing distribution of

---

[36] E.g., *New Zealand Consolidated Stock Act 1877* (NZ); *Loans Fund Amalgamation Act 1879* (NSW); *Public Debt – Loans Act 1872* (Can).

[37] *Alcock v. Fergie* (1867) 4 W W & A'B (L) 285.

[38] The Australian 'claims against the government' legislation is analysed in detail by Finn (1987), *Law and Government in Colonial Australia*, the New Zealand legislation can be found in the *Crown Suits Act 1881* (NZ). For the nineteenth-century Canadian position, see *Windsor & Annapolis Railway Co v. The Queen and the Western Counties Railway Co* (1885) 10 SCR 335.

[39] *British North America Act 1867* (30 & 31 Vict, c 3); *Commonwealth of Australia Constitution Act 1901* (63 & 64 Vict, c 12).

[40] Kennedy (1922); La Nauze (1972), *The Making of the Australian Constitution*.

[41] *British North America Act 1867* ss 102, 53–54; *Commonwealth of Australia Constitution*, ss 52–53, 56, 81, 83. In Australia, the Senate was prevented from 'amend[ing]' a bill for the 'ordinary annual services' of the Commonwealth government: s 53.

financial authority: financial-federalism and judicial review, neither of which effected a material change to the distribution of financial authority exported to their predecessor colonies.

In their fusion of parliamentary government with federalism, the Canadian and Australian constitutions provided for fiscal-federalism in several different ways.[42] The most basic was the express division of legislative powers over financial affairs between federal and regional bodies politic.[43] Another relatively basic federal-financial provision was conferring *ex facie* unlimited constitutional power on the federal governments to make 'grants' to the sub-federal governments.[44] The more complex fiscal-financial provisions obliged the federal polity to make quantitatively fixed payments to regional polities. The *British North America Act 1867* obliged Canada to pay the Provinces prescribed sums and a per capita grant annually,[45] while Australia's *Commonwealth Constitution*'s obligatory federal payments system operated in a tiered fashion.[46]

Those federal-financial provisions share an important similarity: they did not follow American constitutional practices regarding financial federalism. Canadian and Australian senates would not have co-equal power over expenditure, nor would federal parliaments have the financial initiative. That matter is particularly significant given the Canadian and Australian adoption of American precedents regarding the enumeration of divided legislative powers and the clear assumption that the judiciary would be the ultimate guardian of constitutional

---

[42] Broader context can be found in Birch (1955), *Federalism, Finance and Social Legislation*.

[43] Sections 91 and 92 of the *British North America Act 1867* gave the Canadian federal government legislative power over 'public debt and property', 'the raising of money by any mode or system of taxation', 'the borrowing of money on the public credit' and 'currency and coinage', while the provinces were given legislative power over 'Direct Taxation within the Province', and the 'borrowing of Money on the sole Credit of the Province'. Sections 51(ii), (iv), (xii), 90 of the Australian *Commonwealth Constitution* gave the Commonwealth government legislative power over 'Taxation', 'Borrowing money on the public credit of the Commonwealth', 'Currency, coinage and legal tender' and exclusive power to impose 'customs and excise' duties.

[44] *Commonwealth of Australia Constitution*, s 96.

[45] *British North America Act 1867*, s 118.

[46] From 1901 to 1911, the Commonwealth of Australia, was obligated to pay the States 75 per cent of its customs and excise revenue (s 87). From 1902 to 1907, Australia was also required to pay to each State all revenue collected therein, but allowed to keep a residue sufficient to operate government departments in the State (s 89). After 1907, the *Australian Constitution* provided that 'the Parliament may provide, on such basis as it deems fair, for the monthly payment to the several States of all surplus revenue of the Commonwealth' (s 94).

power.[47] In that way, no grievous violence was done to the British model of parliamentary public finance by constitutional mechanisms for fiscal-federalism.

The other opportunity for significant diversion from the distribution of financial authority fixed in British and colonial contexts arose by establishing Canadian and Australian judiciaries as the guardians of the federal division of powers. In neither jurisdiction, however, did federal judiciaries take the opportunity to become more involved in matters of central government finance than their British or colonial predecessors.

No new ground was broken in regard to taxation, as the British judiciary's historically ingrained position regarding taxation disputes was adopted by Canadian and Australian courts in policing the division of taxation power between federal and sub-federal polities.[48] Nor did Canadian and Australian judiciaries develop an entrenched institutional role of resolving disputes regarding appropriation, even where federal boundaries were at stake,[49] thereby replicating the British judiciary's lack of interest in supervising the legality of public expenditure identifiable by the turn of the twentieth century.

Commonwealth Constitutions

From the 1940s to 1980s, a large number of former British colonies obtained independence and adopted written constitutions containing financial provisions modelled on prevailing British practice and the written constitutions of Australia and Canada. Thereby, a form of constitutional boilerplate for financial matters spread throughout the parliamentary constitutional world.

An exhaustive analysis of each constitutional system in the Commonwealth of Nations is beyond the scope of any single work, but

---

[47] Kennedy (1922); Williams (2005), *The Australian Constitution*.

[48] Significant cases in both Canadian and Australian constitutional jurisprudence concern taxation: *Baxter v. Commissioners of Taxation (NSW)* (1907) 4 CLR 1087; *D'Emden v. Pedder* (1904) 1 CLR 91; *Fortier v. Lambe* (1895) 25 SCR 422; *Rattenbury v. Land Settlement Board* [1929] SCR 52.

[49] The most powerful illustration of that reticence is the decision of Australia's High Court, within ten years of Federation, to remove itself from policing expenditure sharing provisions of the *Commonwealth Constitution*, and thereby strip them of any meaningful function: *New South Wales v. Commonwealth* (1908) 7 CLR 179. For some exceptional cases of intervention, see *Reference Re: the Employment Insurance Act* (Can), ss 22 and 23 [1936] SCR 427; [1937] AC 355; *Attorney-General (Vic); Ex rel Dale v. Commonwealth* (1945) 71 CLR 237.

the following survey illustrates how the parliamentary model of public finance assumed a notable uniformity among the nations which broke away from Britain in the twentieth century, and thereby established a remarkably similar distribution of financial authority in parliamentary constitutional systems.

Constitutional Financial Boilerplate

All the written Commonwealth constitutions have a finance chapter, or a discernible set of financial provisions, which contain a strikingly similar set of features.[50] They all make provision for a consolidated fund into which general state revenue flows, prohibitions on expenditure without appropriation, the executive's financial initiative, and (where bi-cameral) the introduction of money bills into the more representative house.[51] Each of those features is familiar from the Australasian and Canadian constitutions drafted in the nineteenth century and the British practice upon which they were drafted.

The mid-twentieth-century Commonwealth constitutions, however, entrenched more of the parliamentary model of public finance than Australian and Canadian pre-cursors. Prominently, many entrenched the 'budget' process by requiring that an 'annual finance statement' be presented to parliaments.[52] That statement typically included 'estimated receipts and expenditure' for that year, as well as a breakdown of the proportion of that expenditure from standing and annual appropriations. Completing those budgetary provisions, many Commonwealth constitutions made provision for supplementary and excess expenditure, as well as votes on account and contingency funding.[53] Many also include an explicit proscription on borrowing without statutory backing,[54] or expressly charged debt repayments on the consolidated funds,[55] while some of the more recent constitutions directly regulate central banks.[56]

---

[50] Except those which derive from civil law traditions: e.g., Mozambique and Cameroon.
[51] E.g., *Constitution of Barbados 1966*, ss 54–55, 107, 109; *Constitution of the Independent State of Papua New Guinea 1975*, ss 209–212; *Constitution of the Kingdom of Swaziland Act 2005*, ss 111–112, 198–199.
[52] E.g., *Constitution of Kiribati 1979*, s 109; *Constitution of Lesotho 1966*, s 112; *Constitution of Malaysia 1963*, s 99.
[53] E.g., *Constitution of Malawi 1966*, ss 177–179; *Constitution of Mauritius 1968*, ss 105–107; *Constitution of Pakistan 1973*, ss 84–85.
[54] E.g., *Constitution of Uganda 1995*, s 159; *Constitution of the Republic of the Seychelles 1993*, s 153.
[55] E.g., *Constitution of Sierra Leone 1978*, s 133; *Constitution of Malta 1964*, s 106.
[56] E.g., *Constitution of Kenya 2010*, s 231.

The additional treatment given to financial matters in the post-War Commonwealth constitutions provide a far greater level of entrenchment of the legal practices, but, in their essence, they replicate the core features of the legal practices developed in the UK, and entrenched in Australian and Canadian federal constitutions. That simple fact can be recognised without making any claim regarding constitutional homogeneity within the Commonwealth. While each former British colony passed through a unique constitution-making process,[57] it is impossible to review those constitutions' finance provisions and ignore the overwhelming commonalities, which were put there intentionally by their drafters.

'Simplified Version of the British System'

In describing the forthcoming *Constitution of Nepal* in 1958, Jennings explained the impact of British precedents on its finance provisions:[58]

> The financial system contemplated is now customary in countries operating parliamentary government, but has been simplified to suit the condition of Nepal.
> There is nothing new in Chapters V [Legislative Procedure] and VI [Financial Procedure] of Part V of the Constitution ... It seems that a simplified version of the British system would best suit the conditions of Nepal. The essence has been retained without the complications which have resulted from a long constitutional history.

The impact of that imperial sensibility is evidenced by the treatment of federal-financial mechanisms within the financial boilerplate of many Commonwealth constitutions. Alike Canada and Australia, those mechanisms were designed to operate within, rather than re-model, the distribution of financial authority between parliaments and executive governments. That point is illustrated by the constitutions of India (independent in 1947), Malaysia (independent in 1957) and Nigeria (independent in 1960).

As a commentator on the *Indian Constitution* noted, 'the broad principles of financial legislation obtaining in *England* have been adopted in

---

[57] Cf Phillips (1985), *West Indian Constitutions: Post-Independence Reform*; O'Brien (2014), *The Constitutional Systems of the Commonwealth Caribbean*; Elias (1962), *The British Commonwealth: The Development of its Laws and Constitutions (Vol 10, Ghana and Sierra Leone)*; Tan (1999), 'A Short Legal and Constitutional History of Singapore'; Harding (1996), *Law, Government and the Constitution in Malaysia*; Basu (1965), *Commentary on the Constitution of India (Vol 1)*.

[58] Kumarasingham (2015), *Constitution-Maker – Selected Writings of Sir Ivor Jennings*, 105, 113 (emphasis added).

our Constitution'.[59] Those principles were entrenched in the 'Finance' provisions of the *Constitution of India*, prominently that 'the Executive cannot raise money by taxation, borrowing or otherwise, or spend money without the authority of parliament' and 'none but a Minister' or 'the Government' can 'make a demand for a grant, ie, either to raise money or to authorise its expenditure'.[60] India's complex federal-financial provisions for the 'Distribution of Revenues between the Union and the States' would operate within those basal principles.[61]

The same embedding of bespoke fiscal distribution provisions within financial boilerplate can be found in the *Constitution of Malaysia*. Commenting on that constitution, Jennings said that there were 'precedents in certain of the Commonwealth Constitutions' which could provide '[m]achinery for consultation between the Central Government and the States and Settlements on certain financial matters'.[62] The written *Constitution of Malaysia* did indeed accommodate the federal compact in its finance provisions.[63] Core federal prescriptions included the division of federal and state expenditure responsibilities, the establishment of a 'National Finance Council' as a forum through which to resolve financial disagreements between federal and state governments,[64] and the allocation of responsibilities concerning the making of 'grants' to the States and the 'assignment of taxes and fees to the States'.[65]

Like India, those bespoke federal-financial mechanisms were located within the familiar parliamentary model of public finance: described by the *Report of the Federation of Malaya Constitutional Commission* as a 'technical matter', but one of 'considerable constitutional importance'.[66] Federal and state 'Consolidated Funds' were established into which '[a]ll revenues and moneys howsoever raised or received by the Federation[or State] shall, subject to [law] ... be paid into and form one fund, to be known as the Federal [or State] Consolidated Fund'.[67] The Federal Consolidated Fund was charged with 'pensions', 'all debt charges for which the Federation is liable' and 'any moneys required to

---

[59] Basu (1965), 692 (original emphasis).
[60] Ibid., 638.
[61] *Constitution of India 1950*, ss 268–273.
[62] Kumarasingham (2015), 79.
[63] Vohrah, Koh and Ling (2004), *The Constitution of Malaysia*, 383–431.
[64] Harding (1996), 176–179.
[65] *Constitution of Malaysia 1957*, ss 82, 98, 108–110.
[66] Reid Commission (1957), [151].
[67] *Constitution of Malaysia*, s 97.

satisfy any judgment ... against the Federation'.[68] The remaining features of the boilerplate provisions were also enacted, including provision for: the 'annual financial statement', 'supply bills', 'supplementary and excess expenditure', a 'contingencies fund' for 'urgent and unforeseen' expenditure, a prohibition on withdrawing money from any consolidated fund without statutory authorisation, audit of public accounts by an Auditor-General, and a prohibition on public borrowing otherwise than by 'federal [or state] law'.[69]

The *Constitution of Nigeria* also brokered the necessary compromises between regional and central finance within the broader context of the financial boilerplate provisions. That constitution provided for a detailed revenue sharing arrangement, including requiring the federal government 'to pay to each Region [50 per cent] of the proceeds of all mining royalties and rent accruing therefrom' and 'the proceeds of all excise duties on tobacco, motor spirits or diesel oil, less those ... attributable to Lagos, are paid to the regions [sic] in proportion to the estimated distribution for consumption in each Region'.[70] Like India and Malaysia, that revenue sharing scheme was embedded in boilerplate financial provisions: a consolidated fund, prohibitions on taxing or spending, provision for an annual financial statement, a public debt charge on the consolidated fund, supplementary and excess appropriation, contingencies and audit.[71]

Commonwealth judiciaries adopted a similarly light-touch attitude to the review of the central governments' major finance activities. Echoes of the British judiciary's reluctance to become embroiled in policing the boundaries of appropriation legislation can be heard throughout the common law world: including, the Supreme Court of Papua New Guinea, the High Court of Sri Lanka and the Supreme Court of India.[72] Examples of more forthright judicial engagement with public

---

[68] *Constitution of Malaysia*, s 98.
[69] *Constitution of Malaysia*, ss 98–111.
[70] Elias (1967), *The British Commonwealth: The Development of its Laws and Constitutions (Vol 14, Nigeria)*, 254; *Constitution of Nigeria 1963*, chapter IX, part 2.
[71] Elias (1967), 258–260. The same retention of the essential aspects of the legal practices concerning public money, despite the existence of various amendments to suit local circumstances, can be seen in Sri Lanka (Cooray (1973), *Constitutional and Administrative Law of Sri Lanka (Ceylon)*, 154–170).
[72] *Reference by Executive Council of the Enga Provincial Government* [1990] PNGLR 532; *Ipatas v. Balakau* [1996] PNGLR 248; *Kariapper v. Wijesinha* (1966) 68 NLR 529; *Bahad v. Union of India* [1970] SC 530; *Balaji v. Government of Tamil Nadu* [2013] INSC 658.

expenditure,[73] and even sovereign borrowing,[74] can be found, but they are remarkable as variations from the wider trend of judicial restraint.

Public Finance in the Parliamentary Tradition

In its export throughout the parliamentary constitutional world public finance law maintained a strikingly similar structure and distribution of financial authority. Thereby, the distribution of financial authority between different constitutional institutions (parliaments, executives and judiciaries) in the UK, dealt with in Chapters 2 and 3, was replicated throughout the British Empire.

All taxation, expenditure and borrowing required legislative authorisation, but locating the financial initiative in executive governments continued to limit the power of parliaments to behave as financial assemblies. Appropriation practice facilitated high degrees of flexibility by treasury departments, which also obtained largely free rein in the acquisition of sovereign debt. Auditors-General remained reliant on treasury departments and judges never took up the opportunity to rule on the legality of spending under appropriation legislation.

Other variations in constitutional structure did not materially affect that model. Constitutional federal-financial provisions operated within the auspices of British, rather than US, constitutional models and federal judiciaries exhibited no greater inclination for involvement in disputes concerning public money than their British and colonial predecessors. Constitution-makers in the decolonised parliamentary world followed a strikingly similar path on the basics of financial organisation, despite other significant divergences from Westminster constitutional practices.

Given the durability of the British model of parliamentary public finance, if Dicey's idea of parliamentary control failed to explain British practice in the nineteenth century, it also failed to describe the concentration of financial authority in executive governments which emerged from the collapse of the British Empire.

Developments in ideas of public finance and public administration in the twentieth century would further concentrate the extent of financial authority held by executive governments.

---

[73] *Dalavai* v. *State of Tamil Nadu* [1976] SC 1559; *Permanent Secretary of the Department of Education of the Government of the Eastern Cape Province* v. *Ed-U-College* 2001 (2) SA 1.
[74] *Abe* v. *Minister of Finance* [1994] 2 LRC 10.

5

History (IV): Public Finance in the Modern State

By the mid-twentieth century, the core features of parliamentary public finance were well established.

Parliamentary legislation underpinned all taxation, expenditure and sovereign borrowing, but executive departments, mainly treasuries and finance ministries, were responsible for generating the economic content of that legislation, could veto its enactment and held wide discretionary power over sovereign debt. Judiciaries were only peripherally involved in public finance, exercising no established jurisdiction over disputes regarding appropriation legislation or sovereign borrowing, and resolved taxation disputes in a manner which explicitly condoned tax evasion.

Within those broad parameters, select parts of the parliamentary model continued to develop throughout the twentieth century. The most profound changes occurred in response to the fiscal expansions necessitated by the World Wars and the welfare state. Total war's crushing financial demands drove the enactment of sovereign borrowing legislation which decoupled treasuries' legal powers to issue debt from annual parliamentary processes. Public expenditure on universal welfare provision was legally structured through standing, rather than annual, appropriation legislation. Responding to fiscal crises of the welfare state, judiciaries revised their attitude to taxation legislation, ushering in revenue-protecting principles for tax disputes. In those ways, the growth of state functions drove significant developments in the distribution of constitutional authority over public finance.

As the twentieth century progressed, wholly public central banks were given 'independence' and their public finance functions became less visible. Central banks' debt management functions were removed in-house to treasuries and their monetary financing powers received no meaningful legislative attention: further distributing debt and monetary financing authority away from parliaments. Towards the close of the twentieth century, new philosophies of public administration grew in influence, and the legislative mechanisms for implementing their deficit controlling aims further reduced parliamentary authority.

Thereby, the twentieth-century experience of parliamentary government shunted an even greater share of financial authority towards executive governments and away from parliaments, maintaining the nineteenth-century trajectory.[1]

Wars and Welfare

The World Wars and the development of the welfare state in the first half of the twentieth century fundamentally altered the financial profile of the public sector.

Total war required total financing commitment, and fiscal activity increased enormously between 1900 and 1947.[2]

Taking the UK as an exemplar, between 1913 and 1915, expenditure moved from ~10 per cent to ~50 per cent of British GDP. Between 1940 and 1946, it rose from ~20 per cent to ~70 per cent of GDP. Tax receipts increased on a similar (but less extreme) trajectory: moving from

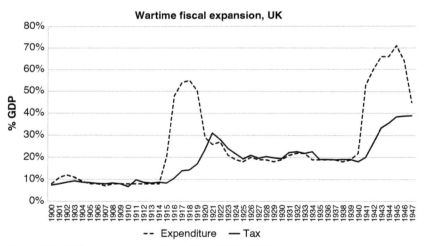

Figure 5.1 UK expenditure and taxation (1900–1945)

---

[1] As with other chapters, the focus throughout is on 'central' government. The reason for adopting that focus is explained in the introduction to Part II.
[2] The data in Figures 5.1 and 5.2 were collected from *BHS*, chapters XI and XVI.

HISTORY (IV): PUBLIC FINANCE IN THE MODERN STATE   97

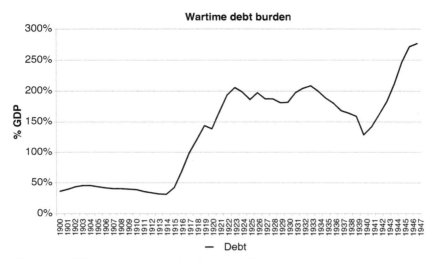

Figure 5.2 UK sovereign borrowing (1900–1945)

~10 per cent to ~15 per cent of GDP between 1914 and 1918, and then from ~20 per cent to ~40 per cent between 1940 and 1945.

Total war also saw extreme spikes in public debt reliance.

The UK's gross debt increased from under 50 per cent of GDP in 1914 to ~150 per cent by 1919. It spiked again from an inter-war low of ~140 per cent of GDP in 1920 to ~270 per cent in 1946.

However, the twentieth century witnessed a more general fiscal expansion, disconnected from financing total war. The scale of that non-military fiscal expansion is vividly illustrated when the growth of expenditure and tax revenue (as a percentage of GDP) is corrected to remove the distortions of total war financing.[3]

Throughout the parliamentary constitutional world, expenditure and tax revenues finished the twentieth century consuming double their late-nineteenth-century share of GDP. In each jurisdiction, expenditure started the twentieth century at between 9 and 18 per cent of GDP, and finished between 35 and 45 per cent. Taxation grew to meet that sustained increase in spending: rising from 9 to 17 per cent of GDP around 1900 to 35–40 per cent by the 1990s.

---

[3] The data concerning expenditure and sovereign borrowing in Figures 5.3-5.5 were drawn from Tanzi and Schuknecht (2000), *Public Spending in the 20th Century*, chapters II and III.

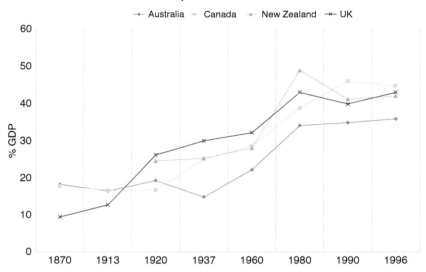
Figure 5.3 Twentieth-century fiscal expansion

The steady increase in tax revenue during that period reduced reliance on debt finance. In 1920, the UK's gross sovereign debt stood at ~132 per cent of GDP. After rising to ~190 per cent in 1937, it continued to fall through the 1970s and 1980s to stand at ~40 per cent in 1990. Australia's and New Zealand's gross debt burden followed a similar trajectory, hitting an inter-war peak of ~155 per cent of GDP in 1937, then dropping throughout the 1970–1980s to ~20 and ~60 per cent of GDP respectively. The fate of sovereign debt financing after the 1990s is dealt with in detail in Chapter 7.

The twentieth century's non-military fiscal expansion is largely explained by the financing requirements of welfare state programmes, as unemployment insurance, pensions, public health and education became the most significant spending activities of governments.

The absolute and relative increases in welfare state expenditure in Australia (~2–18 per cent of GDP) and the United Kingdom (~4–19 per cent of GDP) are reflective of expenditure profiles in advanced economies throughout the twentieth century, including other parliamentary constitutional systems like Canada and New Zealand.[4]

---

[4] Which is the argument presented in Tanzi and Schuknecht (2000).

HISTORY (IV): PUBLIC FINANCE IN THE MODERN STATE

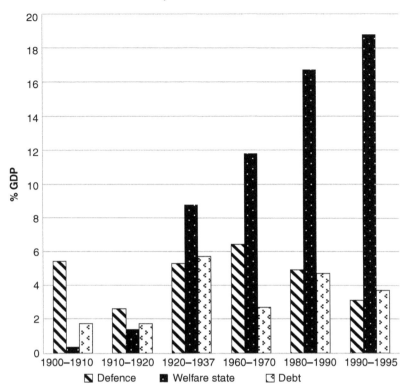

Figure 5.4   UK public expenditure by category (1900–1990)

Much of that fiscal expansion was operationalised via financing mechanisms adopted during wartime. During the First World War, the status of income tax changed from a low-yield to a systemically critical source of national revenue.[5] As the demands of war ebbed, income tax endured as a re-distributive tool of the welfare state. The importance of other wartime financing mechanisms waxed as hostilities ceased. A prime example was Britain's use of monetary financing. During the First World War and its aftermath, Ways and Means Advances from the Bank of England to the Consolidated Fund 'assumed ... a permanent character'.[6]

---

[5] Clark and Dilnot (2002), 'Long Term Trends in British Taxation and Spending'; *Income Tax Act 1915* (Cth); *Income War Tax Act 1917* (Can).

[6] Wormell (1999), volume III, 291.

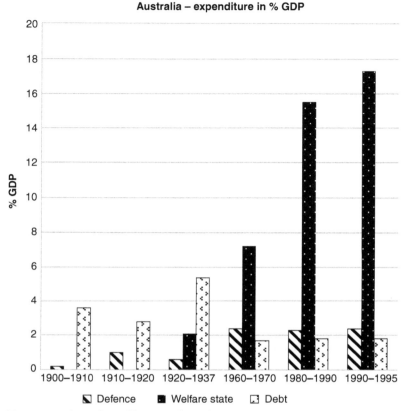

Figure 5.5 Australia public expenditure by category (1900–1990)

In 1917, the Bank advanced ~£160 million to the Treasury: amounting to 126 per cent of customs and excise receipts, 78 per cent of income and property tax and 28 per cent of total public income.[7] In 1919, the Bank advanced over ~£240 million to the Treasury: amounting to 85 per cent of customs and excise, 82 per cent of income and property tax and 27 per cent of total public income.[8] Those enormous monetary injections occurred without noticeable changes to the legislative practices of monetary finance.[9]

---

[7] Ibid.
[8] Ibid., 295 recording fortnightly drawings as high as £26.5 million.
[9] Discussed in Chapter 2.

Parts of the parliamentary model of public finance did, however, change to accommodate the twentieth century's fiscal expansion, most notably sovereign borrowing legislation and a significant growth in the proportional share of expenditure understanding appropriation legislation. Judiciaries supported those legislative developments by disavowing their explicit support for tax evasion.

Authorising War Debt

From the perspective of the constitutional distribution of financial power, the major consequence of total war concerned sovereign borrowing.[10] The critical ground broken was the enactment of legislation conferring standing authority on treasuries to raise money by borrowing, without any pre-set quantitative restrictions.

Prior to the World Wars, treasury departments had wide discretionary power to issue debt, but a weak legal connection remained between sovereign debt issues and annual parliamentary processes.

That connection was strongest in relation to long-term public borrowing where ultimate legal authority to borrow was generally contained in annual legislation or special purpose Acts. In the UK, long-term borrowing authority was contained in *Supply* or *Appropriation Acts*, which conferred authority on the Treasury to borrow up to a limit which matched the lump sum amount of public spending authorised as 'supply'.[11] In Australia, New Zealand and Canada, a similar model was followed, with sovereign borrowing authorisation contained in annual *Loan Acts* which conferred authority to borrow pre-set amounts and, occasionally, pre-set purposes.[12] Those legal frameworks did, however, delegate authority to treasury departments to determine when to issue sovereign debt and the commercial structure of debt issues (maturity,

---

[10] Post-War reconstruction in the UK also saw the enactment of a statutory basis for contingencies expenditure: the *Miscellaneous Financial Provisions Act 1946* (9 & 10 Geo VI, c 40). That Act prescribed the purposes for which contingencies expenditure from the Consolidated Fund could occur, which added to conventional limitations on contingencies spending (see, House of Lords: Select Committee on the Constitution, *The Pre-emption of Parliament* (2013), chapter 2; and HM Treasury, *Managing Public Money* (2013), Annex 2.4), including temporal and quantum limitations which were modified by later legislation (*Miscellaneous Financial Provisions Act 1955* (4 & 5 Eliz II, c 6); *Contingencies Fund Act 1970* (UK); *Contingencies Fund Act 1974* (UK)). For a critique of the Act's design see McEldowney (1988).
[11] The history of *Supply* and *Appropriation Acts* is explained in Chapter 2.
[12] Matters discussed in Chapter 3 above.

interest, denomination, etc.). Thereby, the final composition of a central government's sovereign debt profile arose via executive government decision-making, although the total level of debt was linked to annual legislation.[13]

The fiscal burden of the First World War broke that tradition. Early in the War, the UK Parliament enacted the *War Loan Acts* which conferred authority on the Treasury to borrow 'any money required for raising the supply' for 1915 and 1916.[14] The only quantitative limitation on the assumption of public debt would be the total expenditure needs of the fiscal year and the Treasury was given untrammelled power to determine the price and maturity structure of debt instruments. In accordance with (by then) well-established practices, the repayment of debt issued under the *War Loan Acts* was charged on the Consolidated Fund, and thereby linked to Britain's total tax revenue.

Those features of the *War Loan Acts* severed any meaningful parliamentary link to sovereign borrowing, accelerating the trend set by the late nineteenth century.[15] The magnitude of that development became clear during the inter-war period, when protests were raised in the Commons that Parliament had 'part[ed] with its control', by leaving 'Treasury's ... power uncontrolled by this House ... [t]o create a new debt'.[16] Despite those protests, similarly broad borrowing powers were conferred on the Treasury during the Second World War,[17] beginning a trajectory towards ever-greater delegation of sovereign borrowing authority to treasury departments through the latter twentieth century.

---

[13] Authority for short-term borrowing was largely disconnected from the annual parliamentary process, but of less enduring constitutional significance given the lower financial burden assumed by money-market debt instruments. The UK Treasury was armed with the generous powers conferred by the *Exchequer and Audit Departments Act 1866* (29 & 30 Vict, c 39) and the *Treasury Bills Act 1877* (40 & 41 Vict, c 2), which gave standing power to issue short-term debt and similar versions of that legislative model appeared elsewhere in the Commonwealth: *Treasury Bills Act 1914* (Cth); *Loans Securities Act 1919* (Cth); *Commonwealth Inscribed Stock Act 1911* (Cth); *New Zealand Loans Act 1953* (NZ); *Consolidated Revenue and Audit Act 1931* (Can).

[14] *War Loan Act 1914* (4 & 5 Geo V, c 60); *War Loan Act 1915* (5 & 6 Geo V, c 55).

[15] An earlier example of the same phenomenon was evident during the Boer War: *Loan Act 1901* (1 Edw VIII, c 12).

[16] HC Deb, 14 March 1934, c 519 (John Hills, former Financial Secretary to the Treasury).

[17] *National Loans Act 1941* (4 & 5 Geo V, c 18); Wormell (1999), volume VI, 245. Similar war-debt driven legislative delegations were identifiable in Australia, Canada and New Zealand: *War Loan Act 1914* (Cth); *Loan Act 1942* (Can); *War Purposes Loan Act 1917* (NZ).

Plenary Borrowing Powers

The wartime trajectory of conferring all meaningful authority over sovereign borrowing to treasury departments accelerated throughout the mid-twentieth century. The UK moved first, and most deliberately, to delegate sovereign debt to treasuries, but other parliamentary jurisdictions eventually adopted the same position. Constitutionally, the net impact was to delegate mostly plenary power on executive governments over sovereign borrowing.

In 1968, the UK entrenched the legislative delegation of public borrowing power with the enactment of the *National Loans Act 1968*, which gave the Treasury standing power to borrow any money needed to finance a cash shortfall or fiscal deficit on any terms as to interest or maturity it considered necessary.[18] The only link between annual parliamentary processes and sovereign debt was a connection between the 'National Loans Fund' (into which debt finance flowed and was repaid) and Britain's Consolidated Fund. The two funds were balanced daily: shortfalls in the Consolidated Fund were topped up by the National Loans Fund, and *vice versa*. That link further undermined parliamentary authority over sovereign borrowing: it automatically funnelled cash surpluses to Britain's credit account, which were then automatically applied to debt servicing costs.

Further delegated power over sovereign borrowing was conferred in the 1980s. The *Finance Act 1982* (UK) inserted the underlined text into s 12 of the *National Loans Act*:

12 Power of Treasury to Borrow

(1) *Any money* which the Treasury consider it expedient to raise for the purpose of promoting sound monetary conditions in the United Kingdom and *any money required* –
  (a) *for providing the sums required to meet any excess of payments out of the National Loans Fund over receipts into the National Loans Fund; and*
  (b) *for providing any necessary working balance in the National Loans Fund,*

may be raised in such manner and on such terms and conditions as the Treasury think fit, and money so raised shall be paid into the National Loans Fund.

---

[18] *National Loans Act 1968* (UK), s 12.

The proffered justification for the addition of the new borrowing power was that the deficit financing limit on borrowing imposed by s 12 prevented the issue of new sovereign debt for the sole purpose of monetary policy operations.[19] So the government explained to the Commons:[20]

> When the constraint imposed by section 12 of the Act, which has no coherent relationship with monetary policy, is reached, the Government of the day would be unable to vary debt sales to influence monetary conditions, with adverse consequences for the conduct of monetary policy ... It is quite inappropriate that a section in the National Loans Act should impose such an incidental limitation on our freedom of action in this connection.

Additional to impugning its economic merits,[21] the opposition attacked the constitutional impact of the Treasury's new borrowing powers:[22]

> The clause gives the Chancellor of the Exchequer a new power, not merely to fund the differences between Government revenues and expenditure, but to borrow without limit, providing that his purpose is linked to the purpose of promoting sound monetary conditions in the United Kingdom. There is no definition of sound monetary conditions in the United Kingdom. Therefore, it is a wholly open-ended clause, granting unlimited powers to the Chancellor to borrow money for any purpose that he thinks fit, provided only that the label 'promoting sound monetary conditions' is attached. It is a remarkable extension of Treasury power with no limit written into the clause.

Despite that opposition, the amendment to the *National Loans Act* was carried, and s 12 (as amended) continues to underlie the UK's sovereign debt issuance.[23]

Other jurisdictions gradually followed a similar path in broadening financial executives' statutory borrowing powers. In 1989, New Zealand conferred a quantitatively unlimited authority to borrow and issue sovereign debt 'if it appears to the Minister to be necessary or expedient in the public interest to do so'.[24] By the mid-1990s, Canadian public borrowing authority was limited only by reference to a pre-set 'debt ceiling' and

---

[19] Selling that debt in particular quantities and prices in order to influence the money supply.

[20] HC Deb, 12 July 1982, vol 27 sc 657, 659.

[21] The core disagreement was whether the supply of broad money had 'any real effect on what has happened to the real economy' (HC Deb, 12 July 1982, vol. 27 c 671 (Joel Barnett)).

[22] HC Deb, 12 July 1982, vol. 27 c 662 (Peter Shore).

[23] As discussed further in Chapter 7.

[24] *Public Finance Act 1989* (NZ), s 47.

Australia adopted the same approach to sovereign borrowing legislation after 1997.[25]

In each context, all meaningful authority over sovereign borrowing was delegated by parliaments to treasury departments. A similarly broad delegation of financial authority flowed from the growth of the welfare state.

Financing the Welfare State

The growth of the welfare state had two major impacts on the law of public finance.[26]

The first, and most direct, concerned the use of standing appropriation legislation to authorise welfare state expenditure. That development significantly reduced the relevance of annual parliamentary processes. The second, and less obviously connected to the welfare state's growth, was the judiciary's disavowal of its earlier approval of tax evasion. That development removed a block on the collection of tax revenue and boosted parliamentary fiscal authority.

Standing Authority for Welfare State Expenditure

From the post-War period, welfare state expenditure became the largest single spending objective of government and legal authority for that spending was severed from the annual parliamentary process, via standing legislation establishing a 'welfare fund' model.

Although often marked to the mid-1940s, statutory welfare funds pre-existed both World Wars. The British model dated from the *National Insurance Act 1911*,[27] which established a system of 'national health' and 'unemployment' insurance.[28] The financing of health and unemployment benefits would be met from direct contributions, from potential beneficiaries and employers, and money annually voted by Parliament.[29] Receipts were paid into two funds. Health benefits would be paid from

---

[25] Cf *Borrowing Authority Act 1996-1997* (Can).
[26] The enactment of the *Parliament Act 1911* (1 & 2 Geo V, c 13) could also be understood as a response to the growing push for universal welfare provision. As a political event, that development was monumental, but major jurists described the *Parliament Act 1911* as 'merely [giving] statutory force to existing practice': Anson (1912), 'The Parliament Acts and the British Constitution', 681. For countervailing views of its importance, see McLean (2009) and Jaconelli (1991), 'The Parliament Bill 1910-1911'.
[27] *National Insurance Act 1911* (1 & 2 Geo V, c 55).
[28] Micklethwait (1976), *The National Insurance Commissioners*, 7.
[29] *National Insurance Act 1911*, ss 3 and 85.

the 'National Health Insurance Fund' and unemployment benefits would be paid from the 'unemployment fund',[30] with any deficit to be filled from general revenue. Payments from those funds would not require annual parliamentary approval. In that way, the earliest national insurance legislation partially separated the funding of welfare benefits from annual parliamentary financial processes.

Implementing the Beveridge Report's recommendations,[31] the *National Insurance Act 1946* created a 'National Insurance Fund'. Contributions from employers, insured persons and annually voted supply would flow into that fund, and all expenditure necessary for the payment of benefits would flow out.[32] Thereby, the revenue and expenditure sides of welfare funding were authorised by standing, rather than annual, legislation.[33] In the UK, that basic system would endure through many iterations of unemployment insurance and pension legislation.[34]

A slightly different path was taken in relation to UK public health financing. The *National Health Act 1946* did not establish a fund akin to the National Insurance Fund.[35] Instead, the funds necessary to operate the National Health Service (NHS) were to be paid 'out of moneys provided by Parliament'.[36] Thereby, public health services were to be funded from general taxation, and the expenditure on those services would be provided through the annual supply process. However, from the establishment of the National Insurance Fund proportional contributions to the NHS would be made from national insurance contributions,[37] a funding line which only received explicit statutory support in 1957.[38] From that time, a proportion of public health funding was linked to the welfare fund created by standing legislation and (thereby) removed from the annual parliamentary financial process.

---

[30] *National Insurance Act 1911*, ss 54 and 92.
[31] Which scaled and replicated the 1911 model: Beveridge, 'Social Insurance and Allied Services' (1942), 109.
[32] *National Insurance Act 1946* (9 & 10 Geo VI, c 67), s 35. The latter *National Assistance Act 1948* (11 & 12 Geo VI, c 29) (establishing means tested entitlements) relied on the financing provisions of the *National Insurance Act 1946*.
[33] With the qualification that a supplement (from annually voted expenditure) in the event of a shortfall remained a legal possibility.
[34] E.g., *National Insurance Act 1965* (UK), ss 2, 83.
[35] (9 & 10 Geo VI, c 8).
[36] *National Health Act 1946*, ss 52–54.
[37] HC Deb, 24 March 1958, c 54.
[38] *National Health Contributions Act 1957* (5 & 6 Eliz II, c 54); *National Health Service Contributions Act 1965* (UK).

A similar preference for standing authorisation of expenditure underpinned other major welfare state financing legislation. The Australian *National Welfare Fund Act 1943* established a 'National Welfare Fund' and a standing appropriation of the Australian Consolidated Revenue Fund to the credit of that fund to the lesser of £30 million or ¼ of the total personal (i.e., non-company) income tax collected in a fiscal year.[39] The fund would source expenditure for 'health services, unemployment or sickness benefits, family allowances, or other welfare or social services',[40] including invalid and old-age pensions, maternity allowances and 'pharmaceutical benefits'.[41] Eventually, Australia's welfare state expenditure was removed from a welfare fund model, but the standing authority which originated in that model endured as Australia enacted standing (rather than annual) appropriation legislation for most of its welfare state expenditure.[42]

Matters were more complicated in Canada and New Zealand. Welfare state programmes in Canada were executed through cooperative federal schemes, with national and provincial governments each contributing funding and institutional support for social insurance. Despite that intergovernmental complexity, the preference for standing, rather than annual, appropriation was identifiable: funding for pensions and unemployment insurance was provided by standing charges on the Canadian consolidated fund.[43]

New Zealand represents something of an outlier. Of the nations which enjoyed independent parliamentary government at the inception of welfare state policies, only New Zealand moved from a standing to an annual appropriation model of expenditure authorisation. In 1938, New Zealand established a welfare fund similar to that established by the UK's *National Insurance Act 1946*,[44] but in 1964 welfare expenditure was thrown back onto New Zealand's annual supply process.[45]

---

[39] *National Welfare Fund Act 1943* (Cth), s 5.
[40] *National Welfare Fund Act 1943* (Cth), s 6.
[41] *Invalid and Old-Age Pensions Act 1943* (Cth), s 18; *Maternity Allowance Act 1943* (Cth), s 3; *Pharmaceutical Benefits Act 1944* (Cth), s 17.
[42] *National Welfare Fund Repeal Act 1985* (Cth).
[43] *Old Age Security Act* (RSC 1985), s 45; *Canadian Pension Plan* (RSC 1985), s 108; *Employment Insurance Act* (SC 1996), ss 72–77. Canada's welfare legislation created a much more complex funding system of interlinked federal and provincial grants, which defies easy summary and is put aside here: Federal-Provincial-Territorial Directors of Income Support: *Social Assistance Statistical Report* (2016).
[44] *Social Security Act 1938* (NZ), ss 103 and 106.
[45] *Social Security Act 1964* (NZ), s 124.

Fiscal Nullities

As the twentieth century progressed, the heavy fiscal demands of the welfare state compounded: by the early 1980s, it was common to speak of the fiscal 'crisis of the welfare state'.[46] Those fiscal developments coincided with the common law judiciary's reversal of its explicit approval of tax evasion.

Walking-back *Westminster*

By the mid-twentieth century, the judiciary's taxpayer-protecting approach to tax legislation had grown two limbs.[47] One required a 'strict interpretation' of tax statutes. The other limb required courts to characterise complex transactions by reference to their legal form, rather than their economic substance.[48] Described as the *Westminster* doctrine,[49] that bespoke attitude to tax legislation was discernible throughout the common law world,[50] and evidenced a permissive approach by the judiciary to tax evasion.

From the 1980s, common law judiciaries disavowed the *Westminster* doctrine. The seminal 1982 case *WT Ramsay Ltd* v. *Inland Revenue Commissioners*[51] involved circular transactions designed to avoid tax on capital gains from sales of real property:[52] whereby assets performed a series of legal steps, but remained in the same economic place. Both aspects of the *Westminster* doctrine were jettisoned. The strict interpretation approach to tax legislation was simply written out of the law books:

> What are 'clear words' is to be ascertained upon normal principles: these do not confine the courts to literal interpretation. There may, indeed should, be considered in the context and scheme of the relevant Act as a whole, and its purpose may, indeed should, be regarded.

The legalistic approach to commercial transactions was displaced in a classically crabwise piece of common law reasoning. Lord Wilberforce

---

[46] Joppke (1987), 'The Crisis of the Welfare State, Collective Consumption, and the Rise of New Social Actors', 237.
[47] Its origins were described in Chapter 2.
[48] *Inland Revenue Commissioners* v. *McGuckian* [1997] 1 WLR 991, 999.
[49] *McGuckian* (1997), 1001.
[50] *Anderson* v. *Commissioner of Taxes (Vict)* (1937) 57 CLR 233 and *Mullens* v. *Federal Commissioner of Taxation* (1976) 135 CLR 290 (Australia); *Buckley & Young Ltd* v. *Commissioner of Inland Revenue* [1978] 2 NZLR 485 (New Zealand); *Pioneer Laundry & Dry Cleaners Ltd* v. *The Minister of National Revenue* [1939] SCR 1 and *Covert* v. *Minister of Finance of Nova Scotia* [1980] 2 SCR 774 (Canada).
[51] [1982] AC 300.
[52] Under the *Finance Act 1965* (UK).

described the *Westminster* doctrine as 'cardinal' and then proceeded to explain why it had been misapplied for half a century:[53]

> While obliging the court to accept documents or transactions, found to be genuine, as such, [the Westminster doctrine] does not compel the court to look at a document or a transaction in blinkers, isolated from any context to which it properly belongs. If it can be seen that a document or transaction was intended to have effect as part of a nexus or series of transactions, or as an ingredient of a wider transaction intended as a whole, there is nothing in the doctrine to prevent it being so regarded.

The 'context' to which Wilberforce referred was that tax law 'was created to operate in the real world, not that of make-belief'.[54] Given that the taxpayer in *Ramsay* had received a letter from his accountant stating that 'the scheme is a pure tax avoidance scheme and has no commercial justification',[55] the approach newly birthed in *Ramsay* led the revenue to victory.

That approach eventually crystallised into a discrete legal doctrine: 'steps inserted which have no commercial (business) purpose apart from the avoidance of a liability to tax ... are to be disregarded for fiscal purposes'.[56] That doctrine would eventually be labelled 'fiscal nullity'[57] and mirrored (with local adaptations) in other common law jurisdictions.[58] Starkly reversing course, judges openly chastised the lawyers and accountants who thrived on tax evasion as engaging in 'disingenuous' and 'dangerous' behaviour.[59]

Limits of Fiscal Nullity

Despite their importance, the total significance of *Ramsay* and *Furniss* was limited in several ways.

Old habits died hard in lower courts staffed by tax specialists, who continued to apply a taxpayer-protecting approach, despite admonitions to the contrary from judges at the apex.[60] Additionally, much tax

---

[53] *Ramsay* (1982), 324–325 (emphasis added).
[54] Ibid., 326.
[55] Ibid., 328.
[56] *Furniss (Inspector of Taxes)* v. *Dawson* [1984] AC 474, 527.
[57] *Craven (Inspector of Taxes) Appellant* v. *White* [1989] AC 398, 423.
[58] *John* v. *Federal Commissioner of Taxation* (1989) 166 CLR 417 (for Australia); and *Canada Trustco Mortgage* [2005] 2 SCR 601 (for Canada).
[59] *Inland Revenue Commissioners* v. *Burmah Oil Co Ltd* [1982] STC 30, 32–33.
[60] Complicated outcomes often resulted, see e.g., *Sherdley* v. *Sherdley* [1986] 1 WLR 732, 738, describing *Westminster* as the 'true test' and then being overturned by *Sherdley* v. *Sherdley* [1988] AC 213.

legislation had been drafted in response to the (highly technical) *Westminster* doctrine, with the result that a purposive approach to tax legislation often required using pre-*Ramsay* techniques of interpretation.[61] Finally, statutory cognates of the 'fiscal nullity' doctrine had begun to appear in general anti-avoidance rules (GAARs).[62] An exemplar GAAR was introduced in 1988 by s 245 of the Canadian *Income Tax Act*, which operated to 'deny a tax benefit' to a person who used an 'avoidance transaction', which was defined to mean 'any transaction' or 'series of transactions':

> that, but for this section, would result, directly or indirectly, in a tax benefit, unless the transaction may reasonably be considered to have been undertaken or arranged primarily for bona fide purposes other than to obtain the tax benefit.

In jurisdictions which enacted GAAR legislation,[63] common law doctrines of fiscal nullity operated only as back-up principles, where legislation did not close the tax-evading loophole.[64]

Despite those limitations, from the 1980s it was clear that common law judiciaries had abandoned the extremities of the taxpayer-protecting approach which had ruled tax disputes since the nineteenth century.[65] The financial effect was to empower revenue agencies to adopt strategies for the maximum enforcement of tax. The constitutional effect was to remove the judicial block on the collection of public revenue.

Constitutional Impact

The financing needs of total war and the welfare state had profound impacts on the distribution of financial authority in parliamentary systems of government.

---

[61] A matter explicitly pointed out by the Supreme Court of Canada: *Canada Trustco Mortgage* (2005), 11.
[62] See generally: Fernandes (2016), 'A Principled Framework for Assessing General Anti-Avoidance Regimes'.
[63] E.g., Australia (*Income Tax Assessment Act 1936* (Cth), Part IVA), Hong Kong (*Inland Revenue Ordinance*, chapter 112), Malaysia (*Income Tax Act 1967*, s 140), New Zealand (*Land and Income Tax Act 1954*, s 108) Singapore (*Income Tax Act*, chapter 134) and South Africa (*Income Tax Act 1962*, s 80A).
[64] The UK did not obtain a GAAR rule until 2013: *Finance Act 2013* (UK), part 5.
[65] Although it experienced something of a renaissance in the early twenty-first century, as explained in Chapter 8.

Severing treasuries' power to borrow from the annual supply process conferred standing authority to determine the economic terms on which debt finance would be obtained. When that authority was combined with the standing appropriation for debt servicing costs, parliaments were excluded from decision-making regarding a large portion of public financial activity: assuming and paying sovereign debt.

The establishment of standing authority for welfare finance saw an even greater delegation of financial power to executive governments. As the twentieth century progressed and welfare state expenditure increased, the standing appropriations provided by welfare fund models would permit the authorisation of ever-larger swathes of public expenditure outside the annual parliamentary process.

The shift in the judicial attitude to tax legislation (away from the taxpayer-protecting approach) changed the position of the judiciary vis-à-vis parliamentary fiscal policy enacted into legislation. As judges became less concerned with protecting taxpayers from the 1980s, the prospect of an effective enforcement mechanism for parliamentary fiscal policy increased.

Money and Public Management

The other major changes in public finance law during the twentieth century grew from changing attitudes towards monetary institutions and public administration.[66]

Post-War, central banks were established by statute as the institutions with principal responsibility for the stability of the monetary system, obtaining very broad powers to issue credit mainly to private banks, but also to executive governments. Those responsibilities were largely conferred without any explicit legislative regulation of monetary finance,[67]

---

[66] In a number of parliamentary states a major topic of public financial interest was expenditure equalisation programmes, which could be operated domestically (transferring money from central to non-central governments) or internationally (transferring money outside the nation-state to supranational governments, like the European Union, or international organisations, like the International Monetary Fund). For more information on both types of programmes in the UK, see McEldowney (2015), 'Public Finance and the Control of Public Expenditure', 351; McLean and McMillan (2003), 'The Distribution of Public Expenditure Across UK Regions', 45–46; European Union (2014), *European Union Public Finance*, chapter 8.

[67] During the same period, administrative and scholarly attention focused increasingly on the 'constitutional position of the central bank' through the prism of 'monetary policy', rather than direct provision of finance to government: e.g., Goodhart (2003), 'The Constitutional Position of the Central Bank'.

leaving central bank and treasury officials uncontrolled by legislation in deciding the terms upon which central banks would provide credit to central governments.

As the twentieth century drew to a close, New Public Management philosophies drove large changes in public accounting, fiscal responsibility and appropriation legislation. Prominently, 'fiscal responsibility laws' were enacted which sought to impose a particular view of budget discipline on the formulation of national budgets and sovereign debt policy. Approached with the constitutional distribution of financial authority in mind, fiscal responsibility laws did nothing to bolster parliamentary authority of annual budgets or sovereign debt issues. To the contrary, the deficit control objective of fiscal responsibility laws further diminished the significance of annual parliamentary processes.

Both developments distributed financial authority further away from parliaments.

Central Banking and Public Finance

The development of central banking in the twentieth century has been the subject of a very large secondary literature,[68] and caution should attend any attempt to draw general conclusions regarding the constitutional position of central banking and their functions.

Some core themes are, however, discernible.

Between the 1930s and 1960s, Australia, Canada, New Zealand and the UK established central banks, as wholly public institutions, with legislative monopolies on the issue of high-value currency, capacities to transact with commercial banks and authority to act as sovereign debt managers.[69] Each central banking statute provided for a governance structure under which the bank would be managed by

---

[68] Entry points are Singleton (2011), *Central Banking in the Twentieth Century* and Capie, Goodhart and Schnadt (1994), 'The Development of Central Banking'.

[69] E.g., *Reserve Bank of New Zealand Act 1933* (NZ) (establishing the Reserve Bank of New Zealand); *Bank of Canada Act 1934* (Canada) (establishing the Bank of Canada); *Bank of England Act 1946* (9 & 10 Geo 6, c 27) (nationalising the Bank of England, and continuing its functions, including its statutory monopoly on the issue of paper currency conferred by the *Bank Charter Act 1844* (7 & 8 Vict, c 32)); *Reserve Bank Act 1959* (Cth) (re-constituting the existing Commonwealth Bank of Australia, created as a trading bank by the *Commonwealth Bank Act 1911* (Cth), as a public central bank).

a board that would report to, consult with, or be directed by, treasuries.[70]

The core function of those central banks was regulating the private credit system, including by influencing the price and volume of credit offered by commercial banks, as well as banks' prudential practices. As the twentieth century progressed, the label 'monetary policy' attached to those functions. Despite significant variation in the economic theories underlying monetary policy,[71] central banks mostly executed monetary policy by manipulating interest rates offered on short-term credit to commercial banks.

For much of the post-War period, central banks co-ordinated their monetary policy functions with treasuries and were, in that sense, not 'independent' of the executive government. Worries about the role of politicised central banks contributing to inflation pushed central banks towards formal 'independence' from treasuries.[72] Although the precise form of central bank independence varied by jurisdiction,[73] it coincided with the removal of debt management functions from central banks and the creation of debt management 'agencies' within treasuries.[74] Another public financial plank of central bank independence was to strip central banks of their functions as managers (and often issuers) of sovereign debt.

The UK's experience illustrates the trend.[75] In 1998 legislation gave the Bank of England operational independence over monetary policy, while relocating its debt management functions to the statutory 'Debt

---

[70] *Bank of England Act 1946*, s 4; *Reserve Bank Act 1959* (Cth), s 11; *Reserve Bank of New Zealand Act 1933* (NZ), s 23; *Bank of Canada Act 1934* (Can), ss 7-13.

[71] An illuminating discussion of the complex shifts in monetary policy over time can be found in Goodhart, 'The Conduct of Monetary Policy' (1989) 99 *The Economic Journal* 293.

[72] Goodhart (2010), 'The Changing Role of Central Banks'. Other prominent central banks, such as the US Federal Reserve System, obtained de jure and de facto independence much earlier: Eichengreen and Garber (1991), 'Before the Accord: US Monetary-Financial Policy'.

[73] For the UK central bank, independence was secured de jure, as the Bank of England's independence was enshrined in statute: *Bank of England Act 1998* (UK), s 10. In other jurisdictions, like Australia and Canada, central bank independence is a de facto concept.

[74] The Bank of Canada is the notable exception, which retained its debt-management and monetary financing responsibilities under the *Bank of Canada Act 1985*.

[75] Although some jurisdictions came earlier (like New Zealand, which established the New Zealand Debt Management Office in 1988) and later (like Australia, which established the Australian Office of Financial Management in 2001).

Management Account' operated by the Treasury.[76] Administratively, the shift appeared simple: the Treasury's functions would be exercised by a Treasury agency called the 'Debt Management Office'.[77]

Matters were more complex at the level of legal authority.[78] The Bank of England's standing authority to issue short-term debt under s 8 of the *Treasury Bills Act 1877* was abolished and a cognate power was vested in the Treasury.[79] Confusingly, no separate legal entity was created to exercise the Bank's powers over debt management: instead, a form of split legal personality was bestowed on the UK's Treasury:[80]

> Any powers which relate to Treasury securities and which are conferred on the Treasury in a capacity other than issuer may be exercised by them, and no rule of law preventing a person contracting with himself shall prevent them exercising the powers.

That contorted provision was designed to support the shadowy existence of a separate debt managing (i.e., debt issuing) office within the Treasury (the Debt Management Office), without providing for its legal separation from the Treasury. Under that strange system, the Treasury exercised exceptionally broad powers to issue and repay debt.[81] The link between the Bank's 'independence' and the creation of the Debt Management Account was explained as 'avoid[ing] any perceptions of conflicts of interest between ... the Bank's monetary policy operations and Treasury's debt and cash management operations'.[82]

Dwarfing the significance of central banks' debt management functions was their power to provide credit to the government through monetary financing.

---

[76] *Bank of England Act 1998* (UK), ss 10–12; *Finance Act 1998* (UK), ss 158–161. Like the National Loans Fund and Consolidated Fund, the Debt Management Account was daily balanced with the National Loans Fund, essentially to provide arm's-length financing of the credit account of the Consolidated Fund (Schedule 5A, cl 11).

[77] Prosser (2014), 104.

[78] The same changes were made in Australia and New Zealand without discernible amendments to the legislation governing sovereign borrowing and central banking. Canada never stripped its central bank of public debt management functions.

[79] *Finance Act 1998* (UK), s 159; inserting Schedule 5A into the *National Loans Act 1968*.

[80] Section 158 of the *Finance Act 1998*.

[81] Including 'securing over time that sums are available to meet any daily shortfalls in the National Loans Fund and that any daily surpluses in that Fund are used to the best advantage': *National Loans Act 1968*, Schedule 5A cl 1(1)(a)).

[82] HC Deb, 25 Oct 1999, c 710; HM Treasury, *The Future of UK Government Debt and Cash Management* (1997); Treasury Select Committee, *Government's Cash and Debt Management* (2000).

Monetary Finance

Strangely, the position of central banks in *providing finance to central governments*, as opposed to simply acting as a sovereign debt agent, received scant attention in the growth of public central banks and the latter push towards 'independence'.

Canadian legislation marked the high point of monetary finance regulation. The *Bank of Canada Act 1985* (Can) provided that 'the Bank may':[83]

> make loans to the Government of Canada ... but such loans outstanding at any one time shall not ... exceed one-third of the estimated revenue of the Government of Canada for its fiscal year ... and such loans shall be repaid before the end of the first quarter after the end of the fiscal year of the government that has contracted the loan ...

The admirably clear prescription of quantum and maturity conditions imposed by that Canadian provision was anomalous. By the close of the twentieth century, it represented the only detailed statutory limitation on the monetary financing activities of central banks in the parliamentary nations.[84]

In the UK, the total statutory treatment of the Bank of England's monetary financing powers appeared in a terse subsection of the *National Loans Act 1968*:[85]

> The Bank of England may lend any sums which the Treasury have power to borrow under this section, and section 1 of the Bank of England Act 1819 (loans by Bank to Crown to require authority of Parliament) shall cease to have effect.

That provision permitted the Bank of England to finance the UK Treasury whenever there was a fiscal or cash deficit, or when 'sound monetary conditions' required an injection of central bank credit. The Ways and Means Advance, the ancient financing channel between Bank and Treasury remained alive, would be authorised under that provision.[86]

In 1933, New Zealand's Parliament imposed a quantitative limitation on the Reserve Bank of New Zealand's power to grant credit to the central

---

[83] *Bank of Canada Act 1985* (Can), s18(j).
[84] The secondary literature on the legal powers of central banks to provide monetary finance is sparse and unsatisfying: Cottarelli (1993), *Limiting Central Bank Credit to Government*; Jácome, Luis et al. (2012), 'Central Bank Credit to the Government'.
[85] Sub-section 12(7).
[86] Chapter 7 deals in detail with the Bank of England's public financing role in the twenty-first century via its 'quantitative easing' programme.

government. The limit was imposed as a conditional prohibition: 'that it shall not be lawful for the Bank to':[87]

> (i) Grant accommodation, either directly or indirectly, to the Treasury ... by way of discounts, loans, advances, overdrafts, or otherwise, in excess of one-half of the revenue or estimated revenue for the year ... of the Treasury ...

That restriction on monetary financing survived for around thirty years, before being repealed by the *Reserve Bank of New Zealand Act 1964*. Australian legislation governing the Reserve Bank of Australia never dealt explicitly with monetary financing.

'New Public [Financial] Management'

The cluster of approaches to the liberalisation of government administration often called 'New Public Management' (NPM)[88] grew apace throughout the 1990s.[89] NPM has been described as:[90]

> a model of reform which privilege quantification and results and in which accounting has a central role. It is a model in which mimicry of private sector practices is advocated.

NPM practices were not adopted with the same speed or intensity across all parliamentary systems. Australia and New Zealand have been identified as 'high intensity adopters',[91] while Canada's attitude to NPM reform projects has been described as 'extremely slow' and 'less extensive' than 'other Anglo-Saxon countries'.[92] The UK stands somewhere in the middle.[93]

The application of NPM theories had significant effects on the administration of public money. A prominent impact was the conferral of

---

[87] *Reserve Bank of New Zealand Act 1933* (NZ), s 14(i).
[88] Hood (1995), 'The "New Public Management" in the 1980s: Variations on a Theme'.
[89] For pre-1990s developments, Dewar and Funnell (2016), 196–211.
[90] Lapsley, Mussari and Paulsson (2009), 'On the Adoption of Accrual Accounting in the Public Sector', 720. An entry-point to the significant literature on NPM can be found in Ferlie, Lynn and Pollitt (2005), *Oxford Handbook of Public Management*; Cane (2016), *Controlling Administrative Power*, Chapter 12.
[91] Carlin (2005), 'Debating the Impact of Accrual Accounting and Reporting in the Public Sector', 309–336; Day (2009), 'Implementation of Whole-of-Government Reports in Australia', 229–234.
[92] ACCA (2014), Whole of Government Accounts: Who is Using Them', 9 citing Pollitt and Bouckaert, *Public Management Reform* (2004).
[93] Pollitt and Bouckaert (2004), *Public Management Reform*.

'performance' or 'value for money' auditing functions on Auditors-General,[94] which diminished the importance of their role in overseeing the conformity of executive uses of money with parliamentary legislation. Cosmetic changes to financial legislation were also part of the NPM programme. 'Audit' legislation was gradually re-branded as financial 'management' or 'administration' legislation, and the broad supervisory powers enjoyed by treasury departments were re-cast in 'managerial' terms.[95]

A particularly contentious deployment of NPM thinking was the transportation of the private sector model of accrual accounting to the public sector. Rather than simply recording cash debits and credits, accrual accounting records the value of public sector assets and liabilities,[96] thus attempting to capture a snapshot of the value of public sector entities as 'going concerns'.[97] Accounting for cash flow is an element of accrual accounting, but it is mostly obscured by a focus on recording net cash flow and occasionally replaced by measures of 'revenue' and 'expenses', within which real cash flow figures are adjusted to take account of future cash receivables (revenue) or netted off against transaction costs (expenses).[98] In some jurisdictions, the implementation of accrual accounting was backed by legislation;[99] in others, it occurred at the level of administrative practice.[100]

Whatever be its abstract accounting value, the adoption of accrual accounting added layers of complexity and confusion to public sector reporting with no appreciable benefit to parliaments' authority to set the

---

[94] *Audit Amendment Act 1979* (Cth); *Auditor-General Act 1977* (Can); *Public Finance Act 1977* (NZ); *National Audit Act 1983* (UK); Glynn (1985), 'Value for Money Auditing – An International Review and Comparison'; Dewar and Funnell (2017), 201–222.

[95] Prominent examples were Australia's *Financial Management and Accountability Act 1996* (Cth), which replaced the *Audit Act 1901* (Cth), and the UK's *Government Resources and Accounts Act 2000* (UK), which superseded most of the audit provisions of the *Exchequer and Audit Departments Act 1866*. See, generally, Hollingsworth and White (2001), 'Public Finance Reform'.

[96] Connolly and Hyndman (2006), 'The Actual Implementation of Accruals Accounting', 272–273.

[97] E.g., HM Treasury, *Financial Reporting Manual* (2017/18), 5.

[98] E.g., Australian Bureau of Statistics, *Australian System of Government Finance Statistics: Concepts, Sources and Methods* (2005), Chapter 2.

[99] In Australia, accrual accounting was authorised by the *Financial Management and Accountability Act 1997* (Cth). In the UK, it was authorised by the *Government Resources and Accounts Act 2000* (UK). See further, Likierman (2003), 'Planning and Controlling UK Public Expenditure on a Resource Basis'.

[100] Baker and Rennie (2006), 'Forces Leading to the Adoption of Accrual Accounting by the Canadian Federal Government'.

legal conditions of public financial activity.[101] Despite the complications of accrual accounting, treasury departments adopted it in the annual budgets presented to parliaments, which resulted in the enactment of appropriation legislation which used accrual figures as the quantum limits for spending.[102]

Performance auditing, re-branding of audit legislation and accrual accounting each made public financial law harder for non-specialists to understand, but had no significant impacts on the existing distribution of financial authority between parliament and executive. Indeed, the critical institutions of parliamentary public finance survived the flurry of NPM reforms. The basic concepts of supply and appropriation endured,[103] but were often collapsed into a single appropriation Act.[104] Excesses continued to be authorised retrospectively in most parliamentary systems.[105]

More consequentially, NPM-style thinking did impact the distribution of financial authority through the enactment of 'fiscal responsibility legislation' from the early 1990s.

Fiscal Responsibility Laws

Previously, the process of budget planning, which integrates fiscal, debt management and monetary policy, was largely untouched by positive law. At least cosmetically, that situation changed with the passage of legislation which provided for a 'Charter' of 'Budget' or 'Fiscal' 'Responsibility' (in the UK and New Zealand) or 'Honesty' (in Australia).[106]

At the level of strict legal form, each jurisdiction's fiscal responsibility laws are not identical, but their core features are strikingly similar.

---

[101] To take one example, attempting to apply both cash and accrual accounting systems produced enormous variation in net fiscal positions. Australia's experience is illustrative: in FY2000/01, the difference between cash and accrual accounting produced a ~$135 million variation in the fiscal surplus, while in FY2010/11, that difference produced a ~$4.3 billion variation in the fiscal deficit: data drawn from *AGBP*, Supplementary Tables 1 (2001 and 2010).

[102] Webber (2004), 'Managing the Public's Money: From Outputs to Outcomes – and Beyond'. UK appropriation legislation has, however, maintained a cash-accounting legal limit by including an appropriation for 'net cash requirement(s)', determined by reconciling the accrual budget limits to cash.

[103] For the complicated history between supply and appropriation, see Chapter 2.

[104] As they were in Australia and Canada by the early 1990s.

[105] E.g., *Appropriation (Confirmation and Validation) Act 2014* (NZ); *Appropriation Act, No 5 2014–15* (Can).

[106] *Budget Responsibility and National Audit Act 2011* (UK); *Charter of Budget Honesty Act 1998* (Cth); *Fiscal Responsibility Act 1994* (NZ); generally see, Corbacho, and Schwartz (2007), 'Fiscal Responsibility Laws'.

Fiscal responsibility laws announce substantive economic principles relating to public sector finances, orientated towards reducing or eliminating fiscal deficits and burdens imposed by long-term public debt.[107] In Australian and New Zealand legislation, those principles are set in primary legislation,[108] while the UK's version confers power on the Treasury to set the relevant standards of budget 'responsibility' which must be approved by Parliament.[109] Although appearing anodyne, those principles are generally orientated towards reducing the relative size of the public sector. '[T]he Government is to ... manage financial risks faced by the Commonwealth prudently ... [including] ... risks arising from ownership of public trading enterprises.'[110]

Second, fiscal responsibility laws provide a set of disclosure rules, requiring government bodies to publish reports indicating their compliance with the substantive economic principles.[111]

The enactment of fiscal responsibility laws coincided with an historic reduction in economic volatility in Western industrialised countries, a period referred to as the 'great moderation' by scholars and policymakers.[112] Their prime objectives, of controlling deficit and ensuring debt sustainability, were orientated entirely towards executive governments, rather than parliaments. In that sense, fiscal responsibility laws reflected the overwhelming distribution of financial planning away from parliaments.

When viewed against the existing legal practices regarding financial authorisation of fiscal activities, the salient features of fiscal responsibility laws are a failure to interlock with the processes for statutory authorisation of revenue and expenditure, nor impose any hard legal limitation on executives' use of public money. The substantive norms in FRLs are concerned with the economic efficiency and effectiveness of public finance, rather than the parliamentary processes of legislative authorisation of fiscal activity. While the disclosure norms provide a deal of useful

---

[107] Thornton (2009), 'Do Fiscal Responsibility Laws Matter?'.
[108] *Charter of Budget Honesty Act 1998* (Cth), ss 1, 4 and 5; *Public Finance Act 1989* (NZ), s 26G.
[109] *Budget Responsibility and National Audit Act 2011* (UK), s 1.
[110] *Charter of Budget Responsibility Act 1998* (Cth), ss 5(1)(a) and (2)(a).
[111] *Budget Responsibility and National Audit Act 2011* (UK), ss 2–4 (disclosure occurring mainly through the 'Office of Budget Responsibility'); *Charter of Budget Honesty Act 1998* (Cth), Part 5 (disclosure occurring directly by the treasury and finance departments to Parliament).
[112] E.g., Bernanke, 'The Great Moderation' in Koenig (ed.), *The Taylor Rule and the Transformation of Monetary Policy* (Hoover Institute Press, 2012), 145.

information regarding a government's economic viability, they do not link that viability to a government's compliance with (say) appropriation legislation.

In that way, the battery of fiscal responsibility law enacted throughout the 1990s did nothing to re-concentrate financial authority in parliaments. By focusing on one particular form of fiscal discipline, those laws were concerned exclusively with minimising economic deficits, rather than parliaments' capacity to authorise taxation and expenditure. At base, they were wholly unconcerned with the constitutional relationship between parliaments and executives.

In total, NPM amendments (may have)[113] improved the quality of economic management, but they further relegated parliaments' financial functions.

Public Finance in Modern Parliamentary Government

The tasks of government changed fundamentally in the twentieth century, and the legal structure of public finance changed with them. The state would become a major (sometimes, the primary) provider of social goods to the populace, a major economic actor and a general regulator of the monetary system. Accommodating that expansion in government power required a concentration of financial authority in executive governments and their agencies, rather than parliaments. In that fashion, the pre-twentieth-century shift of constitutional power towards executives, observed in Chapters 2 and 3, continued in the twentieth century.

Mobilising the total resources of the state for military purposes created precedents for the wholesale delegation of sovereign borrowing authority to treasury departments which were eventually adopted in peacetime. The broad-spectrum provision of pensions, health, education and employment insurance by central governments was supported legally by the adoption of standing authorisation for the largest single spending activity of the public sector: welfare state programmes. Each of those developments reduced the significance of annual parliamentary processes and increased the authority delegated to executive governments. Together, they shifted the balance of financial authority further away from parliaments. Some measure of authority was distributed back to parliaments when the judiciary abnegated its explicit support for tax

---

[113] Lapsley, Riccardo and Paulsson (2009), 'On the Adoption of Accrual Accounting in the Public Sector'.

evasion in the 1980s, no longer obstructing the revenue collecting activities of tax agencies. The path dependency of tax law did, however, reduce the pro-parliamentary impact of those judicial developments.

By the end of the 1990s, the centre of gravity in public finance had shifted completely away from parliamentary authorisation and towards optimal economic efficiency. Central banks were established and given independence, and their capacity to provide monetary finance to central governments was never meaningfully regulated – leaving the terms on which monetised expenditure would occur wholly outside the ambit of parliament, and largely in the transacting discretion of central bank and treasury officials.

As philosophies of public management shifted towards a market emulation model, 'fiscal responsibility' laws were established which purported to limit the size and scale of public expenditure, with concomitant reductions in the importance of the annual budgetary process and parliamentary expenditure authority. Those latter developments were driven by a desire to professionalise and 'managerialise' the public sector's economic activities, but they did nothing to bolster parliamentary authority over public finance.

Essentially, the nineteenth-century trend to delegate financial authority to executive governments accelerated throughout the twentieth century. Armed with that conclusion, the next three chapters turn to a closer examination of the operation of public finance law in two parliamentary jurisdictions within a concrete time frame: Australia and the UK between 2005 and 2016.

PART II

Parliamentary Public Finance in Operation

The distribution of financial authority in parliamentary systems of government is not entirely static. Like the financial fortunes of government, it varies as social and economic conditions shift. While the design of public finance law allocates the preponderance of authority to executives *qua* treasury departments, the extent of that allocation changes as economic and financial conditions change.

Periods of economic abundance produce a windfall of tax revenue, reduce the need for public spending on social services and eliminate the need for short- or long-term debt issues. A sudden, but mild or confined, contraction in economic output may shrink tax receipts, trigger increased spending on unemployment insurance and require the issue of short-term debt to fill the cash deficit. Extreme economic dysfunction, both acute and chronic strains, has a vivid impact on public finances. Tax revenues plummet as incomes and transactions disappear. Expenditure spikes as governments subsidise ailing commercial ventures and welfare state programmes replace the private sector in providing basic goods. Vast quantities of sovereign debt instruments, of all maturities, are issued. When all other pools of funding are drained, central banks, usually acting covertly, make emergency payments to governments.

The following three chapters are devoted to providing a detailed explanation of the way that law distributes financial authority between parliaments, executives and judiciaries, which incorporates the impact of those shifting economic and financial sands. Chapter 6 focuses on tax and public expenditure, while Chapter 7 concentrates on sovereign debt and monetary finance. The rationale for that division is to follow the distribution of financial authority up to (Chapter 6) and then beyond (Chapter 7) the point of fiscal balance. Chapter 8 appraises the impact of judicial power on the distribution of financial authority.

Those analyses take place within jurisdictional and temporal boundaries: the Commonwealth of Australia and the UK between 2005 and 2016.

Australian and UK Constitutions, Law and Public Finance

The Australian and UK constitutional traditions, legal practices and economic experiences concerning public money provide rich illustrations of shared and distinct issues concerning the distribution of financial authority in parliamentary constitutional systems. The two jurisdictions are selected for their dissimilarity as much as their similarity.

At the level of constitutional background, the dissimilar features are famous. The UK is a unitary (but partially devolved) constitutional system, while Australia is a federation. Australia has a seminal written constitutional instrument, the UK does not. Australia has a well-established tradition of constitutional judicial review of legislation, while judicial review in the UK tends to focus on the validity of executive action.[1] Points of significant similarity are, however, identifiable: both operate under a system of responsible cabinet government; and in both systems the separation of powers doctrine is almost entirely confined to the institutional independence of the judiciary from the political branches of government. Most importantly, the Australian constitutional treatment of public money is strikingly similar to the UK's, as Chapters 4 and 5 explained.

Despite the variations in constitutional design, Australian and UK public finance law and administration are significantly similar. Both jurisdictions share the same apex financial institutions: Westminster-style parliaments,[2] treasury departments,[3] Auditors-General[4] and central

---

[1] Cf *R (Jackson)* v. *Attorney-General* (2006); *R (Bancoult)* v. *Secretary of State for Foreign and Commonwealth Affairs (No. 2)* (2009); *R (Miller)* v. *Secretary of State for Exiting the European Union* (2017).

[2] Following this book's focus on 'central' government (explained in Chapter 1 above), the relevant institutions are the Parliament of the Commonwealth of Australia and the UK Parliament sitting at Westminster.

[3] In 1976, Australia split its treasury into a Finance Ministry (which administers public expenditure) and a Treasury (which formulates economic policy, administers sovereign borrowing and engages with the Australian central bank). Together, those departments exercise the functions inherited from the UK's treasury as explained by Chapter 4, as illustrated by Section 7 of the *Acts Interpretation Amendment Act 1976* (Cth) which deemed references to the Australian treasury in existing audit legislation to extend to the newly created finance department. See further, Hawke and Wanna (2010), 'Australia After Budgetary Reform', 69; O'Faircheallaigh and Wanna (1999), *Public Sector Management in Australia*, 76.

[4] Which exercise their powers through the administrative medium of national audit offices: the 'Australian National Audit Office' and the UK's 'National Audit Office'.

banks.[5] Additionally, both jurisdictions follow the same basic financial processes concerning taxation, appropriation and sovereign borrowing, for which full details are given in Chapters 6 and 7.

Public Finance between 2005 and 2016

During the years 2005–2016, Australia and the UK, along with the rest of the world, passed through interesting economic times: starting with a moment of overheated abundance, then experiencing an extreme financial crisis, before moving into a period of slow economic recovery (or stagnation). Over that timeframe, the Australian and UK economies sat at opposite ends of the macroeconomic spectrum.

From 2005 to 2007, both Australian and UK economies boomed: GDP growth sat between 2.1 per cent and 3.4 per cent in the UK and 3.2 per cent and 3.8 per cent in Australia. Those years represent a *Boom Phase*. Between 2008 and 2011, both economies suffered significant shocks. British GDP growth shrunk from 2.4 per cent in 2007 to -4.2 per cent in 2009. In the same period, Australian growth dropped from 3.8 per cent to 1.9 per cent. Popularly labelled the 'financial crisis',[6] those years represent the *Bust Phase*. From 2011, both economies began digging themselves out of trouble, but never reached pre-Bust levels of output. Between 2012 and 2016, Britain's GDP began growing at between 2.1 per cent and 3.1 per cent and Australia's at between 2.1 per cent and 3.9 per cent: the *Recovery Phase*.

Those economic events had vivid impacts on public finances, which are best viewed graphically.[7]

Figure II.1 shows the relationship between changes in economic output and public financial activities. The right axis tracks UK annual GDP growth (as a percentage): displaying the massive contraction in FY2008–2009, followed by a slow recovery. The left axis tracks gross annual central government expenditure, tax revenues and debt issue (£billions). It displays the opening of a large fiscal deficit in FY2008/09, as tax revenues drop, expenditure increases and debt spikes. From FY2009/

---

[5] The Reserve Bank of Australia and the Bank of England. See Chapters 2 and 4 for historical accounts of both institutions.

[6] For a legal account, see Black (2010), 'The Credit Crunch and the Constitution', 93. For an economic and political account, see Tooze (2018), *Crashed*.

[7] Data for the following figures are drawn from the datasets at *ONS PFS* (2005–2016); *ONS NA* (2005–2016); Debt Management Office, *Gilt Market: Gross and Net Issuance History* (2017); Debt Management Office, *Money Markets: Issuance of Treasury Bills and Treasury Bill Stock* (2018); *ABS GFS* (2005–2016); *ABS NA* (2005–2016); Australian Office of Financial Management *Historical Data Tables* (2005–2016).

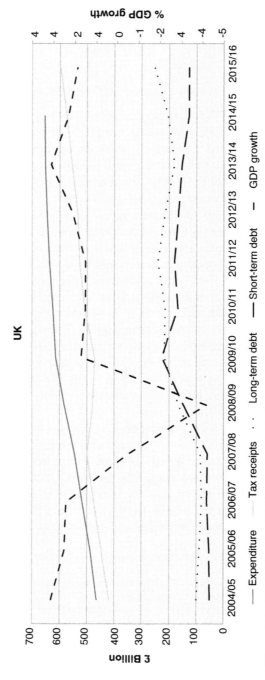

Figure II.1 UK GDP and public finance (2005–2016)

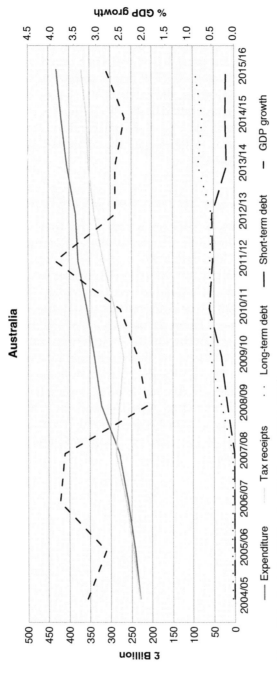

Figure II.2 Australia GDP and public finance (2005–2016)

10, the fiscal deficit begins to close slowly as GDP rebounds: tax yields begin to increase, expenditure drops and debt reliance eases.

The same relationship between economic output and financial activity appears in Australia. The fiscal deficit opens in FY2008/09, as GDP drops and debt reliance increases. As GDP begins to recover around FY2011/12, the fiscal deficit narrows, although debt reliance does not wholly diminish, because of a second GDP dip in FY2012/13.

Those shifting economic and financial conditions provide a vivid backdrop against which to investigate the operation of public finance law in Australia and the UK.

Advantages and Limitations of Case Study Analysis

Two analytical benefits, and one limitation, accrue from investigating the constitutional aspect of public finance within the case studies of Australia and the UK between 2005 and 2016.

The first benefit is that the timeframe traverses a sufficiently large sample of public financial activity to avoid in-year generalisations: like, '50 per cent of expenditure occurs pursuant to standing appropriations', when the actual balance of annual/standing appropriations is constantly shifting. The second is that the sampled timeframe contains sufficiently diverse economic conditions to flush out the relationship between macroeconomic volatility and the distribution of financial authority.

The limitation is that any detailed claim regarding the distribution of financial authority is limited to Australia and the UK. However, the extent to which that claim can be generalised to other parliamentary constitutional systems is broached in Chapter 9, and some tentative conclusions are offered.

6

Fiscal Authority

Fiscal authority, the legal authority to tax and spend, is unevenly distributed between parliaments and executive governments. Parliaments have formal power to enact taxation and appropriation legislation, but very limited power to control the content of that legislation. In contrast, executive governments have exclusive power to originate appropriation and taxation legislation, exercise broad fiscal powers where that legislation provides standing, rather than annual, authority and are largely untrammelled in fixing the public sector's accounting basis. Where necessary, executive governments can, and do, spend money without any parliamentary authority via 'excess' expenditure, the technical jargon for unlawful government spending in violation of appropriation legislation.

In some respects, the lopsided distribution of fiscal authority is static: whatever the economic and social conditions, appropriation and taxation legislation gives wide authority to executive departments to spend and tax without parliamentary involvement. So too does legislation concerning public budgets and accounting systems.

In other respects, the balance of parliamentary and executive authority shifts in response to economic and financial conditions. As economic output contracts, the relative amount of fiscal activity passing through annual parliamentary processes diminishes, in response to increased reliance on welfare state programmes, sovereign borrowing and commercial subsidies. Faced with economic emergencies, treasury departments can, and do, spend in flagrant breach of parliamentary authority.

This chapter illustrates those *static and variable aspects of fiscal authority* by reference to the financial behaviour of the Australian and UK central governments between 2005 and 2016.

Fiscal Background

Before starting the legal analysis, it is worth briefly observing the highpoints of Australia's and the UK's fiscal profiles.

In both jurisdictions, most public expenditure occurred in relation to five general categories: welfare state, including social security benefits, health, education, housing and recreation (62 per cent of total expenditure in Australia, 64 per cent in the UK); economic affairs, including, debt servicing and investment (5 per cent in Australia, 10 per cent in the UK); defence (6 per cent in Australia, 7 per cent in the UK); and fuel, transport and agriculture, and civil order (each under 5 per cent in both jurisdictions).[8]

Both Australia and the UK authorised their expenditure pursuant to standing and annual appropriation legislation, although the respective shares varied significantly between the jurisdictions.[9] Australia authorised 76 per cent of its expenditure through standing appropriations, while the UK only authorised 26 per cent. The dominant reason for the difference between Australia's and the UK's balance of standing and annual appropriations is that Australia authorises ~86 per cent of its welfare state expenditure through standing appropriations, while the UK authorises only ~30 per cent.[10]

Despite the substantial share of standing appropriations, both jurisdictions authorised most of their central government staff salaries and operational expenditure through annual, rather than standing, appropriation. Australian central government staff expenditure averaged 8 per cent of annual expenditure, while the UK's was 16 per cent.

Although the precise proportions of their tax mixes differ, Australia and the UK shared fundamentally similar profiles from fiscal receipts. In both jurisdictions, the largest share of fiscal receipts accrued from individual (rather than company) income tax payments: 46 per cent in Australia, 30 per cent in the UK.[11] Because of the UK's system of hypothecated social welfare contributions, the proportional contribution of income tax was lower than Australia, where Social Security revenue is not segregated from general tax revenue. If the UK's National Insurance

---

[8] Data from *PESA* (2005–2016) datasets 6.1–6.6; *ABS GFS* (2005–2016).

[9] All figures concerning annual and standing appropriations in this chapter are drawn from the following sources (unless otherwise indicated): *AGBP* (2005–2016); HM Treasury, *Consolidated and National Loans Fund Accounts* (2005–2016); HMRC, *National Insurance Fund Accounts* (2005–2016); HM Treasury, *Contingencies Fund Accounts* (2005–2016); Department for Culture, Media and Sport, *National Lottery Distribution Fund Accounts* (2005–2016).

[10] Additionally, Australia authorises a large portion of its domestic equalisation transfers through standing appropriations, whereas the UK's devolution grants are authorised through annual appropriation legislation.

[11] Tax receipt data collected from *ONS PSF* (2005–2016) and *ABS GFS* (2005–2016).

Contributions (NICs) are classified as a form of income tax receipt,[12] the balance evens.

Adopting that convention, both jurisdictions collect ~80 per cent of their fiscal receipts from the same four sources: income tax, 'value-added' or 'goods and services' tax (~15 per cent in Australia, ~20 per cent in the UK), corporation tax (~21 per cent in Australia, ~8 per cent in the UK), and consumption taxes on petrol, alcohol and tobacco (collectively ~12 per cent in Australia, 11 per cent in the UK).

Delegated Fiscal Authority

Throughout the studied timeframe, 2005 to 2016, parliaments in Australia and the UK delegated significant amounts of fiscal authority to executives through standing (i.e., non-annual) appropriation and taxation legislation. In one respect, that delegation appears to be 'static', in the sense of being unaffected by changes in the economic and social context in which public expenditure occurs. In another respect, the extent of authority delegated to executive governments varied in response to economic and social circumstances: as output contracted, the amount of fiscal activity passing through parliaments diminished. Both static and variable varieties of fiscal delegation evidence a very significant distribution of fiscal authority to executive governments, and away from parliaments.

Static Delegation of Fiscal Authority

Irrespective of economic conditions, a large measure of fiscal authority was delegated to executive governments, most prominently through standing appropriation legislation.

In both Australia and the UK, standing appropriation legislation took two types: appropriations which were tethered and untethered to parliamentary conditions for payment.

Tethered Standing Appropriations

Tethered standing appropriations provided standing authority to spend money on activities, and in amounts, which were directly prescribed by statutory conditions for payment.

---

[12] Which may occur if reform proposals to fully integrated NICs into the UK's income tax system succeed: Commons Library, 'National Insurance Contributions (NICs)' (2017).

Australia and the UK used that type of appropriation legislation for the authorisation of the majority of employment insurance and pension payments, which were legally authorised via appropriation provisions which conferred authority to make payments to recipients who met statutorily defined eligibility criteria.[13] UK legislation for the payment of public health expenses operated by reference to a quantitative ceiling expressed as a percentage of NICs.[14] Broadly similar legislation supported the payment activities of tax authorities in both jurisdictions.[15]

Other than removing those payments from the annual parliamentary process – those forms of standing appropriation represented a low level of delegation to the executive, because the ultimate legal basis for payment was a legislative, rather than executive, decision.

Untethered Appropriations

Untethered standing appropriations provided standing authority for public expenditure, which was untethered to any meaningful statutory limits, because the quantum of any payment was fixed according to the discretionary authority of an executive officer. Untethered standing appropriation legislation represented a very high level of delegation to executive governments.

In both the UK and Australia, untethered standing appropriation legislation authorised debt servicing expenditure.[16] The same form of standing legislation provided authority for UK contingences expenditure for 'urgent services',[17] and for bank bail-outs 'if the Treasury are satisfied that the need for the expenditure is too urgent to permit' reliance on annual parliamentary processes.[18] Australian legislation provided

---

[13] For the UK, see *Social Security Administration Act 1992* (UK) s 163. Eligibility criteria were provided by the *Social Security Contributions and Benefits Act 1992* (UK). A standing appropriation was also provided for 'Social Fund' payments by s 168 of the former Act for payments under s 138 of the latter. For Australia, see *Social Security (Administration) Act 1999* (Cth), s 242; *Superannuation Act 1990* (Cth), s 18 and the *Social Security Act 1991* (Cth).

[14] *Social Security Administration Act 1992* (UK), s 162, which authorised ~24 per cent of the UK Department of Health's annual expenditure between 2005 and 2016. Australia adopted a similar regime until 2009: *Health Care (Appropriation) Act 1998* (Cth).

[15] *Commissioners for Customs and Revenue Act 2005* (UK), s 47; and *Taxation Administration Act 1953* (Cth), s 16.

[16] *National Loans Act 1968* (UK), s 12(4); *Commonwealth Inscribed Stock Act 1911* (Cth), s 13AA; *Loans Securities Act 1919* (Cth), s 4; *Treasury Bills Act 1914* (Cth), s 6.

[17] *Miscellaneous Financial Provisions Act 1946* (9 & 10 Geo VI, c 40) and the *Contingencies Fund Act 1974* (UK).

[18] *Banking Act 2009* (UK), s 228.

similarly broad standing appropriation for 'investments'.[19] Intergovernmental payments in both jurisdictions were authorised by untethered appropriation legislation which delegated the amount and precise identity of the funding recipient to executive agencies. UK transfers to the European Union were dependent on international agreements fixed by the executive, as were Australian fiscal federal transfers.[20] None of those provisions imposed a quantitative limit on the amount lawfully expended.

Australian public health legislation authorised payments for medical services, pharmaceutical products, aged care facilities, private health insurance, and primary, secondary and tertiary education by conferring broad authority on an executive entity to determine the relevant subsidy and then a standing appropriation for the payment of those subsidies.[21]

If Australia's untethered standing expenditure items (debt servicing, health, education and inter-governmental transfers) are aggregated, they contributed ~54 per cent of average total standing expenditure (and ~41 per cent of average total expenditure) over the period 2005–2016. Whereas, the UK's untethered standing expenditure items (health, contingencies, debt servicing and inter-governmental transfers) only contributed ~40 per cent of total standing expenditure (and ~10 per cent of total expenditure). Despite those differences, in both jurisdictions untethered standing appropriations supported substantial levels of public expenditure, whether measured in absolute or relative terms.

Standing Taxation Authority

Around 65 per cent of UK and 100 per cent of Australian tax receipts were authorised by standing, non-annual, legislation.

The largest source of standing UK tax receipts flowed from value added tax, or (VAT): ~20 per cent of total receipts.[22] NIC provided the UK's second largest standing source of fiscal receipts: ~19 per cent of total

---

[19] *FMA Act 1997* (Cth), s 39 and the *PGPA Act 2013* (Cth), s 58.
[20] *European Communities Act 1972* (UK), s 2; *New Tax System (Commonwealth-State Financial Arrangements) Act 1999* (Cth); *Federal Financial Relations Act 2009* (Cth).
[21] *Health Insurance Act 1973* (Cth) ss 46AC, 125; *Health Insurance (General Medical Services Table) Regulation 2016* (Cth); *National Health Act 1953* (Cth) s 137; *Aged Care Act 1997* (Cth) and the *Private Health Insurance Act 2007* (Cth); *Australian Education Act 2013* (Cth), s 126 (schools); *Higher Education Support Act 2003* (Cth), s 238-12 (University funding and student fee subsidies).
[22] *Value Added Tax Act 1994* (UK), s 1. The standard rate of VAT was set by s 2(1) as 20 per cent / per supply, the reduced rate was set at 5 per cent by s 29A.

receipts.[23] After NICs and VAT, three excises constituted the UK's most significant source of standing tax revenue: fuel (~5 per cent); tobacco (~2 per cent); and alcohol (~2 per cent) duties.[24] The remaining ~7.5 per cent of standing tax revenue stemmed from a jumble of council tax, business rates, stamp duties, inheritance tax and capital gains tax.[25]

All major Australian taxes were authorised by standing legislation: income tax (including individual, company, and capital gains components),[26] GST, and excises and customs duties.[27] Annual legislation was enacted to amend the standing tax statutes to reflect variations in budget policy,[28] but did not make the taxes they amended 'annual' in any meaningful sense.

Around 35 per cent of the UK's total average fiscal receipts during the reference period derived from two annual taxes: income tax (~28 per cent); and corporation tax (~8 per cent). Both taxes are imposed by legislation that was intimately connected with parliamentary financial procedure and lapses at the conclusion of the fiscal year in which it is enacted.[29]

Constitutional Significance of Standing Fiscal Legislation

The constitutional significance of standing appropriation and taxation legislation may be measured in different ways.

One measure may focus on the capacity of executive governments to undertake fiscal activity if parliament were not convened or failed to pass any tax or appropriation legislation in a given fiscal year: the 'executive's self-financing capacity'. On that measure, there is a greater extent of fiscal

---

[23] *Social Security Contributions and Benefits Act 1992* (UK), which provided four different liability rules for each 'class' of NIC: Class 1 NICs were payable on earnings from employment (s 6), classes 2 and 4 on profits from self-employment (ss 11 and 15), while class 3 contributions were voluntary but were necessary to qualify for certain defined benefits (s 13).

[24] *Hydrocarbon Oil Duties Act 1979* (UK), s 2; *Tobacco Products Duty Act 1979* (UK), s 2 and the *Alcohol Liquor Duties Act 1979* (UK), ss 5, 36, 45, 62.

[25] *Local Government Finance Act 1992* (UK), s 6; *Local Government Finance Act 1988* (UK), s 54; *Finance Acts 2003* (UK) and *1986* (UK); *Taxation of Chargeable Gains Act 1992* (UK), s 1; *Inheritance Tax Act 1984* (UK), s 1.

[26] *Income Tax Act 1986* (Cth).

[27] *A New Tax System (Goods and Services Tax) Act 1999* (Cth); *Excise Act 1901* (Cth); *Excise Tariff Act 1921* (Cth); *Customs Act 1901* (Cth) and *Customs Tariff Act 1995* (Cth).

[28] E.g., *Tax and Superannuation Laws Amendment (2014 Measures Act No. 5) 2015* (Cth).

[29] A combination of Commons resolutions and legislation provided the lawful foundation for the imposition of income taxation: *Provisional Collection of Taxes Act 1968* (UK). Company tax follows the same pattern, but has a standing legislative framework for collection and assessment: s 2 of the *Corporations Tax Act 2009* (UK) and s 3 of the *Corporations Tax Act 2010* (UK).

authority delegated in Australia than in the UK. If the Australian Parliament failed to enact any taxation or appropriation legislation, Australia could continue collecting 100 per cent of its taxation and meet ~70–80 per cent of its expenditure needs on a very large set of welfare state activities (health, education, welfare) and debt servicing. In contrast, if no taxation or appropriation legislation were enacted by the UK Parliament, the UK executive government would lose legal authority for ~25–30 per cent of its tax receipts (income and corporation tax) and only lawfully be able to meet ~20–30 per cent of its total expenditure (confined to payment of welfare benefits, pensions, a minority of public health expenditure and some debt servicing).

Another measure could focus on the share of untethered standing appropriations relative to total expenditure. Again, on that measure, the level of fiscal authority delegated to executive governments in Australia was greater than in the UK between 2005 and 2016. Australia's aggregate untethered standing expenditure items (debt servicing, health, education and inter-governmental transfers) contributed ~54 per cent of average total standing expenditure and ~41 per cent of average total expenditure. Whereas, the UK averaged untethered standing expenditure items (health, contingencies, debt servicing and inter-governmental transfers) only contributed ~40 per cent of average total standing expenditure and ~10 per cent of total expenditure. Despite those differences, in both jurisdictions untethered standing appropriations supported substantial levels of public expenditure, whether measured in absolute or relative terms.

A significant qualification must, however, be recorded to both of those measures of the extent of fiscal authority delegated to executive governments by standing fiscal legislation. In both jurisdictions, public servant salaries and departmental operating expenses were approved through annual appropriations in Australia (exclusively) and the UK (predominately).[30] The practical consequence is that although the executive could finance many social programmes through standing appropriations, it could not finance the administrative structure through which they are operationalised.

Even with that qualification, it is clear that in both Australia and the UK, fiscal legislation delegates a significant degree of financial authority away from parliaments and towards executive governments.

---

[30] Accommodating the possibility that the standing NHS contribution could be used to pay staff salaries.

Variable Delegation of Fiscal Authority

Economic conditions also impacted the extent of delegated fiscal authority in both Australia and the UK between 2005 and 2016.

Compared to periods of economic expansion during periods of sharp economic contraction, the proportion of expenditure authorised by standing appropriations, increased relative to annual appropriations, an effect which lingered throughout periods of economic recovery. In both jurisdictions, the main cause of the shifting balance was the increased reliance on untethered standing appropriations (concerning debt servicing and contingencies) relative to other standing appropriations (financing welfare state expenditure and tax credits) and annual appropriations. That proportional increase in expenditure through untethered standing appropriations shrunk the total amount of economic resources available for approval through the parliamentary process.

Shift in Balance of Standing/Annual Expenditure

Throughout the turbulent economic circumstances between 2005 and 2016, both Australia and the UK evidenced a common pattern.

As economic output shrunk during and after the financial crisis, relative levels of unemployment, business failure, welfare provision and government debt increased. The impact on public finance was predictable: spending grew on unemployment insurance, subsidies to the private sector, public health and housing, and debt-servicing. Because those types of public expenditure were authorised by standing appropriations, the share of public expenditure approved outside the annual parliamentary process also grew. Because the total amount of public expenditure in any given year is finite, the relative amount of money authorised through parliaments' annual budget process shrunk. Put differently, as economic output contracted and the fiscal deficit widened, appropriation legislation operated to shrink the size of parliaments' potential authority to influence financial or economic policy.

In Australia, standing appropriations grew from a low share of ~70 per cent in 2005 to a high of ~79 per cent in 2015. In the UK, the share of standing appropriations grew from ~19 per cent to 23 per cent over the same period. Across the eight years from 2008 to 2016, the UK experienced a slightly higher average growth in the share of standing appropriations (~2 per cent) than Australia's (~1.4 per cent). The origin of that proportional increase in standing appropriation expenditure lay in the financial crisis.

The impact of the change in economic conditions following the financial crisis is revealed when the percentage growth in standing appropriations is charted chronologically and in comparison with percentage GDP growth.

Although the precise trajectory of the increase in the proportional share of standing appropriation varies in Australia and the UK, that share spiked at two points in both jurisdictions.

The first spike occurred during and immediately after the financial crisis: in FY2008/09 Australia recorded a ~6 per cent and the UK an ~8 per cent increase in the proportional share of expenditure under standing appropriations. The second spike occurred in FY2010/11, with Australia recording a ~3 per cent increase and the UK, a ~15 per cent increase.

Both of those spikes resulted from increased reliance on standing appropriation legislation to respond to contractions in economic output. The UK's ~8 per cent spike in FY2008/09 occurred largely as a result of one factor: emergency spending by the UK Treasury on bank bailouts. In that year, ~£10.9 billion was spent in reliance on the standing appropriation governing use of the Contingencies Fund, ~£8.4 billion of which was spent by HM Treasury on various bank bailouts.[31] The Treasury also relied on the bank-bailout-specific standing appropriation in the *Banking Act* to spend ~£1.6 billion on bank bailouts.[32] When aggregated, those payments amount to ~2.7 per cent of total expenditure in FY2008/2009, a very significant increase from the 0.6 per cent of total expenditure spent from the Contingencies Fund in FY2007/2008.

The second ~15 per cent spike in the relative share of standing appropriation expenditure in FY2010/11 occurred as a result of the spending from the National Loans Fund on debt servicing. Between 2009 and 2011, debt spending from that fund began a slow march upwards, increasing from ~£21 billion to ~£38 billion in absolute terms and from ~4 per cent to 6 per cent of total expenditure. As debt servicing costs compounded, that proportional share remained relatively steady between 2011 and 2016 at ~6 per cent of total expenditure.

---

[31] HM Treasury, *Contingencies Fund Account* (2008–2009), 13, 14; HM Treasury, *Annual Report and Accounts* (2008–2009), 149, 222.
[32] HM Treasury *Annual Report and Accounts* (2008/09), 173.

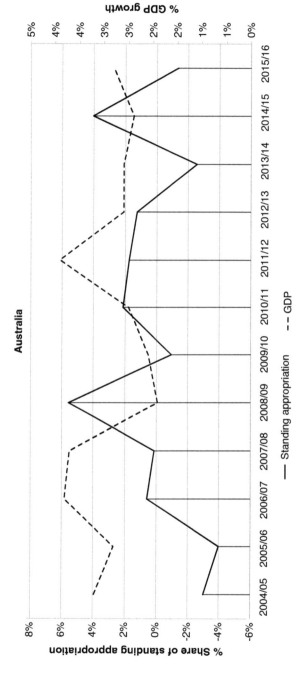

Figure 6.1 Australia balance of standing/annual appropriation (2005–2016)

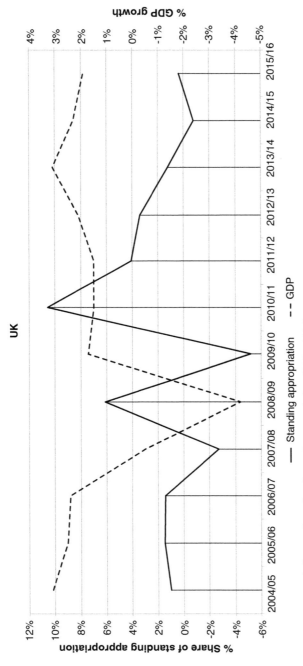

Figure 6.2 UK balance of standing/annual appropriation (2005–2016)

Post-crisis sovereign borrowing also explains the relative increase of Australian standing appropriations. The initial (FY2008/09) increase occurred as a result of Australia's commencement of a substantive sovereign borrowing programme during the financial crisis, as debt servicing costs moved from ~2 per cent to 8 per cent of standing expenditure and ~1 per cent to ~3 per cent of total expenditure. The second FY2014/15 spike in standing expenditure occurred as a result of a debt servicing costs.

Economic Contractions and Annual/Standing Balance of Expenditure

Although both jurisdictions experienced the same shift in the balance of standing and annual appropriation, the precise extent of that shift in the distribution of financial authority in Australia and the UK was not static.

Different measures produce different results. Australia experienced a higher absolute increase in the share of standing appropriations over the period (9 per cent). The UK's increase was smaller (4 per cent), although the UK's average annual growth in the share of standing appropriations was slightly higher (~2 per cent) than Australia's (~1.4 per cent). On either measure, it is clear that economic conditions had a non-negligible impact on the distribution of financial authority away from parliaments and towards financial executives.

In one sense, that impact can be understood as the legal consequence of the economic reality of increased debt issues during a downturn: a larger amount of total economic resources is devoted to debt servicing because the amount of sovereign debt spending has increased proportionally to total spending.

While that is a trite economic explanation, matters are more complicated at the level of legal authority. The automatic diversion of debt servicing expenditure (and the proportional reduction of the total amount of economic resources passing through the annual parliamentary process) only occurred because of a legislative decision to authorise debt repayment by a standing, rather than an annual, appropriation. If debt servicing appropriations were not standing, then parliaments would have a greater capacity to decide the conditions under which debt repayment occurred and, thereby, the proportional allocation of financial resources to debt servicing as opposed to other expenditure programmes through the annual appropriation process.[33]

---

[33] The other side of that counter-factual is examined in Chapter 7: that a lower degree of financial authority would be distributed away from parliament if it had a meaningful role in authorising debt issues.

The relationship between economic conditions and the distribution of fiscal authority can also be seen in relation to government spending in violation of appropriation legislation: excess expenditure.

Excess Expenditure

All governments spend in excess of budget limits set by appropriation legislation, as did Australia and the UK during the studied period 2005 to 2016.

The most common type of excess spending is unavoidable: it results from unpredictable surges in the demand for public, mainly welfare, programmes. Another type of overspending, resulting from errors in legal and administrative processes, is unavoidable because human errors are ineradicable. Yet another type of overspending is more sinister, resulting from conscious, strategic decisions of executive officials to spend without parliamentary approval.

The first two types of excess expenditure were clearly identifiable in Australia and the UK, but the third, sinister, type was only seen in the UK during the depths of the financial crisis.[34]

Demand-Driven Overspending

The most common type of excess expenditure in both Australia and the UK occurred as a result of failed forecasting projections for demand-driven spending programmes. Those excesses were identifiable throughout the radically different economic conditions experienced between 2005 and 2016.

In FY2004/05, the UK Department for Work and Pensions recorded a ~£188 million 'overspending on housing benefits': 0.3 per cent over its total main estimate. Of that amount, ~£41 million was overspent on an unanticipated increased uptake (~60 per cent) by 'temporarily homeless people' of 'more expensive, leased accommodation rather than bed and

---

[34] Legal and financial detail for British retrospective appropriations can be found in 'Statement[s] of Excesses' presented by the UK's Treasury to Parliament (via the Public Accounts Committee, reporting annually to the House of Commons), the annual *Appropriation Act* (before 2011) and the annual *Supply and Appropriation (Anticipation and Adjustments) Act* (from 2011). From the late 1990s, Australia ceased retrospectively authorising its excess expenditure, citing highly dubious, legal advice that such authorisation was a breach of the written *Commonwealth Constitution*. Unparticularised details of Australia's excess expenditure can be found in Australian Auditor-General's reports: Auditor-General, *Financial Statement Audits* (2005–2017).

breakfast accommodation' as provided by local authorities 'in line with government policies'. The remaining ~£146 million was overspent as a result of failed forecasting of recovering benefit payments, maintenance for non-resident parents, irregularly obtained.

In FY2005/06, excesses of ~£788 million were recorded by the NHS pension scheme, representing: (i) ~£586 million spending beyond forecast for hospital services of general practitioners; and (ii) ~£202 million on lower-than-forecast receipts (i.e., payments into the pension scheme).[35] Both were results of actuarial re-adjustments. In FY2006/07, excesses of ~£81 million were recorded for the Teachers' Pension Scheme, resulting mainly from higher than anticipated 'service costs': ~1 per cent over main estimates. In the same year, ~£20.8 million of excess expenditure was recorded by the Ministry of Defence: ~0.06 per cent over its main estimate. The 'main contributing items were the firing ... of a greater number of Hellfire missiles in Afghanistan than originally forecast'.[36]

In FY2011/12, Australia spent ~$1.4 billion without legislative authorisation across nine agencies,[37] with the large majority of those excesses resulting from the provision of misleading information from members of the public 'including personal information such as estimates of income and employment status' in relation to 'payments such as welfare benefits and superannuation entitlements'. Those excesses were economically insignificant (~0.4 per cent of total expenditure), and, like the UK, excesses appeared to arise from the difficulty of administering a complex bureaucracy.

Overspending through Administrative Errors

The next most common type of excess expenditure was the result of errors in the administration of public funds.

In most cases, excesses from administrative errors were not economically significant. In FY2005/06, the UK Assets Recovery Agency (covering civil confiscation) overspent by ~£6.7 million due to mistaken advice that the agency could apply confiscated sums to pay expenditure, and failing to appreciate 'that parliamentary approval was also required through the Supply process'.[38] In FY2007/08, the UK Department for Transport

---

[35] HM Treasury, *Statement of Excesses* (2005–2006), 2.
[36] HM Treasury, *Statement of Excesses* (2006–2007), 2–3.
[37] Auditor-General, *Audit Report No. 16 2012–13* (2012), 75.
[38] HM Treasury, *Statement of Excesses* (2005–2006), 3.

overspent by ~£3 million as a result of an administrative error in drawing funds for works on the Crossrail project. The Department had lawfully obtained an advance from the Contingencies Fund in anticipation of the enactment of the *Crossrail Act 2008* (UK) for FY2005/06. Those funds were lawfully used for that year, but in FY2007/08, the Department again spent on Crossrail projects without legal authority under the annual *Appropriation Acts* or the Contingencies Fund legislation.[39]

Administrative errors did, however, cause some very large excess spending. A truly stunning example was the ~£200 billion spent by the UK Ministry of Defence between 2007 and 2013 in breach of legislative authority.

Between 2007 and 2013, the supply vote for the Ministry of Defence was conditioned on a maximum number of members of the Reserve Naval Forces under the *Reserve Forces Act 1996* (UK): the size of which varied, but ranged between: 1,139 and 2,020 troops.[40] That troop limit was a limitation on the Ministry's annual expenditure imposed by the relevant *Appropriation Acts* between 2007 and 2013. Each year, that limitation was breached by between 1,600 and 1,900 personnel: roughly, double the troop limit. The cause of the breach was a failure to count members of the Reserve Fleet Auxiliary as Special Members of the Reserve Naval Forces.

After the Ministry of Defence reported those excesses in 2013,[41] the 'token' sum of £1,000 was retrospectively appropriated for each financial year the troop limit was breached by ss 6–11 of the *Supply and Appropriation (Anticipation and Adjustments) Act 2014* (UK). That token sum concealed the total size of economic resources affected by the Ministry's unlawful expenditure. From 2007 to 2011, the troop limit applied to an annual average ~£30 billion of the Ministry's appropriated budget: ~86 per cent of the average total defence appropriation of ~ £35 billion. From 2012 to 2013, the troop limit applied to an annual average of £36 billion: being ~73 per cent of the average total defence appropriation of £49 billion. The aggregate amount affected (directly and indirectly) by the breach of the troop limit was ~£814 billion, which represented ~140 per cent of the total prospective appropriations in the

---

[39] HM Treasury, *Statement of Excesses* (2007–2008), 3.
[40] See (the unpaginated) Ministry of Defence, *Excess votes 2007–08 – 2012–13* (2014).
[41] Ibid. The following figures relating to Ministry of Defence appropriations calculated from *Appropriation Acts 2007–2010*, Schedule 2 and *Supply and Appropriation (Main Estimates) Act 2011–2013*, Schedule.

144   PARLIAMENTARY PUBLIC FINANCE IN OPERATION

Supply and Appropriation (Main Estimates) Act 2014 (UK), and ~115 per cent of total UK public expenditure in FY2014/15.

Deliberate Overspending

Only one example of deliberate overspending emerged during the studied period: the UK's ~£24 billion overspend on a bank bailout at the height of the financial crisis. Understanding how it transpired requires decoding a rather obscure set of financial events.

The overspending occurred as a result of the UK Treasury's underwriting of the Asset Protection Scheme,[42] which was designed to provide government support for insolvent UK banks during the financial crisis.[43] In late 2008, the Treasury provided ~£30 billion of direct funding to several ailing commercial banks, including Royal Bank of Scotland (RBS). By early 2009, it was clear that RBS would require an additional £25 billion to avoid insolvency. The Treasury agreed to provide that funding (and a guarantee of £282 billion of distressed assets) in exchange for a ~84 per cent interest in the bank.

That £25 billion payment to support RBS violated the annual statutory limit on the UK Treasury's expenditure by ~£23.8 billion, or 119 per cent in excess of the legal limit originally imposed on the Treasury.[44] That illegal expenditure represented ~6 per cent of the total statutory appropriation for the entire UK central government in FY2008/09 (~£429.9 billion) by the main estimates. Recording a qualification of its audit opinion, the National Audit Office (NAO) indicated that the Treasury's decision not to seek authorisation from Parliament through the normal process of parliamentary supply was deliberate. The Treasury justified its excess expenditure as necessary because it 'could not estimate' the total amount of solvency support for RBS until it was 'too late ... to seek extra resources from Parliament'.[45] However, the Comptroller and Auditor General explained that the Treasury 'knew from the outset that [the Asset Protection Scheme] would result in a significant loss'.[46]

---

[42] HM Treasury, *Annual Report and Accounts* (2008–2009), 169.
[43] National Audit Office, *The Asset Protection Scheme* (2010), 4, 14–15; HM Treasury, *Annual Report and Accounts* (2008–2009), 172–173, 241, 243.
[44] The original total resource limit was ~£20.9 billion and actual total expenditure was ~44.8 billion: HM Treasury, *Annual Report and Accounts* (2008–2009), 172.
[45] HM Treasury, *Annual Report and Accounts* (2008–2009), 173.
[46] Ibid., 173.

In absolute and relative terms, the size of the Treasury's FY2008/09 overspend was enormous. It was also a desperate financing measure, given that the Treasury had exhausted all other lawful forms of emergency finance: including drawing on the Contingencies Fund to its maximum extent, and executing virements from other sub-heads of ~£980 million.[47] While (arguably) economically necessary, that expenditure represented a low point of the UK Parliament's financial authority, because no question of maladministration arose: the Treasury simply decided to spend ~£23.8 billion without parliamentary approval because it took the view that such payment was too urgent to be slowed down by parliamentary processes.

Excess Expenditure in Constitutional Perspective

Excess expenditure represents a hard case for an analysis of the distribution of financial authority.

Viewed with maximum optimism, the fact that parliaments retrospectively appropriate unlawful expenditure evidences their authority to censure executives that behave unlawfully. Viewed less optimistically, retrospective appropriation of excesses illustrates the practical limitations of parliaments' authority over public expenditure: compliance or non-compliance is entirely in the hands of executive officials. Where non-compliance is accidental, the executive's (*qua* treasury department's) own limitations over public expenditure are revealed. Where non-compliance is deliberate, the hard limits of parliaments' financial authority are revealed.

Executive Control of the Structure of Public Finances

Both constitutional phenomena, the delegation of fiscal authority and excess expenditure, occur inside a broader institutional context in which treasury departments hold plenary authority to determine budgetary limits, accounting standards and the ultimate structure of appropriation legislation.

Financial Initiative

Predictably, the impact of the executive's possession of the financial initiative between 2005 and 2016 was profound: it gave Australian and

---

[47] Ibid., 149, 194, 222.

UK executive governments authority to determine the economic plans underpinning, and legal content of, expenditure and taxation legislation.

Expenditure planning and financial forecasting was undertaken in both jurisdictions by financial executives through multi-year 'spending reviews' or 'expenditure review committees',[48] which were a mixture of technical economic forecasting and policy execution which carried heavy structural implications for the public and private sectors.[49] As Prosser observed of the UK spending review process, parliamentary involvement was minimal: 'the estimates approved by Parliament reflected decisions already taken in the spending review process, which had received hardly any Parliamentary scrutiny'.[50]

The legislative impact of the financial executives' initiative is best illustrated by reference to a reform project undertaken in the UK between 2007 and 2011, which fundamentally altered the UK's annual parliamentary financial processes.[51] In 2007, the *Governance of Britain* Green Paper proposed simplifying 'the reporting of Government expenditure to Parliament': a proposal followed by a Treasury memorandum in 2008 under the title *Alignment 'Clear-Line-Of-Sight' Project* (CLOS). CLOS's stated aim was to align the presentation of financial information in departmental accounts, estimates presented to, and expenditure legislation passed by, the UK Parliament.

It effected two salient changes to the legal practices of fiscal activity.

The first change was to declutter the UK estimates. Prior to CLOS, annual estimates presented a hotchpotch of information regarding public sector expenditure. They included the core accrual accounting concepts of current (resource) and 'capital' expenditure, split between 'departmental' and 'managed' expenditure.[52] But those concepts did not express the legal limits of voted expenditure. Instead, those limits were expressed as 'requests for resources' (RfR), although the 'subhead' of each estimate referred to departmental, managed, resource and capital expenditure. After CLOS, the references to RfR were scrubbed, and estimates simply expressed legal limits on voted expenditure by reference to the core

---

[48] The UK conducted its spending reviews in 2007, 2010 and 2015. The Australian expenditure review committee met annually.
[49] Prosser (2011), '"An opportunity to take a more fundamental look at the role of government in society": the Spending Review as regulation', 598.
[50] Ibid., 607.
[51] Australian annual legislative practices regarding financial legislation did not experience the same seismic shift during the reference period.
[52] Some discussion of the adoption of accrual accounting in the UK appears in Chapter 5.

accrual accounting concepts. The change was mostly cosmetic, but did clean the estimates of confusing detail and aligned the presentation of information to the UK Parliament with information in departmental accounts.

The second change was more thoroughgoing. CLOS replaced the over 300-year-old system of separate *Supply* and *Appropriation Acts* with two annual expenditure Acts.[53] The *Supply and Appropriation (Main Estimates) Act*, which granted 'supply' and then 'appropriated' the totality of the main estimates for the impending financial year. The *Supply and Appropriation (Anticipation and Adjustments) Act* granted supply and appropriated the supplementary estimates and retrospectively appropriated excess spending.

CLOS is a powerful illustration of the contemporary potency of the financial executive's initiative concerning expenditure legislation. The UK Parliament's role in enacting annual expenditure legislation remained in place, but the form and content of that legislation was radically altered. Those radical alterations were conceived and instituted by the UK's Treasury, with only minimal consultation from the UK's Parliament.[54]

Accounts and Estimates

Australian and British legislation conferred total power on treasury departments to determine the form and content of public accounts, and required Auditors-General to use those accounts as the basis of public audit. Thereby, parliaments abnegated all authority over the core accounting concepts underpinning public sector budgets.

In the UK, the *Government Resources and Accounts Act 2000* (UK) commanded a 'government department for which an estimate is approved by the House of Commons' to prepare 'resource accounts ... in accordance with directions issued by' the UK's

---

[53] The history is contained in Chapter 2.
[54] See 'Financial Scrutiny: Parliamentary Control over Government Budgets' (2009) in response to HM Treasury, 'Alignment (Clear Line of Sight) Project' (2009). CLOS was also significant for what it failed to reform. It did not require that the legislative basis for standing expenditure be identified in estimates, leaving a reader to search the statute book to find a possible Act to authorise 'non-voted' expenditure. Nor did it clarify the legal basis for devolution payments, which simply appeared as 'Non-budget voted expenditure' in the *Main Estimates* and *Anticipation and Adjustments Acts*. Additionally, CLOS selectively presented critical 'financing aggregates' in estimates, omitting any accurate comparison of the total amount of estimated expenditure authorised by annual and standing legislation.

treasury.[55] In Australia, the same effect was achieved by requiring executive agencies to prepare public accounts in accordance with subordinate legislation made by the Australian Finance Department.[56] In both jurisdictions, the detailed accounting rules imposed on executive government departments were fixed by the relevant treasury departments.[57]

The system of accounts established by treasury departments in both jurisdictions formed the basis for audit by Auditors-General. The British Comptroller and Auditor-General's mandate to 'examine resource accounts to ensure' they 'present a true and fair view' was contingent on the UK's Treasury providing a system of accounts which permitted those conclusions to be reached.[58] In Australia, the Auditor-General's audit of 'annual financial statements' was similarly dependent on the accounts prepared in accordance with the Australian finance ministry's directions.[59] In that fashion, Auditors-General in both jurisdictions were legally obliged to rely on executive governments' own systems of accounting in determining the regularity of public expenditure.

The accounting system selected by treasury departments also determined the content and structure of Australian and UK estimates, appropriation legislation, and framed the financial reports of executive governments.

Reporting on the Public Funds

Australian and UK legislation imposed no obligation on executive officials to provide a detailed report of compliance with financial legislation.

Some UK legislation did provide for a piecemeal reporting on the use of public 'funds'. Section 21 of the UK *National Loans Act 1968* required that accounts of the Consolidated Fund, National Insurance Fund and National Loans Fund be presented to Parliament, and an annual

---

[55] *Government Resources and Accounts Act 2000* (UK), c 20, s 5. Those directions were transmitted in a 'Dear Accounting Officer' letter sent by the Treasury.

[56] *Financial Management and Accountability Act 1997* (Cth), s 49 and the *Public Governance Performance and Accountability Act 2013* (Cth), s 42.

[57] For the UK, see the HM Treasury, 'The Government Financial Reporting Manual 2019-20'; for Australia, see *Public Governance, Performance and Accountability (Financial Reporting) Rule 2015* (Cth).

[58] *Resources Act 2000*, s 6.

[59] *FMA Act 1997* (ss 56–57) and the *PGPA Act 2013* (ss 43–44). The UK's Comptroller and Auditor-General's reports were appended to departmental reports laid before the UK's Parliament, while the Australian Auditor-General simply appended a 1/2-page audit 'opinion' to departmental annual reports.

Commons order imposed the same requirement on the Contingencies Fund accounts.[60] While those accounts represented the major sources of fiscal receipts and outlays,[61] there was no legal requirement, or administrative practice, to report their relationship with annual or standing appropriation legislation. Nor was any provided by the various 'fiscal responsibility laws' enacted in both jurisdictions.[62]

The critical observation is that no legislation in either jurisdiction required the reporting of absolute figures regarding the aggregate balance of expenditure pursuant to annual and standing appropriation legislation.[63] Nor was such aggregate information presented via annual budget processes or 'whole of government' accounts. The only way to arrive at those figures was to extract financial data from the individual accounts of funds (in the UK) and budget papers (in Australia), and then independently perform the necessary arithmetic.

Conclusion

The design and operation of public finance law in Australia and the UK between 2005 and 2016 evidenced a significant distribution of fiscal authority away from parliaments and towards financial executives.

Broad swathes of fiscal authority were delegated to treasury departments through standing taxation and appropriation legislation, particularly appropriations which were untethered to legislatively fixed criteria for payment. Although Australia had a higher level of expenditure under standing appropriations and taxation, executive governments in both jurisdictions increased their proportional reliance on standing appropriations as economic conditions soured.

---

[60] E.g., House of Commons Paper No. 56 of 2015–16, 'That there be laid before this House an Account of the Contingencies Fund, 2015–16, showing (1) a Statement of Financial Position, (2) a Statement of Cash Flows and (3) Notes to the Accounts'.

[61] Accounts were also presented to Parliament for the 'National Lottery Distribution Fund' (which financed between 0.2 and 0.4 per cent of total expenditure) and the 'Exchange Equalisation Fund', which did not provide for domestic finance: *Exchange Equalisation Account Act 1979* (UK).

[62] *Finance Act 1998* (UK); *Fiscal Responsibility Act 2010* (UK); *Budget Responsibility and National Audit Act 2011* (UK); *Charter of Budget Honesty Act 1998* (Cth); *Government Resources Act 2000* (UK).

[63] No legislation in either jurisdiction required treasury departments to report on the use of their powers to refuse to pay money requested by departments.

Significant overspending also occurred in both jurisdictions, with the largest total overspend occurring in the UK as a result of the economic contraction stemming from the financial crisis. That overspending reveals the practical inability of parliaments to constrain the broader executive to the legal limits set in appropriation legislation.

Importantly, the Australian and UK experience between 2005 and 2016 indicates that governments fail to comply with expenditure legislation in good and bad economic fortune as a result of maladministration and forecasting difficulties. The experience of the UK indicates that in extreme economic circumstances financial executives will deliberately refuse to comply with legal limitations in financial legislation. In that sense, parliaments' financial authority is observably weaker in times of economic emergency.

7

Debt and Monetary Authority

Parliaments have no meaningful role in the authorisation and acquisition of debt finance from private financial markets, and monetary finance from central banks.

Legislation delegates all meaningful authority over sovereign borrowing to executive government agencies. Treasury departments hold plenary power to determine whether to issue sovereign debt and the commercial structure of debt securities. No discernible legislative framework governs the issue of monetary finance, leaving central bank and treasury officials largely unshackled by positive law in deciding the terms on which public expenditure will be monetised. Thereby, the vast preponderance of financial authority over sovereign borrowing and monetary finance is distributed to executive governments, rather than parliaments.[1]

Broader economic conditions impact the distribution of authority over sovereign borrowing and monetary finance. As executive governments experience financial stress, they exercise their broad powers over debt and monetary finance in ways which illustrate the absence of any meaningful parliamentary involvement in those types of finance. In economic emergencies, treasury departments and central banks are largely autonomous in gathering debt and monetary finance.

This chapter argues for those claims by continuing the case study analysis of Chapter 5: analysing Australia's and the UK's legal and financial behaviour between 2005 and 2016 concerning sovereign borrowing and monetary finance. Within the book's total scheme, this chapter's objective is to analyse the way that public finance law distributes financial authority over debt and monetary finance between parliaments and executives within a concrete timeframe.

---

[1] Exercising that authority, treasury departments have established various methods of oversight of sovereign borrowing, some of which involve the release of financial information to parliaments, but none of them disturb treasuries' historically settled position as the custodians of debt financing power discussed in Chapters 2, 4 and 5.

The chapter commences by introducing the technical details of sovereign borrowing and monetary finance, which may be less familiar to jurists than they are to finance specialists. After those financial preliminaries, the case study analysis resumes by focusing on two signal issues regarding the distribution of financial power over debt and monetary finance. The first is the extremely broad statutory delegation of authority over sovereign borrowing to executive agencies. The second is the absence of any meaningful legislative regulation of monetary finance. The chapter concludes by reflecting on the constitutional implications of parliaments' exclusion from sovereign borrowing and the public financing activities of central banks.

Sovereign Borrowing

The broad expression *sovereign borrowing* encompasses short- and long-term debt finance obtained by central government. Almost exclusively, that finance is obtained by the issue of tradable debt securities. Shorter-term debt securities generally mature within one year: described as 'bills' or 'notes' which trade in the money market.[2] Long-term sovereign debt securities generally mature over longer durations (between one and fifteen years): described as 'bonds' or 'gilts' which trade in the bond market.[3] Governments use short-term debt to finance shortfalls in projected fiscal receipts (tax 'smoothing' or 'cash management') and long-term debt to finance the gap between planned expenditure and fiscal receipts (a 'fiscal' or 'structural' deficit).[4]

A government's reliance on debt markets varies with its economic fortunes. Obviously, governments in financial distress, with large, multi-year, fiscal deficits, require both short-term debt (to smooth tax receipts) and long-term debt (to finance expenditure, including debt servicing costs). Less financially distressed governments, with small or no fiscal deficits, may still issue short-term debt to plug cash flow gaps. Governments in extremely lucky financial fortunes, running multi-year fiscal surpluses, may have no need for short-term debt (because of accumulated tax receipts and dividends from sales of public assets, like commodities), but require long-term debt for reasons having little to do with public financing (such as allowing the

---

[2] Choudhry (2001), *The Bond & Money Markets*, 513.
[3] Ibid., 203–247, 513.
[4] Williams (2013), 'Debt and Cash Management'.

execution of monetary policy through the sale and re-purchase of sovereign bonds).

At various points between 2005 and 2016, Australia and the UK relied on sovereign borrowing in each of those ways.[5] Before the financial crisis, both the UK and Australia's debt finance activities were relatively modest, reflecting the fact that neither government was plunging into severe deficit spending, nor experiencing cash flow problems. Australia's fiscal surpluses obviated the need for any meaningful debt issues and no short- or long-term debt was issued between 2005 and 2009.

The financial crisis precipitated a predictably profound increase in Australia's and the UK's reliance on long- and short-term debt finance.[6]

For both figures, the left axis tracks gross debt issues compared to GDP growth on the right axis. Figure 7.1 shows the enormous increase in

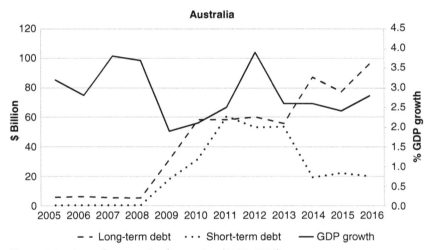

Figure 7.1 Australia sovereign borrowing (2005–2016)

---

[5] Lower-yield forms of debt finance may be raised through 'retail' offerings to the general public, such as the UK's 'National Savings and Investments' programme, which provided under 5 per cent of total annual debt receipts in 2016 (National Savings & Investments, *Annual Report and Accounts* (2015–2016)) and was authorised under a legislative regime delegating broad authority to issue, and determine the cost of, debt: *National Savings Bank Act 1971* (UK); *National Debt Act 1972* (UK).

[6] Data for Australian and UK sovereign borrowing were drawn from ONS PFS (2005–2016); ONS NA (2005–2016); Debt Management Office, *Gilt Market: Gross and Net Issuance History* (2017); Debt Management Office, *Money Markets: Issuance of Treasury Bills and Treasury Bill Stock* (2018); ABS GFS (2005–2016); ABS NA (2005–2016); Australian Office of Financial Management *Historical Data Tables* (2005–2016).

Australian long-term debt from below $5 million in FY2007/08 to almost $60 billion in FY2010/11, and short-term debt from $0 to over $60 billion in the same period. Figure 7.2 shows a similar growth trend of long-term debt from ~£70 billion to over £230 billion between FY2007/11, and short-term debt growing from ~£90 billion to over £250 billion in the same period. The far larger absolute size of the UK's annual debt issues reflects the UK's lack of a fiscal surplus and the sharper contraction of fiscal receipts in comparison to Australia.

However, when sovereign debt issues are viewed through the prism of annual growth, the similarities in the Australian and UK debt burden are revealed. Between 2008 and 2009, long-term debt grew in Australia by around 510 per cent and by around 140 per cent in the UK. Short-term debt grew by over 300 per cent in the UK and annual Australian short-term debt grew from $0 to $180 billion. The important (albeit predictable) constitutional observation is that executives' use of their very broad powers to borrow and issue sovereign debt spikes as economic conditions contract.

Reliance on debt finance relaxed, but did not cease, as the financial crisis abated. Between 2012 and 2016, both Australia and the UK continued to issue large amounts of short- and long-term sovereign debt, although both trended towards reduced reliance on debt financing. Despite that trend, the cost of debt servicing remained high and, in the UK, those debt servicing costs drove a sustained monetary financing programme, as will be explained shortly.

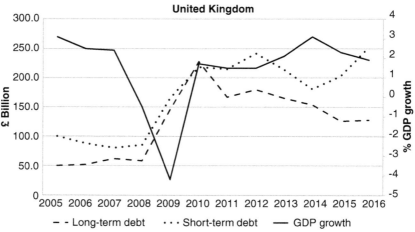

Figure 7.2 UK sovereign borrowing (2005–2016)

Monetary Finance

Central banks provide two kinds of monetary finance to governments: ordinary and exotic monetary finance.

The most visible form of finance provided by a central bank is the transfer of cash proceeds of central bank operations to government, the central bank's 'dividend' to government.[7] Central bank dividends are the paradigm case of ordinary monetary finance. They provide a relatively insignificant amount of finance to central government which represents the yield of the conventional functions of central banks: printing money, settling inter-bank transactions, supervising the financial sector and engaging in monetary policy operations.

Central banks may also provide far less visible monetary finance to governments. Long-standing examples include the provision of short-term credit, or overdraft, facilities to treasuries. Depending on the conditions under which they are used, central bank overdrafts may be entirely conventional, especially where the quantum of credit granted is small, at market rates of interest, and repayable overnight. Central bank overdrafts to government will be exotic where the amounts advanced are large, at low interest (or interest free) and perpetual, in the sense of having no fixed maturity date. Very exotic monetary finance occurs through absolute cash transfers to government with no statutory obligation to repay.

The more exotic types of monetary financing are contentious because of the economic thinking concerning their inflationary effects. So it goes, funding public expenditure with money supplied by a central bank increases the money supply, increasing prices and debasing the currency.[8] That economic thinking, orthodox through much of the 1990s, is reflected in some legal instruments regulating or prohibiting monetary finance.[9] Reflecting that economic orthodoxy, central bank credit to treasury accounts tends to occur only when both fiscal and short-term debt receipts cannot fund planned expenditure and there is no generally acceptable framework within which (very exotic) outright cash transfers should occur.

---

[7] Capie, Goodhart and Schnadt (1994), 'The Development of Central Banking', 55.
[8] The technical economic arguments are collected in Turner (2015), 'The Case for Monetary Finance'.
[9] The most prominent example is Art 123 of the *Treaty on the Functioning of the European Union*, which prohibits most European central banks from issuing any form of monetary finance.

Both kinds of monetary finance did, however, occur in the UK during and after the financial crisis.[10] In late 2008, the UK's Treasury drew down ~£19.5 billion from its standing overdraft facility at the Bank of England, the Ways and Means Advance,[11] in an attempt to bail-out an insolvent commercial bank.[12] The size of that monetary injection can only be appreciated in relative terms. The ~£19.5 billion monetary injection by the Bank of England was +200 per cent of the UK's monthly income tax receipts in the preceding month (~£9 billion) and ~300 per cent of the UK's monthly VAT receipts (~£7 billion) in the same month.

The repayment burden imposed on the UK's government by that monetary injection is also best appreciated in comparative perspective. In the 12 months surrounding the ~£19.5 billion Ways and Means Advance injection, the Treasury repaid around ~£24 billion to the Bank of England.[13] Shortly before the 2008 Ways and Means Advance monetary injection, ~£13 billion of the Treasury's outstanding overdraft was repaid. The last month of those payments (March 2008) saw public expenditure on repaying the Ways and Means Advance standing at almost ~97 per cent of central government staffing costs and ~120 per cent of total national insurance benefit payments. After the 2008 Ways and Means Advance monetary injection, ~£9 billion was repaid, consuming a lower (but still significant) proportion of relative public expenditure: ~40 per cent of staffing costs and ~48 per cent of national insurance benefits.

In addition to supplying monetary finance via a short-term overdraft, the Bank of England also provided the most exotic form of monetary finance: direct cash transfers with no obligation to pay interest and no maturity date. From 2013, the Bank of England began making direct cash transfers to the UK's Consolidated Fund, which represented the surplus of the Bank's quantitative easing programme (QE Transfers).

Initially, the QE Transfers made a very significant contribution to the UK's public receipts.[14] During the first ten months of 2013, QE Transfers

---

[10] Data for the Ways and Means Advance in the figures throughout this chapter are drawn from the dataset entitled BoE, *B72A Ways and Means Advance: Weekly and Quarterly Outstanding figures: 2006-2017* (2017). Fiscal data is drawn from ONS PSF.
[11] The history of the Ways and Means Advance is canvassed in Chapter 2.
[12] Cross, Fisher and Weeken (2010), 'The Bank's Balance Sheet during the Crisis', 36.
[13] Reflecting an outstanding balance of ~£13.5 billion at January 2008.
[14] Data for the QE Transfers in the figures throughout this chapter are drawn from *ONS PSF, PSA9 Bank of England (BoE) Asset Purchase Facility Fund (APF) including Term Funding Scheme (TFS)* (2017).

stood at a monthly average of 31 per cent of income tax, 46 per cent of NICs and 41 per cent of VAT receipts.

Compared to less significant, but still economically critical, receipts, the scale of monetary finance provided by QE Transfers is fully revealed. From January to October 2013, QE Transfers stood at a monthly average of 184 per cent of corporation tax receipts, and 106 per cent of total excises (being the aggregate of 495 per cent of alcohol, 659 per cent of tobacco and 182 per cent of fuel duties). The enormous scale of the 2013 QE Transfers was the consequence of unpaid accumulation of cash balances in the Bank of England's QE account between 2009 and 2013.

After those, initially enormous, monetary injections, the relative contribution to consolidated revenue of QE Transfers diminished, although it still outpaced lower-yield fiscal receipts. Between FY2013 and FY2017, QE Transfers stood at an annual average of 9 per cent of income tax, 13 per cent of NICs and 12 per cent of VAT receipts. Over the same four-year period, QE Transfers stood at an annual average of 137 per cent alcohol, 154 per cent tobacco, 53 per cent fuel duties and 817 per cent of National Lottery receipts.

The long-term monetary finance programme executed via the QE Transfers cannot be viewed in isolation from the enormous debt burden assumed by the UK after the financial crisis. As will be explained, the Treasury's public explanation for the QE Transfers focused on debt servicing. Assuming that explanation to be true, for the calendar years 2013–2016, the contribution of QE Transfers to net interest repayments on UK debt stood between a high of 80 per cent in 2013, and a stable ~20 per cent for the following years.

Delegated Debt Finance Authority

One constitutionally significant aspect of Australian and UK sovereign borrowing legislation was its delegation of authority to assume sovereign debt in a manner which was entirely unconnected to any meaningful parliamentary processes of authorisation.

Plenary Borrowing Authority

UK and Australian legislation conferred authority on executive agencies to borrow money and issue securities for those borrowings in extremely broad terms. The UK's sovereign borrowing legislation expressed that breadth of power via a combination of s 12 and Sch 5A items 3 and 4 of the *National Loans Act*:

12 Power of Treasury to borrow

(1) Any money which the Treasury consider it expedient to raise for the purpose of promoting sound monetary conditions in the United Kingdom and any money required –
  (a) for providing the sums required to meet any excess of payments out of the National Loans Fund over receipts into the National Loans Fund, and
  (b) for providing any necessary working balance in the National Loans Fund,
may be raised in such manner and on such terms and conditions as the Treasury think fit, and money so raised shall be paid into the National Loans Fund.

...

(2) For the purpose of raising money under this section the Treasury may create and issue such securities, at such rates of interest and subject to such conditions as to repayment, redemption and other matters (including provision for a sinking fund) as they think fit.

...

Financial instruments

3(1) For the purposes of exercising their functions with regard to the Debt Management Account the Treasury may –
  (a) acquire (and arrange to acquire) and hold securities issued under section 12 of this Act;

...

Borrowing

4 (1) If the Treasury consider it expedient to raise money for the purpose of exercising their functions with regard to the Debt Management Account they may raise it in such manner and on such terms as they think fit, and money so raised shall be paid into the Account.

Together, those provisions conferred power on the UK Treasury to borrow money and issue securities for that borrowing through the Debt Management Account. As Chapter 5 explained, that function was de facto carried out by an agency of the UK Treasury, the Debt Management Office.

Australian legislation conferred similarly broad sovereign borrowing authority on the executive government. Australian sovereign debt legislation developed significantly between 2005 and 2016 in response to the financial crisis, but the final power to borrow and issue securities was contained in ss 3A and 4 of the *Commonwealth Inscribed Stock Act*:

3A Authority to borrow
(1) *The Treasurer may, from time to time, borrow money on behalf of the Commonwealth by issuing stock denominated in Australian currency.*
...

4 Power to create stock
(1) *The Governor-General may, by writing signed by him or her, create stock, Treasury Bonds, Treasury Notes or other prescribed securities from time to time for:*
(a) *raising money by way of loan* ...

Those provisions conferred authority to borrow and issue debt of relatively similar breadth to those conferred by the *National Loans Act*.

Commercial Structure of Sovereign Debt

In addition to the largely plenary power to borrow, sovereign borrowing legislation also conferred exceptionally broad authority on treasuries to determine the commercial structure of sovereign debt and the administrative structure of the sovereign debt market.

Sovereign debt securities come in a variety of different forms. Short-term debt may be issued as 'discount instruments' (like Treasury Bills): when the Treasury issues a £10 million three-month treasury bill at 5 per cent, the counterparty pays £9.5 million to the Treasury, and receives £10 million from the Treasury three months later.[15] Long-term debt instruments (like gilts and bonds) often have a different commercial structure. When Australia issues a $10 million fixed-rate 2 per cent long (15 years) bond, the counterparty pays $10 million to the Australian Treasury, and receives $20 thousand every year for 15

---
[15] Choudhry (2001), 513.

years (in interest), and then $10 million at maturity, from the Treasury.[16]

Australian and UK legislation concerning sovereign debt wholly delegated authority over those matters of commercial structure to treasuries. The *National Loans Act* simply provides that the 'the terms and conditions' of borrowing and rates of 'interest and ... conditions as to repayment, redemption and other matters' are to be determined as the Treasury think fit'.[17] The Australian *Commonwealth Inscribed Stock Act* similarly provides (s 7) that the:

> *manner in which, the prices at which and the terms and conditions (including terms and conditions as to redemption and interest) on which stock may be issued and sold shall be as directed by the Governor-General [on advice from the Treasury].*

Australian and UK sovereign borrowing legislation also gave treasuries total freedom to determine the currency in which sovereign debt may be issued. The *National Loans Act* provided 'for the avoidance of doubt' that:

> *it is hereby declared that the power to raise money under this section extends to raising money either within or outside the United Kingdom and either in sterling or in any other currency or medium of exchange, whether national or international.*

A similarly broad power to determine the currency of issue was contained through the inter-linking of the broad borrowing authority contained in the *Commonwealth Inscribed Stock Act* and the *Loans Securities Act 1919* (Cth), the latter of which provided:

> **6A Currency in which moneys may be borrowed**
> *Where under an Act the Treasurer has authority to borrow moneys, the Governor–General may authorise the Treasurer to borrow the moneys in whole or in part in currency other than Australian currency, and, in that case, the Treasurer is empowered to borrow the moneys accordingly.*

Australian and UK treasuries exercised those powers by issuing debt securities denominated in non-domestic currencies. A particularly striking example was UK Treasury's issue of a long-term debt product in 2014 denominated in the national currency of the People's Republic of China:

---

[16] Australian Office of Financial Management, *Information Memorandum Treasury Bonds* (2014).
[17] Sub-sections 12(1) and (3).

a renminbi bond.[18] That renminbi-denominated debt security was issued for three years (2014–2017), for CY3 billion (~£340 million) at a rate of 2.7 per cent interest. Its terms and conditions provided that the 'creation and issue of the [bond] was authorised pursuant to the National Loans Act 1968'.[19]

Finally, Australian and UK sovereign borrowing legislation provided no legal framework for the operation of the primary market in sovereign debt.

In the UK, only a select group of financial institutions were permitted to purchase gilts from the UK's Treasury: 'Gilt Edged Market Markers' (GEMMs). The eligibility criteria to be appointed a GEMM (and the attendant privilege of having access to the UK's primary gilt market) are determined by the Treasury without any legislative direction. The apparent financial rationale for the enclosure of the primary sovereign debt market for GEMMs is to guarantee a total subscription of each debt issue,[20] but the effect is to confer significant commercial privileges on a select group of private financial organisations to determine the terms of the secondary market in government debt. Australia had a less restrictive primary sovereign debt market policy, selling to both large financial institutions, and other registered organisations, but the majority of debt is still sold wholesale through intermediaries.[21] Alike the situation in the UK, the Australian Treasury was un-limited by law in choosing the market participants in the primary market for its debt.

Critically, Australian and UK sovereign borrowing legislation was wholly disconnected from annual parliamentary processes: treasuries in neither jurisdiction were legally required to obtain parliamentary approval, annual or otherwise, before any debt issue.

To that observation, it could be retorted that there is a de facto link between annual parliamentary processes because treasuries' sovereign borrowing powers are limited, in fact, to deficit financing, and thus to the expenditure approved by annual parliamentary processes. The actual behaviour of Australian and UK treasuries during the studied

---

[18] Although described as 'Notes' in its offering circular, the renminbi bond's maturity period (three years) was rather 'bond-like': HM Treasury, *Offering Circular* (17 October 2014), 1.
[19] Ibid., 18.
[20] Choudhry (2001), 216.
[21] Through 'Registered Bidder Agreements': OECD (2013), *Sovereign Borrowing Outlook* (OECD).

period illustrates, however, that sovereign borrowing is not limited by deficit financing. As will be explained shortly, the Australian Treasury began issuing long-term debt while still running a fiscal surplus prior to the economic contraction of the financial crisis. The UK's issue in 2014 of a Chinese currency-denominated debt security was only justifiable as a promotional activity to boost London's position as a global centre for financial intermediation, rather than deficit financing.

Variable Delegation of Financial Authority

Variations in economic conditions had vivid impacts on the degree of debt finance authority delegated to Australian and UK treasuries.

Obviously, the immense economic contractions caused by the financial crisis led to a very robust exercise of treasury powers to issue sovereign debt: treasuries in both Australia and the UK borrowed more as cash and fiscal deficits opened. Economic conditions also had a more subtle impact on the delegation of sovereign borrowing authority in Australia, which was initially disconnected to deficit financing.

From 2008 to 2016, Australia fundamentally altered its sovereign borrowing legislation five times, to accommodate the massive expansion of its sovereign debt portfolio. During that period, the annual compound growth rate of Australia's sovereign debt issue was 44 per cent and the size of its sovereign debt portfolio increased 400 per cent.

Prior to 2008, Australian legislation authorised long-term debt issues through the passage of an annual *Loan Act*. From 1996, Australia ceased enacting an annual *Loan Act*, as it started a 12-year run of large fiscal surpluses accruing from historically exceptional mineral exports. In 2008, Australia's Parliament fundamentally amended its sovereign debt legislation by conferring a plenary authority on its Treasury to borrow and issue debt securities by amendment of s 3A *Commonwealth Inscribed Stock Act* (set out above).

Perhaps counter-intuitively, Australia's move from annual to standing sovereign borrowing authority was not initiated by the need for deficit financing, because it was commenced before Australia experienced any contraction in fiscal receipts. Instead, the change was the result of lobbying by private financial interests who were seeking to move capital into Australian dollar-denominated assets, because of the turbulence in North Atlantic markets during the financial crisis.

That motive was alluded to in the Australian government's second reading of the Bill to liberalise the Australian Treasury's borrowing powers:[22]

> Over recent months, demand for the bonds has intensified due to the strength of the Australian economy and exchange rate, together with global credit concerns that have increased the demand for high-quality securities.
>
> As a result, the Treasury bonds available on issue have become more tightly held and it has become more difficult for dealers to obtain some lines of stock and maintain an active market in them.

More illuminating was the boast of a senior investment banker that the amendments were exactly 'what we asked for'.[23]

The broad power to issue debt to permit a safe harbour for offshore capital in Australian dollar-denominated bonds was not limited by a deficit financing condition. Instead, Australia inserted a statutory 'debt limit' in s 5 of the *Commonwealth Inscribed Stock Act*:

> The total face value of stock and securities on issue under this Act and the Loans Securities Act 1919 at any time must not exceed $75 billion.

When that debt limit was enacted, in 2008, Australia had issued $49.3 billion in bonds and had a total debt portfolio of $60.4 billion.

Within a year (in 2009), an amendment permitted Australia's Treasury to increase that limit to $125 billion by a written declaration which was not subject to parliamentary veto.[24] By the end of FY2009, $78.4 billion in bonds was outstanding, and the total debt portfolio had risen to $101.1 billion. In 2011, the Act was amended again to lift the debt limit from $75 billion to $250 billion:[25] by the close of FY2011, $161.2 billion in bonds was outstanding, and Australia's debt portfolio had risen to almost $200 billion.

Those expansions of the Australian executive's authority to issue sovereign debt reflected the large fiscal deficit caused by the financial crisis. The trend continued as output gradually recovered. In 2012, a legislative amendment lifted the debt limit to $300 billion,[26] as the

---

[22] Second Reading Speech, *Commonwealth Securities and Investment Legislation Amendment Bill 2008* (2008).
[23] 'Head of debt markets at Macquarie Bank': Parliament of Commonwealth of Australia, Bills Digest No 129 (2007–2008).
[24] *Commonwealth Inscribed Stock Amendment Act 2009* (Cth).
[25] *Appropriation Act (No. 2) 2011–2012* (Cth), s 18.
[26] *Appropriation Act (No. 2) 2012–2013* (Cth), s 18.

amount of outstanding bonds rose to $205.3 billion and the total debt portfolio lifted to $233.9 billion. The debt limit received its *quietus* in 2013 when it was entirely repealed,[27] leaving the Treasury unlimited by any *ex facie* restriction on its capacity to issue sovereign debt. In the fiscal year after its repeal, Australia had almost $300 billion in outstanding bonds and a total debt portfolio position of $319.4 billion.

Sovereign Debt and the Self-Financing Executive

Sovereign borrowing legislation has two wider impacts on the extent of the delegation of total financial authority, both of which were equally present in Australia and the UK.

The first impact is on the expenditure side of fiscal activity. As Chapter 6 observed, Australian and UK sovereign debt servicing expenditure is authorised by standing appropriations. Because the conditions under which sovereign debt is assumed are delegated to treasuries, those standing appropriation provisions are not tethered to any meaningful legislative authority. In that sense, the wide delegation of debt finance authority increases the degree to which expenditure is authorised without parliamentary involvement, thereby shunting financial authority further away from parliaments and towards executives.

The second impact concerns the interlocking of debt finance authority with fiscal authority. Recalling the 'executive self-financing' measure of the extent of delegation of fiscal authority, identified in Chapter 6, the wholesale delegation of legal authority to obtain sovereign debt provides Australian and UK financial executives with a legal basis to continue funding public sector activities without any annual parliamentary legislation, or tax revenue. Of course, economic factors would constrain the extent to which either government could debt finance its activities in the absence of income or corporation taxes. But, the breadth of the legal authority possessed by treasury departments to assume sovereign debt boosts their capacity to self-finance and distributes a greater share of total financial authority away from parliaments.

Autonomous Monetary Finance

In both Australia and the UK, all but the most anodyne forms of monetary finance are almost entirely un-governed by clear legislative

---

[27] *Commonwealth Inscribed Stock Amendment Act 2013* (Cth).

conditions. Thereby, parliaments expressed no statutory view on the provision of monetary finance, leaving officials of treasuries and central banks largely autonomous to negotiate the terms upon which central banks' provide financial accommodation to executive governments.

Dividends, Overdrafts and Cash Transfers

Between 2005 and 2016, monetary finance in Australia and the UK took three distinct types, only two of which had a discernible statutory basis.

Central Bank Dividends

The payment of a divided by the Bank of England was authorised pursuant to s 1(4) of the *Bank of England Act 1946*, which provides for the payment of 25 per cent of the Bank's after-tax profit from its banking functions. A more flexible legislative framework underpinned the Reserve Bank of Australia's dividend payments. Section 30 of the *Reserve Bank of Australia Act 1959* (Cth) provides for so much of the 'net profits' of the Bank to be 'paid to the Commonwealth' as the 'Treasurer, after consultation with the Reserve Bank Board, determines'.

Those provisions left the total amount of the dividend hostage to the fortunes of the relevant central bank's operations, but they did express a clear legislative prescription of a central bank's public financing contribution in ordinary economic circumstances. Despite that clarity, Australian and UK central bank dividends made only a modest contribution to central government finances. Between 2005 and 2016, the Australian Reserve Bank paid an annual average dividend of ~$1.3 billion: being 0.9 per cent of average income tax receipts, and 0.7 per cent of total receipts.[28] Over the same period, the Bank of England paid an annual average dividend of ~£314 million: 0.20 per cent of income tax, 0.05 per cent of total government receipts.[29]

Central Bank Overdrafts

No meaningful legislative treatment attended central bank overdraft facilities in Australia and the UK. Indeed, the legislation governing the Reserve Bank of Australia makes no provision whatsoever for government credit.

---

[28] Australian dividend data collected from Reserve Bank of Australia, *Annual Reports* (2005–2016).
[29] UK dividend data collected from BoE, *Annual Reports and Accounts* (2005–2016).

As Chapter 5 observed, since 1968, UK legislation has provided a very broad authority on the Bank of England to provide credit to the UK's central government. Section 12(7) of the *National Loans Act 1968* provides that the Bank 'may lend any sums which the Treasury have power to borrow under this section'. That provision links the Bank's authority to lend money to the Treasury's powers to borrow money. Accordingly, the Bank may lend to the UK's Treasury the total amount of any cash or fiscal deficit, or to 'promote sound monetary conditions' in the UK. In that way, legislation supported the UK's ancient monetary finance channel, the Ways and Means Advance,[30] which is paid into the National Loans Fund,[31] but it imposes no detailed limitations on the quantum, or commercial structure, of finance provided.

Direct Cash Transfers

No legislation authorised Australia's or the UK's central banks to make direct cash transfers to executive governments. Such transfers were, however, made in the UK following the financial crisis. From 2013, the Bank of England made direct cash transfers to the UK's Consolidated Account, representing the cash surpluses from its quantitative easing programme: described earlier as QE Transfers. Understanding how the Bank of England came to make those direct cash transfers requires explaining the 'unconventional'[32] monetary policy of quantitative easing.

Economically, quantitative easing was the label given to the processes by which a central bank creates monetary units (often described as central bank 'reserves')[33] to purchase assets circulating in the financial system with the objective of increasing the liquidity of private financial markets and thereby increasing the total amount of money circulating in the economy.[34] The assets purchased through quantitative easing programmes were generally government bonds issued by the treasury (and denominated in the currency) of the same state as the central bank

---

[30] The history is provided in Chapter 2.
[31] Bank of England, *Annual Reports and Accounts* (2008–2009), 98.
[32] Joyce, Tong and Woods (2011), 'The United Kingdom's Quantitative Easing Policy: Design, Operation and Impact'.
[33] Some, but not all, of the complexities of these arrangements are explained in McLeay, Radia and Thomas (2014), 'Money Creation in the Modern Economy'.
[34] That description is a simplification and its economic characterisation is contested: cf Borio and Disyatat (2009), 'Unconventional Monetary Policies: an Appraisal'.

carrying out a quantitative easing programme. A number of central banks commenced quantitative easing programmes from 2008.[35]

The Bank of England began its quantitative easing programme in March 2009. Between 2009 and 2016, the Bank's newly created reserves were used to purchase UK bonds (gilts) worth ~£435 billion, and non-government bonds worth ~£10 billion. Through those bond purchases, the Bank of England came to own ~30 per cent of the total portfolio of UK sovereign bonds on issue.[36]

At an economic level, understanding QE requires focusing simply on 'the Bank'. At an administrative and legal level, the picture is more complex. Operationally, quantitative easing asset purchases were carried out by a UK registered corporation (wholly owned by the Bank),[37] the Bank's *QE Subsidiary*, which acquired the almost half a trillion pounds of UK bonds purchased through quantitative easing and would sell those bonds when, or if, quantitative easing is unwound.

At the commencement of the quantitative easing programme, the Treasury and the QE Subsidiary executed a 'deed of indemnity' which provided that 'any financial losses as a result of the asset purchases are borne by HM Treasury, and any gains are owed to HM Treasury'.[38] Since it began operation in January 2009, the QE Subsidiary suffered no losses, but accumulated a large cash surplus on account of the UK's Treasury paying interest instalments on the bonds held on its balance sheet.

The opportunity of using that cash surplus to fund general government expenditure was raised by the Treasury in 2011, when it formally requested that the QE Subsidiary transfer all cash balances in its accounts to the Treasury in order to finance debt repayment:[39]

> holding large amounts of cash in the APF is economically inefficient as it requires Government to borrow money to fund these coupon payments. Transferring the net income from the APF will allow the Government to manage its cash more efficiently, and should lead to debt interest savings to central government in the short term.

---

[35] QE-like processes have been undertaken by the Bank of Japan (since the early 2000s), the US Federal Reserve (from 2008) and the European Central Bank (from 2010): Borio and Disyatat (2009), 9; Lenza, Pill and Reichlin (2010), 'Monetary Policy in Exceptional Times'; Ahearne et al (2002), 'Preventing Deflation'.
[36] National Audit Office, *Evaluating the Government's Balance Sheet* (2017), 46.
[37] Bank of England Asset Purchase Facility Fund Limited.
[38] Bank of England Asset Purchase Facility Fund Limited, *Annual Report and Accounts* (2016–2017), 4.
[39] Osborne to King, *Transfer of Excess Cash from the Asset Purchase Facility to HM Treasury* (9 November 2012) (added emphasis).

A Treasury press release was even more explicit:[40]

> any net coupon income transferred from the APF to the Exchequer should be used solely to pay down government debt.

By early 2017, the Treasury stated that QE Transfers were 'surrendered to the Exchequer to fund the operations of government'.[41] Under those arrangements, the QE Subsidiary transferred ~£72 billion to the Treasury between 2013 and 2017.[42] Those payments were made under a legal framework which did not include any specific legislative authorisation.

The first relevant legal step in the Bank of England's quantitative easing programme was the incorporation, in 2008, of the QE Subsidiary under the UK *Companies Act 2006* (UK) as a wholly owned subsidiary of the Bank, and staffed with officers of the Bank as its directors.[43] Section 3A of the *Companies Act* conferred generic legal powers on the QE Subsidiary to buy, hold, sell and encumber property. Additional powers were conferred by the QE Subsidiary's Memorandum of Association, relevantly including powers 'To enter into any arrangements with any government ... that may seem conducive to the attainment of the Company's object' and '[t]o lend or advance money and to give credit and to enter (whether gratuitously or otherwise) into guarantees and indemnities of all kinds ... in such circumstances and on such terms and conditions as the board of directors thinks fit'.[44]

The second step was the Bank making a 'loan' to the QE Subsidiary, which represented the proceeds of newly created central bank 'reserves'.[45] The third step involved the QE Subsidiary purchasing UK sovereign bonds ('gilts') and corporate bonds on the secondary market using the loan proceeds transferred from the Bank.

The fourth step involved creating a legal framework to govern the QE Transfers to the UK's Treasury. That legal framework was contained in a document executed by the QE Subsidiary and the Treasury, described

---

[40] HM Treasury, *Changes to Cash Management Operations* (9 November 2012).
[41] HM Treasury, *Annual Report and Accounts* (2016-2017), 22.
[42] The Treasury estimates future receipts from the QE Subsidiary of £51.2 billion: Ibid., 16.
[43] Bank of England Asset Purchase Facility Fund Limited, *Certificate of Association* (30 January 2009).
[44] Bank of England Asset Purchase Facility Fund Limited, *Memorandum of Association* (30 January 2009), [3.2.10]; Bank of England Asset Purchase Facility Fund Limited, *Memorandum of Association* (10 February 2009), [3(q)].
[45] There is no express legislative conferral of power on the Bank to create central bank reserves.

in various Bank and Treasury documents as a 'deed of indemnity',[46] the terms of which were not publicly available. The fifth step involves the QE Subsidiary making direct cash transfers, the QE Transfers, into the UK's Consolidated Fund via the Treasury.[47] Beyond those steps, no information was made public regarding the legal basis for the QE Transfers.[48] That leaves very significant gaps in the, publicly available, legal framework governing the public financing aspects of quantitative easing.

Viewed from a constitutional perspective, the critical conclusion is that monetary finance from quantitative easing occurred in the absence of any meaningful parliamentary prescription. The legal basis for the QE Transfers was provided by private law frameworks, particularly UK corporations legislation and general law powers to enter into contracts, acquire and alienate property. None of those frameworks provided any *ex ante* legal conditions regarding the critical financial integers of the QE Transfers: their size, their duration, their relationship to other public financial activities (such as the fiscal deficit, volume of sovereign borrowing or tax receipts). Nor did those private law frameworks provide any legal conditions concerning the transmission of information to Parliament regarding the QE Transfers.

The net distributional result is that all meaningful monetary financing authority was held by Treasury and central bank officials, rather than Parliament.

Conclusion

The design and operation of the legislative practices of debt and monetary finance provided for the distribution of very large shares of financial authority away from the Australian and UK parliaments.

Australian and UK sovereign borrowing legislation effected a strikingly similar delegation of authority over the issue, quantum and commercial structure of debt finance to executive governments. That delegation effected a substantial distribution of financial authority away

---

[46] HM Treasury, *Annual Report and Accounts* (2016-2017), 87-88, 135; Bank of England Asset Purchase Facility Fund Limited, *Annual Report and Accounts* (2016-2017), 4, 6.

[47] HM Treasury, Response to FOI Request (FOI2017/20111).

[48] The *Bank of England and Financial Services Act 2016* (UK) provides for the audit of a 'company in which the Bank has an interest ... where the Treasury gives an indemnity ... in respect of an activity or series of activities undertaken by the company' (s 7C). Reports of the QE Subsidiary appear to have been audited on that basis, but provide no further information about the content of the deed of indemnity.

from parliaments, by depriving them of any meaningful role in the acquisition of sovereign debt and, thereby, increasing the self-financing capacity of financial executives. Legislation in both jurisdictions lacked any meaningful provision for exotic monetary finance, which left executive officials in a position to act largely autonomously of parliaments in obtaining credit from central banks.

The critical distributional point is that the large statutory delegations of debt finance authority and the total absence any legislative framework for monetary finance left the interaction of debt and monetary finance in economic emergencies un-governed by statutory law. To that degree, financial executives (and central banks) are autonomous, in the sense of creating their own rules, in formulating a financial response to economic emergencies.

8

Judicial Power

Judiciaries play a mostly muted role in public finance.

Only a small proportion of public financial activities, those concerning taxation, are the normal subject of judicial attention. Disputes about appropriation legislation, sovereign borrowing, public audits and monetary finance are exemplars of non-justiciable subject matter. Even where tax cases come to court, the capacity of judges to bolster parliament's authority over public finance is very limited. The net constitutional effect is that the presence of judicial power does not substantially impact the distribution of financial authority between executive governments and parliaments.

This chapter opens by explaining the asymmetrical involvement of judiciaries in public finance law: why disputes concerning tax legislation are more justiciable than disputes concerning appropriation, debt and monetary finance. The chapter then analyses a case study of the only modern attempt by a common law judiciary to expand its involvement in disputes concerning public expenditure. That attempt took place in Australia and neatly illustrates the judiciary's inability to effect a meaningful re-distribution of financial authority away from treasury departments and towards parliaments. The chapter closes by examining another case study, this time drawn from the UK, which illustrates the difficulties with viewing common law courts as systemically reliable mechanisms to enforce parliamentary authority over taxation.

At the outset, a caveat must be lodged regarding the following treatment of taxation law. In line with earlier chapters, no attempt is made to synthesise the entire body of enacted and judicially decided law concerning taxation, a task far beyond this book's remit. Instead, the focus is on the attitude of influential apex courts to tax disputes. No such caveat is required for the decided law concerning appropriation, debt or monetary finance, because no discernible body of case law exists on those matters: *QED*.

Asymmetric Judicial Power

The extent of the judiciary's involvement with public finance makes little sense if approached with the Diceyan assumption that all uses of public money 'may become dependent upon the decision of the judges upon the meaning of an Act of Parliament'.[1] Judges regularly pronounce upon taxation disputes, but never upon enactments concerning appropriation, sovereign borrowing or monetary finance, anomalies aside.

A collection of factors accounts for that asymmetric judicial involvement in public finance. Judges have made conscious choices to become embroiled in some public finance activities, like taxation, while avoiding others, like expenditure, debt and monetary finance. Some public finance activities, particularly appropriation, are governed by legislation which is designed in such a way that the judiciary cannot effectively review conformity with its terms. Other public financial activities, particularly debt and monetary finance, occur in a technical context which makes disputes about their legality extremely difficult to submit to the judiciary.

Those factors can be collected under the broad notion of *justiciability*, which can be divided into *principled* and *practical* justiciability where: principled justiciability represents the judiciary's *principled reasons* for restraining from passing judgment on a dispute; and practical justiciability means the *practical capacity* for a dispute to be submitted to the judiciary.

Principled Justiciability

In the common law tradition, justiciability is mainly understood as a principle of 'judicial restraint':[2] a set of standards applied by judges to determine whether they should resolve a particular dispute.[3] As the judiciary's supervision of government expanded during the twentieth century, various doctrines developed to assist judges to identify types of disputes involving government behaviour which were better left alone by the judiciary. Various technical labels exist, including 'justiciability' 'standing' and 'deference'.[4] Although each doctrine has a unique ancestry

---

[1] Dicey (1885), 178.
[2] King (2008a), 'Institutional Approaches to Judicial Restraint'.
[3] King (2007), 'Justiciability of Resource Allocation'.
[4] *Council of Civil Service Unions* v. *Minister for the Civil Service* [1985] AC 374, 410; *Shergill* v. *Khaira* [2015] AC 359, [41]; *R* v. *Inland Revenue; ex parte National Federation of Self-Employed and Small Businesses Ltd* [1982] AC 617; *R (Lord Carlile of Berriew)* v. *Secretary of State for the Home Department* [2015] 1 AC 945, [22]-[34].

and mode of application, they may conveniently be collected here under the broad label of *justiciability*.

Judges justify the deployment of justiciability doctrines in different ways. Occasionally, a crude distinction between 'political judgment' and legal determination is invoked.[5] More often the concept of the separation of powers appears:[6]

> [i]n a ... system ... concerned with the separation of powers ... decisions about social and economic policy, particularly those concerned with the equitable distribution of public resources ... are ordinarily recognised by the courts to be matters for the judgment of the elected representatives of the people.

Applying justiciability doctrines, informed by that justification, often results in the judiciary holding back from resolving disputes concerning matters of social and economic policy or recognising 'a built-in latitude (or margin of discretion)' when ruling on those matters.[7]

Specifically applied to disputes about public finance,[8] justiciability doctrines premised on the separation of powers have been explained as an aggregate of various different 'factors'.[9] Chief amongst which is the existence of an historically grounded constitutional practice of non-judicial institutions having exclusive 'competence'[10] (or custody) over a particular dispute's subject matter. That factor is often explicitly relied upon by judges.[11] A related factor may be the absence of judicial 'expertise' concerning the subject matter of a dispute.[12] That invocation of expertise is related to judicial perceptions of competence or

---

[5] *A v. Secretary of State for the Home Department* [2005] 2 AC 68, [29].
[6] *R (Hooper) v. Secretary of State for Work and Pensions* [2005] 1 WLR 1681, [32].
[7] *R (Public Law Project) v. Lord Chancellor* [2016] AC 1531, [33]. Issues concerning 'the allocation of finite financial resources' have had a broader impact on the development of substantive legal principles: *X (Minors) v. Bedfordshire County Council* [1995] 2 AC 633, 737.
[8] Justiciability doctrines can operate differently elsewhere: *Mohammed (Serdar) v. Ministry of Defence* [2017] 2 WLR 2879, [79]; *Shergill* (2015), [42]; *Prebble v. Television New Zealand Ltd* [1995] 1 AC 321.
[9] See King's 'multi-factorial' and 'institutional' approach to justiciability: King (2008a), 'Institutional Approaches to Judicial Restraint'.
[10] Jowell (2003), 'Judicial Deference and Human Rights: A Question of Competence'.
[11] '[T]he allocation of public resources is a matter for ministers, not courts': *Regina v. Secretary of State for the Environment, Transport and the Regions* [2001] 2 AC 349, 395. '[R]eallocation of resources or additional expenditure' are 'matters for decision by Parliament, not the courts': *In re S (Minors) (Care Order: Implementation of Care Plan)* [2002] 2 AC 291, 297, 314 [43].
[12] Kavanagh (2008), 'Deference or Defiance', 192.

custodianship over disputes concerning public finance: a lack of expertise may arise *as a result of* the historical practice of allocating disputes to another institutional custodian; and a lack of judicial expertise may only be *relative to* the superior expertise of personnel in that other institution.[13]

Yet another factor may be that the 'consequences' of a dispute are exceptionally difficult for judges to foresee or predict. That aspect of judicial restraint saw its most thoughtful expression in Fuller's idea of 'polycentricity':[14]

> *A pull on one strand will distribute tensions over a complicated pattern throughout the web as a whole. Doubling the original pull will, in all likelihood, not simply double each of the resulting tensions but will rather create a different complicated pattern of tensions. This would certainly occur, for example, if the doubled pull caused one or more of the weaker strands to snap. This is a 'polycentric' situation because it is 'many centered' – each crossing of strands is a distinct centre for distributing tensions*

Tellingly, Fuller singled out public expenditure decisions as a prime example of polycentricity:[15]

> *In allocating $100 million for scientific research it is never a case of Project A v. Project B, but rather of Project A v. Project B v. Project C v. Project D ... bearing in mind that Project Q may be an alternative to Project B, while Project M supplements it, and that Project R may seek the same objective as Project C by a cheaper method, though one less certain to succeed, etc.*

On Fuller's account, disputes with strong polycentric elements should be resolved by more deliberative 'parliamentary methods which include an element of contract in the form of the political "deal" ... an accommodation of interests'.[16] To whit, political, rather than judicial, resolution of resource-use disputes should be preferred. Yet another factor lying behind principled judicial restraint is that civil and political rights are more appropriately protected by the judicial system than social or economic rights.[17]

Principled justiciability analysis is a necessary but not sufficient explanation for judiciaries' asymmetric involvement in public finance

---

[13] King (2008a), 423.
[14] Fuller (1978), 'The Forms and Limits of Adjudication', 395; cf King (2008b), 'Pervasiveness of Polycentricity'.
[15] Fuller (1978), 395.
[16] Ibid., 400.
[17] That point is strongly contested by King (2012), *Judging Social Rights*.

disputes. That is so because the bulk of public finance law has never been litigated, indicating the influence of forces beyond judges' principled decision-making.

Practical Justiciability

As a practical matter, it is exceptionally difficult to submit many financial disputes to judicial resolution. For a judge reared on a staple diet of linguistically precise legal documents, appropriation legislation is notoriously nebulous and, therefore, judicially indigestible. Treasury and central bank operations are attended by extreme secrecy and haste, imposing large obstacles to effective litigation about sovereign debt and monetary finance. Those barriers to judicial review exist *dehors* a judge's principled decision to decline to resolve a dispute, and are best explained through the rubric of practical justiciability: the *practical capacity* for a given dispute to be submitted to the judiciary.

Practical matters impacting the judiciary's capacity to resolve a public finance dispute include: (i) the design of financial legislation (*legislative design*), and (ii) technical aspects of financial administration which are external to the legislative or judicial practices (*externalities*).[18] The design of financial legislation may have a negative or positive impact on practical justiciability. Some financial legislation is framed in relatively clear, calculable or 'formal'[19] terms and may contain an express mechanism to funnel disputes regarding financial activity to the judiciary: a *positive legislative design*.[20] Other legislation may be vague, nebulous, or 'informal' and omit any mechanism for funnelling disputes to the judiciary: a *negative legislative design*.[21]

Externalities may also be positive or negative. Some public financial activities take place at low speed and under technical conditions which permit transparency of financial information, together allowing for the meaningful operation of judicial processes before the subject matter of

---

[18] 'Externality' here means 'qualities external to' the design of public finance law, rather than the technical economic meaning of a 'side-effect or consequence (of an industrial or commercial activity) which affects other parties without this being reflected in the cost of the goods or services involved; a social cost or benefit': cf both usages in *Oxford English Dictionary Online*, 'externality, n' (July 2018).
[19] Tamanaha (2004), *On the Rule of Law*, chapter 7.
[20] Cf the contrary view that 'vague' legal standards should not negatively affect the assessment of justiciability: King (2012), 297.
[21] The possibility that vague or nebulous legislation could lead to interpretative disputes and, thereby, provoke judicial review is acknowledged.

the dispute is rendered irrelevant as a matter of economic reality: *positive externalities*. Other public financial activities are so critically time-sensitive and secretive that there is, either, no practical opportunity to notify potential litigants or insufficient time for judicial processes to unfold: *negative externalities*.

No single factor of principled and practical justiciability wholly explains the asymmetric involvement of judiciaries in public finance disputes. Even where legislative design points extremely strongly towards non-justiciability (where jurisdiction is deliberately not conferred on the judiciary) the judiciary retains the power to determine its own involvement: as demonstrated by the history of ouster clause litigation.[22] In that sense, an assessment of justiciability appears not as a binary choice, but as a position on a spectrum of *more or less justiciable* disputes.

More Justiciable Disputes

Of all disputes regarding public finance, taxation disputes are the most clearly justiciable.

All principled factors point strongly to justiciability. The judiciary's historical position as the ultimate custodian of taxation disputes is deeply embedded: so much is evidenced by the concentration of legal expertise concerning taxation.[23] Polycentric concerns are less overt in tax disputes, as the consequences of curial determinations appear to be constrained to the parties before the court, at least insofar as a 'pay first, litigate later' rule is in force.[24] Additionally, taxation disputes directly implicate the protection of private property rights: a classic concern of the common law judiciary.[25]

As a matter of practical justiciability, taxpayer disputes are facilitated by a positive legislative design which expressly provides for judicial review as the end-point of an elaborate statutory review and appeal process.[26] Externalities are also positive. Administrative processes give

---

[22] *Anisminic Ltd v. Foreign Compensation Commission* [1968] 2 AC 14; *Plaintiff S157/2002 v. Commonwealth* (2003) 211 CLR 476.
[23] The historical position is surveyed in Chapter 2.
[24] As is the default in both Australia (*Taxation Administration Act 1953* (Cth), ss 14ZZR, 14ZZM) and the UK (*Finance Act 2014* (UK), c 26, Part 4).
[25] It is less clear whether that classic concern suffices to override the (obvious) counter-point that the outcome of a tax dispute carries large consequences for the broader distribution of wealth, and thus implicates the effective realisation of civil and political rights.
[26] E.g., Smailes (2017), *Tolley's Income Tax 2017–2018*, chapter 5.

taxpayers advance notice of tax collection and highly transparent reasoning processes accompany the assessment of tax liability. Perhaps most importantly, no financial cliff edge is approached in the event that a taxpayer successfully contests tax liability, as executive agencies have ready recourse to alternative methods of revenue-raising: debt and money markets.

For that collection of reasons, taxpayer vs taxman disputes sit at the most justiciable end of the spectrum of justiciability.[27]

Less Justiciable Disputes

Disputes about other public financial activities are far less obviously justiciable.

Disputes concerning appropriation fall towards the less justiciable end of the justiciability spectrum. No settled practice of judicial review of appropriation legislation exists and other institutions have long had custody over the legal limits of appropriation legislation.[28] Since the mid-nineteenth century, it has been clear that treasury departments and Auditors-General have had exclusive custody over executives' compliance with appropriation legislation.[29] That long-standing institutional arrangement has left a void of judicial expertise regarding appropriation legislation. Except in exceptional cases, the consequences of a legal decision regarding public expenditure are intrinsically polycentric, and directly raise questions concerning the distribution of economic resources which lie outside the judiciary's traditional concern with the protection of private property and negative liberty.

Similarly strong obstacles arise regarding practical justiciability. The design of appropriation legislation makes no express provision for funnelling disputes towards the judiciary. Nor is it framed in clear, formal terms, but rather a hotchpotch of legal and non-legal limitations which are designed to facilitate the exercise of wide delegated authority by

---

[27] Other taxation disputes are less evidently justiciable, particularly those where the legality of a tax agency's decisions are challenged by a litigant other than a taxpayer: *R v. Inland Revenue; ex parte National Federation of Self-Employed and Small Businesses Ltd* [1982] AC 617.

[28] There is, of course, a settled practice of judicial review regarding legal entitlements to be paid money by a government (especially, in the form of welfare payments). That practice does not, however, touch the more fundamental question of whether a payment falls within the scope of an appropriation.

[29] The historical detail can be found in Chapter 2.

financial executives.[30] The administration of appropriation legislation is attended by strong negative externalities. Most prominent is the size and complexity of modern bureaucratic government, which can conceal matters critical to determining the legality of the wider executive's compliance with appropriation legislation.[31] Another negative externality is the necessary speed and secrecy attending the economic conditions in which government spending sometimes must occur.[32]

Disputes concerning the legality of debt and monetary finance are even less evidently justiciable than appropriation legislation. As a matter of history, treasury departments, and latterly central banks, have enjoyed sole custody over sovereign borrowing and monetary finance:[33] leaving scant opportunity for the judiciary to develop any expertise in the complex economic thinking underlying sovereign debt management and monetary authority.[34]

Practical non-justiciability factors point even more powerfully towards non-justiciability. The legislative design of sovereign borrowing legislation is characterised by extremely broad discretions, conditioned on states of satisfaction regarding monetary policy and fiscal deficits, while monetary finance occurs in the absence of any meaningful legislative regulation. The negative externalities are overwhelming. Where legal authority to engage in sovereign borrowing is conditioned on the existence of a fiscal or cash deficit,[35] identifying a breach of law requires the judiciary to have access to minute-by-minute cash-management information. Similarly, the speed with which monetary finance may be required and the complexity of modern financial markets make meaningful involvement by the judiciary in disputes about monetary finance wildly impracticable.

For that collection of reasons, disputes concerning debt and monetary finance fall at the least-justiciable end of the justiciability spectrum.

---

[30] As the analysis of the complex history of virement rules in Chapter 2 illustrated.

[31] Examples of that complexity were discussed in Chapter 5, prime amongst which was the accidental breach of annual appropriation legislation by the UK Ministry of Defence each year between 2007 and 2012.

[32] A prominent example of such spending, examined in Chapter 6, was the UK's decision to spend ~£24 billion in excess of annual appropriation legislation on urgent bank bailouts in 2009.

[33] For the eighteenth- to twentieth-century history, see Chapters 2 and 5. For the early twenty-first-century practice, see Chapter 7.

[34] It is an open question whether judicial expertise could be extended to the economic and financial issues which arise in debt management and monetary policy.

[35] As it was in the UK between 1968 and 1983.

Constitutional Consequences

The constitutional consequence is that judicial power has a very limited capacity to impact executives' concentrated authority over public finance.

A certain type of legal traditionalist may object that such a conclusion overlooks the judiciary's inherent power to hold government to account, especially in the teeth of patent legal or constitutional violations.[36] Such an objection relies heavily on a vision of the judiciary as the ultimate superintendent of the executive government. So it would go, any theory that public finance disputes are non-justiciable can be instantly falsified if the judiciary so wishes: viz, a 150-year pattern of judicial exclusion from most public finance activity can be overturned at any time because the judiciary possesses apex institutional authority to ensure that no government official behaves *ultra vires*. Ordinary judicial power suffices to bring errant treasury officials to parliamentary heel.

Weighing the strength of that objection is difficult in the abstract, but, fortunately, a case study exists which illustrates the boundaries of the judiciary's capacity to shift the distribution of constitutional authority over public finance, even when highly motivated.

Expenditure and the Judiciary

As earlier chapters explained,[37] the nineteenth- and twentieth-century precedents were clear: the authority possessed by treasury departments over public expenditure would not be policed by the exercise of judicial power. In the early twenty-first century, the High Court of Australia attempted, but ultimately failed, to change that position.

In hindsight, that attempt followed a discernible trajectory. It began with the Court's recognition that annual appropriation legislation could not be effectively judicially reviewed, leaving the executive unchecked by

---

[36] The '*Pergau Dam*' case is an example of such a dispute (involving a decision to spend public money against all economic advice and in the absence of legal advice), although it did not concern the judicial review of appropriation legislation: *R* v. *Secretary of State for Foreign Affairs ex parte World Development Movement Ltd* [1995] 1 All ER 611. The UK Supreme Court's decision to quash the advice of a British Prime Minister to the Monarch on the ground of improper purpose is another example: *R (Miller)* v. *The Prime Minister* [2019] UKSC 41.

[37] For the history of the common law judiciary's non-involvement in disputes concerning appropriation legislation, see Chapter 3 and for extension of that position to the broader parliamentary constitutional world, see Chapter 4.

law in decisions concerning public expenditure.[38] It continued as the Court formulated a new constitutional rule requiring additional statutory authorisation for public expenditure, displacing the constitutional function of annual appropriation legislation.[39] It concluded as the Court sanctioned a model of public expenditure legislation which replicated the executive's financial predominance.[40] As a case study, the High Court's experience demonstrates the difficulties confronting attempts to bring public expenditure within the purview of judiciaries in parliamentary constitutional systems.

Attempted Judicial Enforcement of Appropriation Legislation

The High Court's attempt to expand the scope of judicial review over public expenditure began in a 2005 challenge to the legality of expenditure for political advertising under an annual appropriation Act: *Combet* v. *The Commonwealth*.

The *Combet* plaintiffs, a Shadow Opposition Front Bencher and the head of a union body, sought declarations that a line item in an annual appropriation Act did not authorise the use of money to advertise the virtues of contemplated industrial legislation. Injunctions were also sought to prevent Australian treasury departments from paying funds from consolidated revenue to fund that political advertising.

The relevant Australian appropriation legislation was heavily influenced by 'New Public Management' philosophies;[41] using highly obscure terminology to set the legal boundaries of public spending. The annual *Appropriation Act (No 1) 2005–2006* (Cth) identified '[h]igher productivity, higher pay workplaces' as an 'outcome' for which funds (called 'Departmental items') could be applied as 'departmental expenditure' of the Department of Workplace Relations.[42] The Department's estimate[43] gave limited further guidance regarding that outcome: 'providing policy advice and legislation development services to government' and 'supporting employers and employees in adopting fair and flexible workplace

---

[38] *Combet* v. *The Commonwealth* (2005) 224 CLR 494; *Pape* v. *Commissioner of Taxation* (2009) 238 CLR 1.
[39] *Williams* v. *Commonwealth (No. 1)* (2012) 248 CLR 156.
[40] *Williams* v. *Commonwealth (No. 2)* (2014) 252 CLR 416.
[41] The historical rise of New Public Management philosophies on fiscal legislation was observed in Chapter 4.
[42] The relevant provisions were ss 4, 7, 15 and Sch 1.
[43] Its 'Portfolio Budget Statement'.

relations practices'.[44] The total amount appropriated was $140,131,000: within the total departmental appropriation of $1,447,552,000. The plaintiffs argued that the use of funds for advertising the virtues of proposed industrial legislation fell outside the statutory description of 'higher productivity, higher pay workplaces'.[45]

The Court (by a 5:2 majority) rejected that argument.[46] Two pathways led to that conclusion. The first was that the *Appropriation Act* imposed no subject-matter limitation on the relevant expenditure. So long as the money appropriated to 'higher pay, higher productivity workplaces' was spent by the relevant department, it did not matter whether the activity funded was indeed orientated towards boosting pay and productivity. Four judges adopted that position, holding that the appropriation Act:[47]

> *imposes no narrower restriction on the scope of the expenditure ... it does not matter whether any part of the $140,131,000 (or the $1,447,552,000) is spent otherwise than on activities leading to higher productivity or higher pay workplaces ..., so long as it is 'departmental expenditure'.*

The other pathway to upholding the validity of the expenditure was that the subject-matter limitation in the appropriation Act was so broad that political advertising fell within its limits. Gleeson CJ adopted that view, explaining that the 'relevant outcome is stated with such breadth' that '[p]ersuading the public of the merits of [industrial] policy and legislation' fell within its terms.[48]

Of greater importance than *Combet's* relatively narrow *ratio*, was the Court's recognition that it was unable to impose meaningful limits on the political and administrative concepts which constituted the *Appropriation Act*'s legal limitation on expenditure. With admirable candour, Gleeson CJ explained that particular difficulty by reference to a statutory line item for the Department of Foreign Affairs and Trade:[49]

---

[44] *Combet* (2005), [27].
[45] The stakes were high. Two years after the litigation the prime minister, who bet his premiership on the proposed industrial legislation, lost both government and his seat in Parliament.
[46] Two dissenting judges held that spending for the advertising program did not fall within the expression 'higher pay, higher productivity workplaces': *Combet* (2005), [36], [172].
[47] Ibid., [128], [163]. That interpretation was based on a 'note' in the *Appropriation Act*, which the Court construed to render the funds listed in the Appropriation Act next to the item for 'higher pay, higher productivity workplace' legally 'notional'.
[48] Ibid., [29].
[49] Ibid., [12].

> The relevant outcome is: 'Agriculture in developing countries and Australia is more productive and sustainable as a result of better technologies, practices, policies and systems'. Plainly, that outcome is likely to be affected by a host of factors beyond the control or influence of the Australian Government. Furthermore, opinions may be divided upon whether agriculture at one time is 'more productive and sustainable' than at another, or upon whether certain technologies, practices, policies and systems have been made 'better'. This is a description, in the broadest political terms, of an objective of governmental activity. Whether a particular form of expenditure on goods or services (output) is likely to contribute to that objective might be contestable. For such a contest to give rise to a justiciable issue, as distinct from a political or scientific controversy, the issue could not be formulated appropriately by stating the outcome and asking whether the expenditure would contribute to it. The generality, and the value-laden content of the outcome would make that impossible.

The example neatly illustrates how the line-item limits in annual appropriation legislation are maladapted to judicial interpretation.

The remainder of the Court was less transparent in its reasoning, but still acknowledged the difficulty of imposing judicially enforceable limitations on the subject-matter restrictions in annual appropriation legislation:[50]

> at least since the mid-1980s the chief means of limiting expenditures made by departments of State that has been adopted in annual appropriation Acts has been to specify the amount that may be spent rather than further define the purposes or activities for which it may be spent.

From that assertion of historical fact, the majority's conclusion that the *Appropriation Act* imposed no legal limitation by reference to subject matter made some sense.

The dispute in *Combet* taught the Australian High Court a simple lesson: annual appropriation legislation could not be subjected to ordinary judicial review. Evidence of that lesson learned appeared in the Australian High Court's next engagement with appropriation legislation, *Pape v. Commissioner of Taxation*,[51] where it decided that annual appropriation legislation did not give a government power to spend money.

Pape concerned a constitutional challenge to the payment of a 'tax bonus' by the Australian government. The tax bonus was a form of direct fiscal stimulus designed to boost Australian consumption as a buffer

---
[50] Ibid., [161].
[51] (2009) 238 CLR 1.

against the economic contraction of the financial crisis.[52] Its statutory basis was the elegantly branded *Tax Bonus for Working Australians Act (No. 2) 2009* (Cth), which empowered the Commissioner of Taxation to credit the bank accounts of taxpayers who paid income tax in the fiscal year preceding the financial crisis.[53] An activist taxpayer sued the Australian government, contending that it had no constitutional power to pay him a tax bonus.

Central to the *Pape* litigation was the question whether payment of the tax bonus was within the constitutional power of the Australian federal government or the States.[54] The Australian federal government's preferred answer was that the provision of the *Australian Constitution* which permitted appropriation 'for the purposes of the Commonwealth' conferred authority to spend money on 'the fiscal management and monetary management of the national economy'.[55] So it went, because the tax bonuses were supported by appropriation legislation designed to respond to an economic emergency, they were constitutionally valid.

The Court disagreed, holding that appropriation legislation did not confer any 'power to spend' money, but merely authorised the 'earmarking' or 'segregation' of funds within Australia's consolidated revenue.[56] Such a holding sat uncomfortably next to several centuries of uncontested practice that appropriation legislation provided a legal basis to spend money. The Court's iconoclasm made more sense when viewed as a sequel to its unhappy attempt to judicially review appropriation legislation in *Combet*: if appropriation legislation imposed no meaningful limits on public spending, then it also did not confer any meaningful legal power to spend.

Combet's significance was openly acknowledged by an influential branch of the Court. Justices Gummow, Crennan and Bell explained that *Combet* 'illustrates' that 'the description given to items of appropriation provides an insufficient textual basis for the determination of issues of constitutional fact and for the treatment of s 81 as a criterion of

---

[52] The stimulus could be described as 'helicopter money': cf Friedman (1969), 'The Optimum Quantity of Money'.

[53] A tax bonus of $900 was payable if taxable income was below $80,000; $600 if below $90,000; and $250 if below $100,000.

[54] Appleby and McDonald (2011), 'The Ramifications of Pape v. Federal Commissioner of Taxation'; Twomey (2010), 'Pushing the Boundaries of Executive Power'.

[55] Section 81: 'All revenues or moneys raised or received by the Executive Government of the Commonwealth shall form one Consolidated Revenue Fund, to be appropriated for the purposes of the Commonwealth'. *Pape* (2009), 9.

[56] Ibid., [133], [366].

legislative validity'.⁵⁷ Justices Hayne and Kiefel described the appropriation legislation they encountered in *Combet* as using 'diffuse ... descriptions of' the purposes for which money would be expended.⁵⁸ Translated from Australian legal diction, those statements amount to an acknowledgement that appropriation legislation was insufficiently precise to create judicially ascertainable standards of conduct.⁵⁹ Given the Australian High Court's commitment to a strict version of judicial supremacy, that was a particularly significant withdrawal of judicial oversight.⁶⁰

Together, *Combet* and *Pape* indicate some of the difficulties faced by common law judiciaries in engaging in judicial review of appropriation legislation. *Combet* illustrates the difficulty *in application*, as the judges struggled to make sense of the 'generality, and the value-laden content' of legal limitations in appropriation legislation.⁶¹ *Pape* illustrates the judges' *principled acceptance* of those difficulties by articulating a general legal position that the judiciary should stop trying to apply ordinary judicial techniques to appropriation legislation.⁶²

The educational dividend for the High Court was that it could not impose effective judicial rules on public expenditure by reference to appropriation legislation. A somewhat large query did, however, remain: what was the legal basis for public spending, if not appropriation legislation? In constitutional terms, that query left an appropriation-legislation-sized gap in the rule of law.

Building New Principles

The Court's response to that rule-of-law gap was to construct a constitutional rule that would require parliaments to enact a new kind of expenditure-authorising statute, additional to appropriation

---

⁵⁷ Ibid., [197].
⁵⁸ Ibid., [296].
⁵⁹ Ibid., [100]. Considerations of the federal division of powers were also relevant to the Court's decision: see Twomey (2010).
⁶⁰ For an insightful critique of Australian public law doctrine, see Taggart (2008), '"Australian Exceptionalism" in Judicial Review'.
⁶¹ That matter has been overlooked: not unreasonably, given that the Court's reasons were 614 paragraphs long and referenced by 725 footnotes.
⁶² The Court had avoided giving definitive answers to this question in the past: *New South Wales v. Bardolph* (1934) 52 CLR 455; *Victoria v. The Commonwealth* (1975) 134 CLR 338; *Davis v. The Commonwealth* (1988) 166 CLR 79.

legislation, in a case concerning the legality of public expenditure on school chaplains: *Williams v. Commonwealth*.

Williams concerned the legality of Australian government expenditure on salaries and expenses of chaplains in primary and secondary schools through the federal Department of Education, Science and Training.[63] Chaplain payments were contemplated by annual appropriation Acts, but not by any programme-specific legislation. The legality of that funding was challenged on the basis, inter alia, that it was contrary to the idea of 'parliamentary control of money' and 'parliamentary control of the executive'.[64] The purported violation hinged on the Court's earlier holdings in *Combet* and *Pape*, that annual appropriation legislation conferred no legal authority on the Australian executive government to spend money.

A bare majority of the Court (4:3) held that such additional legislation was required, and, in its absence, all payments to school chaplains unlawful. Underpinning that surprising outcome was a holding that public expenditure was unlawful in the absence of specific (i.e., non-appropriation) legislation, which was itself based on the need to ensure 'parliamentary control' over the executive and enforce the federal division of powers established by the *Australian Constitution*.

The Court's reliance on the mooted principle of parliamentary control assumed the limitations acknowledged in *Combet* and *Pape* regarding the judiciary's capacity to review compliance with appropriation legislation. It accepted that, post-*Pape*, Australian law considered that appropriation legislation provided no power to spend money and thus provided an insufficient basis for Parliament to control public money.[65] The Court's focus on federal considerations also included a recognition of the difficulties, identified in *Pape*, of undertaking judicial review of appropriation legislation: one judge described the difficulty of judicially reviewing appropriation legislation as a negative 'consequence for the Federation', which could only be rectified by requiring additional legislative authorisation of expenditure.[66]

The weaponisation of 'parliamentary control' in *Williams* could be criticised from many angles. Perhaps the most powerful criticism is

---

[63] *Williams (No. 1)* (2012), [10].
[64] High Court of Australia, Transcript of Proceeding (9 August 2011) [2011] HCATrans 198. Manifold other arguments were raised, none of which assumed significance.
[65] *Williams (No. 1)* (2012), [157], [189], [191], [222], [530], [538].
[66] Ibid., [37]-[39].

that, as a matter of historical fact, any 'control' parliament had over the executive government's expenditure was exercised *through appropriation legislation* rather than anything *additional to* that legislation. Next in line is the long-standing judicial practice of leaving parliaments and financial executives alone to resolve their disputes regarding public expenditure.[67]

Given the weaknesses of the technical reasoning in *Williams*, the case is probably best understood as a response to the rule-of-law gap that opened after *Combet* and *Pape*. Viewed in that way, *Williams* appears as an attempt to fill that gap by requiring that a new form of legislation be enacted authorising public expenditure, which, unlike appropriation legislation, the judiciary could enforce.

Australia's frolic with judicial review of appropriation legislation cannot be understood without reference to the aftermath of *Williams*, which involved the Australian Parliament enacting legislation which delegated all legal responsibility for determining when public money should be spent to the executive:

32B Supplementary powers to make commitments to spend public money etc
(1) If:
    (a) apart from this subsection, the Commonwealth does not have power to make, vary or administer:
        (i) an arrangement under which public money is, or may become, payable by the Commonwealth; [and]. . .
    (b) the arrangement or grant, as the case may be:
        (i) is specified in the regulations; or
        (ii) is included in a class of arrangements or grants, as the case may be, specified in the regulations; or
        (iii) is for the purposes of a program specified in the regulations;
the Commonwealth has power to make, vary or administer the arrangement or grant.

That provision's effect was to confer *ex facie* unlimited power on the Australian executive to make regulations which would, by circular

---

[67] Chapter 2. The Court's reliance on federal considerations to justify an additional legislation requirement was hardly compelling as the existence of legislation had never been a *sine qua non* to effective judicial review of limitations imposed by federal (or any other legal) constraints in a common law legal system, as the well-established practice of judicial review of the prerogative amply demonstrates.

drafting, confer authority 'to make, vary, and administer' funding. The Australian executive quickly exercised that power and began making voluminous regulations to provide specific authorisation for the school chaplain payments and myriad other spending programmes placed in legal jeopardy after *Williams*.[68]

The legality of that legislative fix was challenged in *Williams v. Commonwealth (No. 2)*.[69] A critical issue in that litigation was whether the legislative fix also flouted the principle of 'parliamentary control' by delegating authority to the executive to determine the subject matter and quantum of public spending programmes. Giving sparse reasons, the Court refused to invalidate the legislative fix,[70] and it has been churning away ever since:[71] with Australian Treasury departments determining, as a matter of delegated legislative authority, the legality of public expenditure, behind a façade of 'parliamentary control'.

Failing to Re-distribute Financial Authority

The Australian experience illustrates the durability of the distribution of financial authority in parliamentary systems of government, and the inability of a common law judiciary, at this point in the historical record, to disturb the status quo.

The judiciary's experimentation with review of public expenditure did nothing to allocate a greater share of financial authority to the Parliament. By the end of the *Combet-Pape-Williams* saga, the judiciary accepted that a wholesale legislative delegation of the power to authorise public expenditure to the executive sufficed to secure Parliament's financial rights. For all practical purposes, the *status quo ante* was restored. The Australian Parliament continued to enact annual *Appropriation Acts* which were formulated, approved and administered

---

[68] *Financial Management and Accountability Regulations 1997* (Cth), Item 407.013 of Schedule 2: 'National School Chaplaincy and Student Welfare Program'.
[69] (2014) 252 CLR 416.
[70] Ibid., [36]. The Court also held that the Australian federal parliament had no legislative power to make payments to school chaplain under s 51(xxiiiA) because such payments were not benefits to students and family allowances (*Williams (No. 2)* (2014), [48]). It also refused to re-endorse the 'additional expenditure legislation' requirement from *Williams (No. 1)*, suggesting the shelf life of that doctrine may be rather limited (Ibid., [66], [69]).
[71] The current *Financial Management Regulation* stands at ~200 pages, approving over 800 spending programmes.

by Australia's treasury departments. Those executive bodies also set the conditions for the wider executive's expenditure, with the *ex post* audit oversight of the Auditor-General in the background. The legislative fix to *Williams (No. 1)* was simply appended to those deeply embedded practices by technical amendments to delegated legislation by the same executive organs which formulated, introduced and administered appropriation legislation.

Viewed in the larger context of the legislative practices of public expenditure, such a result seems inevitable. Given the ~150-year gap between the *1872 Treasury Case* and *Williams*, neither the judiciary, nor legal profession, possessed any expertise on the obscure topics of annual appropriation legislation or public expenditure practice generally. During that time, a system of legislative appropriation grew which was often retrospective, accommodated extreme flexibility and relied on Treasury departments to formulate the content of spending proposals, the accounting basis of public financial activity and the supervision of the wider bureaucracy's use of money.[72] Those longstanding institutional features erect exceptionally high obstacles to a judicial attempt to become embroiled in disputes concerning public expenditure.

Taxation and the Judiciary

In light of the judiciary's ancient jurisdiction over tax disputes,[73] it is tempting to understand judicial review as a mechanism for the enforcement of tax legislation against, both, revenue agencies and recalcitrant taxpayers. As sentinels against liberty-encroaching officialdom, judges appear to enforce parliaments' legislative will on tax officials who might otherwise exceed their statutory mandates. When they rule against taxpayers (in civil or criminal proceedings), judges can appear to be supporting the executive in the enforcement of parliamentary fiscal policy. On both views, judges are seen as the enforcers of the letter and spirit of parliaments' authority over taxation.

While that understanding of the judiciary's role vis-à-vis government is relatively orthodox from a strictly legal perspective, matters are not so straightforward if a broader institutional perspective is adopted. Such an institutional perspective would recognise that parliament has selected

---

[72] Explained in Chapters 2 and 3.
[73] Discussed in Chapter 3.

revenue agencies as the institutions with principal responsibility for executing tax legislation and mandated those executive bodies with the maximally efficient collection of public revenue. From that perspective, executive officials, not judges, are mandated to maximise the tax yield.

Judges could, however, be understood as supporting revenue agencies in carrying out the fiscal policy objectives of tax legislation. But revenue agencies do not view judiciaries in this way, and rely on a swathe of other measures in closing tax gaps and thereby increasing compliance with parliamentary fiscal policy.

Accordingly, judicial review of tax disputes does not invariably distribute significant financial authority over taxation to parliament and away from financial executives, as revenue agencies remain the institution with principal authority to enforce tax law. From the perspective of the distribution of financial authority, the core observation is that judiciaries are not a systematic mechanism for enforcing the executive's compliance with the limits of parliamentary fiscal policy enacted in tax legislation, despite their well-embedded role in resolving disputes regarding taxation.

Financial Perspective

Viewed from the vantage point of the revenue agencies charged with enforcing taxation law, judicial power neither significantly obstructs, nor materially assists the maximal enforcement of tax legislation. That point is best illustrated in two ways, by reference to the UK's revenue agency, Her Majesty's Revenue and Customs (HMRC), during the period 2005–2016: the low impact of judicial review on public receipts, and the general irrelevance of the judiciary in closing 'tax gaps'.

Cash Shortfalls and Tax Receipts

Judicial review of taxation decisions *could* have significant impacts on public sector receipts, but the *actual likelihood* of losing material revenue streams as a result of judicial review is low. So much is revealed by the measures taken by revenue agencies to quantify their exposure to legal risk and hedge against it by provisioning for legal claims.

Between 2005 and 2016, HMRC annually provisioned for between ~£19 million and ~£80 million for outstanding legal claims where the amount in dispute was quantifiable, and there appeared to be reasonable certainty of outcome.[74] While those figures may seem substantial, they

---

[74] Data collected from HMRC, *Annual Reports and Accounts* (2005–2016).

are economically insignificant when compared to the total annual receipts of HMRC during the same period (between ~£418 billion and ~£575 billion) and the UK central government's fiscal deficit (between ~ £27 billion and ~£201 billion).

HMRC also reported a larger provision for legal claims of a more speculative nature as contingent liabilities. From 2008 (when quantified contingent liabilities began being reported) to 2015, HMRC provisioned for between ~£7.1 billion (2015) and ~£81.2 billion (in 2010). Annually averaged between 2008 and 2015, HMRC's contingent liabilities provision stood at 5 per cent of total tax receipts and 20 per cent of the fiscal deficit.

The main consequence of those figures is to illustrate the limited importance of judicial review of tax decisions, relative to the total revenue collecting functions of the executive government.[75] The UK tax agency takes the position that the likely quantifiable loss of tax revenue from litigation is economically insignificant and that the only material impact on tax receipts is by highly speculative claims. Several interpretations of that conclusion are available, including that UK tax authorities are: highly compliant with (the judiciary's likely interpretation of) tax legislation, confident that taxpayers are unlikely to robustly guard against unauthorised tax collection, or imprudent in their liability provisioning. On any measure, potential tax litigation does not appear as a material threat to public financial security.

Tax Agency Mitigation Measures

From the perspective of maximising the tax yield, judicial review hardly registers as an enforcement mechanism in comparison to the internal measures adopted by tax agencies to boost taxpayer compliance.

Revenue agencies adopt a range of measures to close 'tax gaps': the spread between tax yields in a world of total compliance with tax legislation and the actual tax yield. HMRC describes its understanding

---

[75] A similar trend is identifiable in other jurisdictions, including Australia. Between 2005 and 2016, the Australian Taxation Office provisioned for contingent liabilities of between ~$8 billion and ~$3 billion relating to tax disputes. The average annual amount was ~$5.9 billion, which stood at ~2 per cent of total average annual tax receipts and ~10 per cent of the annual fiscal deficit between 2009 and 2015 (when Australia swapped its surplus for a deficit): Data collected from Australian Taxation Office, *Annual Reports and Accounts* (2005–2017).

of the tax gap as resting on an idea of maximal enforcement of parliamentary fiscal policy: 'The "theoretical tax liability" represents the tax that would be paid if all individuals and companies complied with both the letter of the law and our interpretation of Parliament's intention in setting law.'[76] The causes of the tax gap are numerous, including: 'criminal attacks', 'evasion', 'hidden economy', 'avoidance', 'legal interpretation', 'non-payment', 'failure to take reasonable care' and 'error'.[77]

The UK's reported tax gap stands at ~6 per cent of total tax receipts, or ~£34 billion. That is a conservative estimate which omits 'ghosts', 'moonlighters', the 'hidden economy' and avoidance measures for income tax, NICs and capital gains tax.[78] That total figure does not spread evenly across all tax categories: for self-assessed 'business taxpayers' of income tax, the tax gap is 26 per cent (£4.8 billion); for 'hand-rolling tobacco duties' it is 32 per cent (£600 million); for corporation tax it is 6.4 per cent (£3.3 billion), of which 8 per cent (£1.9 billion) is attributable to small/medium-sized businesses and 5 per cent (£1.4 billion) is attributable to large businesses.

HMRC takes a number of measures to close those tax gaps, most of which are premised on improving the relationship between tax agencies and taxpayers. A parliamentary review into HMRC's measures identified relationship building with taxpayers and public education as the most important measures. A number of comparative measures may also have 'behavioural'[79] and technological elements: such as focusing on 'enhancing digital services', improving 'data matching capability' and educational programmes including advance alerts to taxpayers who may be facing compliance issues.[80]

While prosecution of criminal violations of tax legislation are nominated as strategies to close the tax gap, ordinary civil litigation (i.e., judicial review of tax decisions) does not feature as an enforcement mechanism. Given the judiciary's ambivalence towards the collection of public revenue, that should come as no surprise.

---

[76] HMRC, *Measuring Tax Gaps* (2017), 12.
[77] Ibid., 16.
[78] HMRC classifies ghosts as 'individuals whose entire income is unknown to HMRC' and moonlighters as individuals 'known to us in relation to part of their income, but have other sources of income that HMRC does not know about': Ibid., 11.
[79] Cf Oliver (2014), *Behavioral Public Policy*.
[80] Australian Taxation Office, *Addressing the Gap* (2017).

Doctrinal Perspective

From, at least, the mid-nineteenth century, British judges adopted a taxpayer-protecting attitude to taxation disputes, through a strict interpretation of taxation legislation and generous attitudes to tax-evasive transactions. By the later twentieth century, the judges had reversed course, adopting revenue-protecting doctrines of statutory interpretation and reversing their endorsement of evasive transactions. Chapters 3 and 5 recount those developments. By the beginning of the twenty-first century, as will shortly be explained, judicial attitudes swung back towards the insulation of wealth from taxation.

Those shifting jurisprudential sands reveal important truths about the judiciary's constitutional position in relation to taxation. Judges select the doctrinal techniques which govern taxation disputes, and those techniques do not invariably support the maximal execution of tax legislation. Occasionally, judges adopt doctrines which support executive agencies in discharging their statutory mandate to collect tax revenue. At other times, doctrines are deployed which hamper revenue agencies from recovering tax. From a purely doctrinal perspective, the most that can be said is that the judiciary may, but will not invariably, support Parliament's authority over taxation.

Resurrecting *Westminster*

Given the judicial strides in the 1980s away from the taxpayer-protecting approach,[81] the judiciary appeared headed towards a revenue-protecting doctrine in tax disputes. However, recent developments in the UK illustrate the limit of that trend.

In *MacNiven* v. *Westmoreland Investments Ltd* the House of Lords disavowed the revenue-protecting doctrines developed in *Ramsay* and *Furniss*, and reinstituted a measure of the taxpayer-protecting approach drawn from *Duke of Westminster*.

Like *Ramsay* and *Furniss*, *MacNiven* concerned a circular transaction where cash moved between different legal entities, but stayed still as a matter of economic substance. The technical legal question was whether a circular payment of interest 'made for no commercial purpose other than gaining a tax advantage'[82] was deductible by virtue of the words 'payments . . . of yearly interest' in the *Income and Corporations*

---

[81] A development dealt with in Chapter 5.
[82] *MacNiven* v. *Westmoreland Investments Ltd* [2003] 1 AC 311, [13].

Taxes Act 1988 (UK). The taxpayer lost at first instance, won on appeal, and won again in the House of Lords.

In the UK's final appellate court, the revenue agency contended that the evasive transaction should be approached on the basis of the, then orthodox, 'fiscal nullity' rule:

> When a court is asked (i) to apply a statutory provision on which a taxpayer relies for the sake of establishing some tax advantage (ii) in circumstances where the transaction said to give rise to the tax advantage is, or forms part of, some pre-ordained, circular, self-cancelling transaction (iii) which transaction though accepted as perfectly genuine (ie not impeached as a sham) was undertaken for no commercial purpose other than the obtaining of the tax advantage in question then [absent contrary legislative language] there is a rule of construction that the condition laid down in the statute for the obtaining of the tax advantage has not been satisfied.

Adopting that principle would have continued the trend against tax evasion set in the 1980s, and spelled disaster for the plaintiff taxpayer, but the UK Law Lords rejected it on a number of bases.

First, it was said that a revenue-protecting rule of statutory construction could not be adopted because 'the courts have no constitutional authority to impose such an overlay upon the tax legislation'.[83] Second, the words 'payments of yearly interest' could not be disregarded 'simply on the ground that [payments occurred] ... solely for tax reasons'.[84] Third, focusing on tax advantages would not 'promote clarity of thought' because tax legislation does not have 'a penumbral spirit which strikes down devices or stratagems designed to avoid its terms or exploit its loopholes'.[85] Together, those reasons amounted to a forthright rebuttal of any general revenue-protecting principle: thereby any role for judicial doctrine as 'a broad spectrum antibiotic which killed off all tax avoidance schemes' was disavowed.[86]

The extent to which the UK judiciary resiled from adopting a revenue-collection doctrine was apparent from later cases. *Barclays Mercantile Business Finance Ltd* v. *Mawson* also concerned a series of payments which 'circulate[d] within the Barclays group', which sought to exploit the purchase price of a sale-and-lease-back agreement as a capital

---

[83] Ibid., [29].
[84] Ibid., [59].
[85] Ibid., [52].
[86] Ibid., [49].

allowance.[87] Although the taxpayer lost in *Barclays*, the UK Supreme Court stridently endorsed *MacNiven*'s holding that there was a 'need to avoid sweeping generalisations about disregarding transactions undertaken for the purpose of tax avoidance'.[88] Speaking extra-curially, a leading UK judge described *MacNiven* and *Barclays* as having 'killed off the *Ramsay* [anti-evasion] doctrine as a special theory of revenue law and subsumed it within the general theory of the interpretation of statutes'.[89]

The relevant 'general theory' was 'the modern approach to statutory construction ... to have regard to the purpose of a particular provision and interpret its language, so far as possible, in a way which best gives effect to that purpose'.[90] Although the purpose of tax legislation may be generally understood to raise revenue for central government, the judicial adoption of a 'purposive' approach to the interpretation of tax legislation does not invariably lead to that simple end.

That result follows from the difficulty of identifying a coherent (or unified) 'purpose' of a given taxation provision:[91]

> To say that its general purpose is to raise revenue is of no rational assistance in solving a problem of interpretation of one of its provision ... the purpose is not to raise as much revenue as possible, regardless of the consequences. The purpose is to raise revenue according to an intricate pattern of fiscal policy, which is almost constantly changing, and some of whose elements may be inconsistent.

To be sure, tax law is not only used to generate revenue for government, but also to structure incentives for economic behaviour by conferring concessional or detrimental tax treatment on certain types of transactions. In that way, many contested provisions of tax legislation will have mixed purposes of generating revenue and manipulating social behaviour. Given those multiple purposes, judges can be 'compelled by necessity to construct potentially fictional legislative intentions in order to interpret laws that are ambiguous, obscure, ... [and] uncertain'.[92] In

---

[87] *Barclays Mercantile Business Finance Ltd* v. *Mawson (Inspector of Taxes)* [2005] 1 AC 684, [18].
[88] Ibid., [37].
[89] Hoffmann (2005), 'Tax Avoidance', 203.
[90] *Barclays* (2005), [28].
[91] Gleeson (2009), 'The Meaning of Legislation', 32.
[92] South (2014), 'Are Legislative Intentions Real?', 854. That idea is derived from a broader (and older) claim that statutory 'purpose' is a flawed idea because of the diversity of political views and compromises which result in a statutory text: Radin (1930), 'Statutory Interpretation', 870.

that sense, statutory 'purpose' provides an uncertain guide to judicial interpretation of tax legislation. When that purposive understanding was applied to the impugned taxation schemes in *MacNiven* and *Barclays*, it resulted in doctrines which were protective of taxpayers who established economically contorted commercial structures in order to evade tax.

That brief review of the fickleness of doctrinal approaches to tax law reveals the significant institutional freedom enjoyed by judiciaries: judges select the doctrinal techniques which will guide their decision-making in taxation disputes. In those circumstances, a claim that the judiciary enforces parliamentary fiscal purpose, enacted in tax legislation, appears illusory. At best, judicial resolution of tax disputes enforces (or protects) tax legislation to the extent of correlation between the judicially selected doctrines of tax law and the revenue-raising policies enacted into legislation, rather than dogged obedience by the judiciary to parliamentary fiscal policy.

Conclusion

A naïve account of the constitutional position of the judiciary in financial affairs would emphasise its role as the guardian of parliament against the executive: enforcing statutory boundaries against officials who might act *ultra vires*. Such an account cannot survive an encounter with the historical and contemporary experience of judicial review and public money.

Judges abnegated any role in resolving disputes concerning appropriation legislation over a century ago, and recent attempts to re-enter that field have resoundingly failed. Practical and principled reasons stand firmly in the way of judicial involvement in disputes concerning sovereign borrowing and monetary finance. Judiciaries only have a meaningful role in relation to tax disputes, and, even in that limited context, they do not play the role of a systematic enforcement mechanism.

In total, the distribution of the predominance of fiscal, debt and monetary finance authority to executive governments (and away from parliaments) is materially unaffected by the presence of judicial power.

PART III

Evaluating Parliamentary Public Finance

The descriptive conclusion of the forgoing chapters is that the preponderance of financial authority in parliamentary systems of government is distributed to executive governments, rather than parliaments. It now falls to explain the impact of that conclusion on prevailing constitutional thinking.

Can parliaments still 'control' public finance if they have given away most of their financial authority? If parliamentary control of public money is a poor description of constitutional arrangements, what should replace it? Are parliament and executive financially interdependent, is the executive firmly in control, or is yet another description of the constitutional aspect of finance appropriate? Where does the democratic control of public resources fit in each of those models?

Those questions are answered in Chapter 9, which concludes that an idea of parliamentary ratification best describes the constitutional aspect of public finance, and that such an idea protects a relatively low level of democratic control of public finance.

Chapter 10 concludes by reflecting on three select issues facing future engagements with constitutionalism and public finance. The first is the complex set of empirical and normative issues which attend proposals that parliaments should have greater financial power. The second is the relevance of the 'rule of law' to legislative regimes which are both foundational to constitutional government, but fall outside the judiciary's purview. The third issue is the complex interplay of public and 'private' finance in constitutional arrangements

9

Failure of Parliamentary Control

'Parliamentary control of public finance' is a wholly unsatisfying constitutional idea. Plainly put, it fails to describe the manner in which financial authority is distributed between parliaments, executive governments and judiciaries. Whether viewed from the perspective of the formal design of public finance law, or the institutional context in which governments carry out their financial activities, there is a large deficit of parliamentary control over public finance.

More satisfying descriptions of the distribution of financial power have been proffered: that parliament and executive are financially 'interdependent', or that the executive is firmly in control in public money. While both come closer to describing the financial aspect of parliamentary government, they are not entirely convincing. If parliaments should be located at the constitutional centre of public finance, the best that can be said is that they ratify executive plans and use of public money. Whatever descriptive label is selected, it is clear that the legal and institutional arrangements governing public finance secure a relatively low level of democratic control over the state's use of financial resources.

This chapter argues for those claims. It begins by settling on an analytical framework for assessing whether parliament does indeed 'control' public finance by reference to an idea of 'financial self-rule'. That framework is then applied to the legal and institutional practices which were observed in the case study of Australia and the UK between 2005 and 2016: concluding that parliaments cannot be said to have control of public finance in either jurisdiction. After discussing how broadly that conclusion can be generalised, the chapter moves on to consider different descriptive models of public finance in parliamentary constitutions: executive control, financial interdependence and parliamentary ratification. The chapter concludes that the latter 'ratification' model is most compelling and explains why that model secures a rather low level of financial self-rule.

Assessing 'Parliamentary Control'

Parliamentary control must mean more than the sum of all legal norms governing public finance existing at any one time. That simply accords with the way constitutional participants (politicians and judges) use the idea of parliamentary control as a yardstick to assess the desirability of a development of the legal practices: enacting, repealing or amending 'law X threatens or protects parliamentary control'. Additionally, it cannot sensibly be said that parliamentary control exists where *any* parliamentary legislation is enacted concerning public finance: no 'control' would be evidenced by a parliament's enactment of a single-section statute providing that 'the Treasury may raise and spend money as it considers necessary'.

Similarly, parliamentary control must mean more than the distribution of financial authority between parliaments and executive governments. Simply observing that a large proportion of financial authority is distributed away from parliaments by public finance law does not answer the question of 'control', because the idea of control could still accommodate a very lopsided distribution of financial authority. Perhaps, parliaments could remain in financial control despite losing all authority over debt and monetary finance to treasuries and central banks, but maintaining all authority over fiscal activities. Or, perhaps, parliamentary control only requires parliaments to retain authority over the accounting basis of public financial activity, and could accommodate the distribution of all substantive financial activities to treasury officials.

Further complicating the picture is the reality that financial control may be exercised *ex ante* and *ex post* any particular use of public money. A form of *ex post* control appears in the accountability functions of Auditors-General and parliamentary public account committees. *Ex ante* control appears in the statutes which govern taxation, expenditure, sovereign borrowing and monetary finance which all assume that parliamentary authorisation (by statute) precedes any lawful use of public money.[1]

A useful way of addressing those complications is to build a framework of parliamentary control which is both 'normative' (incorporating the reasons why parliamentary control is valuable) and 'practical' (calibrated to the institutional realities of modern parliamentary government). Such a framework recognises that constitutional ideas (even used in

---

[1] It could also be contended that a parliament's power to force a government from office which cannot secure supply is a form of *ex ante* control.

a descriptive or explanatory mode) are not simple descriptions of human practices – they are normative, in the dual sense of being value-rich and guides to action.² It also incorporates *ex ante* and *ex post* forms of control.

For present purposes, that requires identifying the values which parliamentary control could serve, explaining how an idealised model of control would secure those values and then calibrating that idealised model to the institutional context of modern parliamentary constitutional systems. The resulting framework can then be used as a way to evaluate whether the idea of parliamentary control succeeds in explaining the distribution of financial authority effected by the design and operation of the legal practices of public money.

The Value of Financial Self-Rule

The idea of parliamentary control of public money is valuable because it promises a form of *financial self-rule*: ensuring that the primary representative institution has the authority to control the economic activities of the body politic. Ultimately, that form of representative control is desirable because parliaments are the apex democratic institutions of state.

Removed from the thin air of political philosophy,³ democracy *qua* self-rule is intimately tied up with representative parliaments. Although they are imperfect, '[e]lected legislatures are most directly subject to influence by the public' and for 'that reason, they have a natural primacy',⁴ as democratic institutions. Objections to parliaments' democratic primacy have focused on the practical constraints of modern electoral systems (providing only sporadic 'verdict[s] of the people')⁵ and the tendency of majoritarian electoral systems to lead to oppression of electoral minorities.⁶ While those objections are certainly meaningful, they do not entail giving 'up on the idea that the ordinary lawmaking operations of government instantiate rule by the people'.⁷

---

² Loughlin (1992), *Public Law and Political Theory*, 56.
³ Wherein many different models of democratic government can be found: ranging from 'a general equality of status, or a rough equality of economic condition' (Waldron (2012) 'Democracy', 187) to 'deliberative democracy', which itself contains an intricate substratum of models including 'liberal deliberativism', 'civic republicanism' and 'radical democracy': Talisse, 'Deliberation' (2012), 214.
⁴ Richardson (2002) *Democratic Autonomy*, 179.
⁵ Cf Manin (1997), *The Principles of Representative Government*, chapter 5.
⁶ E.g., Dworkin (1998), *Law's Empire*, 356.
⁷ Richardson (2002).

Importantly, scepticism of parliaments' democratic bona fides has not disconnected the bond between parliaments and democratic self-rule in much juristic constitutional thinking.[8] As has been written about the UK's constitution:[9]

> The ideological basis of the United Kingdom constitution consists in the notion of the political sovereignty of the people. Political power rests, in the last resort, with the electorate: Parliament exercises its legal sovereignty in recognition of its supreme political authority.

On that view, parliaments lie at the core of democratic notions of self-rule, whether expressed as 'rule by the people'[10] or 'self-governing'.[11] In a world of limited economic resources, parliamentary self-rule necessarily entails that parliaments have institutional primacy over the economic resources consumed by the functions of governing. Therein lies the *financial* aspect of self-rule.

Financial self-rule is valuable from a number of different substantive perspectives on government. For those interested in protection of private property, it is critical that representative bodies have the sole capacity to permit expropriation of private property in the form of taxation. For similar reasons, financial self-rule is also valuable to those primarily interested in re-distribution of wealth and public investment. In that sense, the value of financial self-rule is not tethered to a particular economic model, but safeguards the institutional mechanism through which representative democracy determines the state's financial (and macroeconomic) activity.

Focusing solely on the abstract value of representative democracy produces a highly idealised form of financial self-rule wherein parliaments must have total control over the use of economic resources by public officials in order to carry out political projects involving the allocation (or re-distribution) of economic resources. At a practical level, that would require parliaments to formulate and execute the detailed metrics of all financial proposals: the desired levels of taxation, expenditure, debt and monetary finance, integrated into wider macroeconomic policy. It would also require parliaments to execute and enforce those financial proposals; entailing practical power over the

---

[8] Although highly sceptical accounts exist: Harden (1993), 'Money and the Constitution: Financial Control, Reporting and Audit', 33.
[9] Allan (1985), 'Legislative Supremacy and the Rule of Law', 129.
[10] Waldron (2012), 188.
[11] Talisse (2012), 212.

disbursement of public funds, the collection of taxes, the negotiation of public debt and the conditions under which any instance of monetary finance occurred.

Attractive though that ideal form may be *in theory*, a framework of parliamentary control that is designed to evaluate the *real* distribution of financial authority must calibrate the ideal form to the contextual facts of life in parliamentary constitutional systems. Three contextual facts are critical to that exercise: parliaments are neither 'governments' nor 'enforcement' institutions and public financial activity takes place in highly variable economic and social conditions.

Facts of Parliamentary Life

In the (increasingly) distant past, parliaments had a set of functions which gave them a reasonable share of practical governing power, including passing private legislation on personal and local matters.[12] While some vestiges of those functions remain,[13] modern parliaments' primary function is debating and voting on legislation of general application and their subsidiary functions are supervising government agencies and convening hearings into matters of general public importance.[14]

Departments and agencies of the executive government perform practical governing functions: administering legislation, making delegated legislation, independently formulating administrative programmes in the absence of legislative direction and managing the conduct of the large mass of public sector employees. The last function (managing public sector employees) is particularly significant, as it demonstrates the, absolute and relative, differences in institutional size and complexity between parliaments and the wider public sector.

In 2017, 5.2 million people were employed in the UK public sector (or ~17 per cent of total UK employees).[15] In Australia over the same period, ~2 million people (or ~16 per cent of total Australian employees) were employed in the public sector.[16] The UK Parliament seats ~1,400 members (~750 in the Lords and ~650 in the Commons), and employs ~2,000 people. The Australian Parliament seats 226 members (151 in the House

---

[12] See Sayles (1988), *The Functions of the Medieval Parliaments of England*.
[13] Like their penal jurisdiction: Blackburn and Kennon (2003), *Griffith & Ryle on Parliament: Functions, Practice and Procedures*, 133–135.
[14] Horne and Le Sueur (2016), *Parliament: Legislation and Accountability*.
[15] Office of National Statistics, *Public and Private Sector Employment; Headcount* (2018).
[16] Australian Burea of Statistics, *DO001_2016–17 Employment and Earnings, Public Sector, Australia, 2016–17* (2017); Australian Bureau of Statistics, *Labour Force, Australia* (2018).

of Representatives and 76 in the Senate), and employs around ~1,200 people. That enormous disparity in the personnel of parliaments and the wider public sector illustrates the reality of parliaments' non-governing role. Nor are modern parliaments enforcement institutions. Despite vestigial judicial functions, such as contempt powers and quasi-judicial committees, parliaments do not possess formal or practical responsibility for enforcing legislation (undertaken by parts of the executive) or resolving legal disputes (the responsibility of the judiciary).[17]

The other critical contextual fact of parliamentary government is that economic conditions do not remain invariably stable. Whether caused by the financing needs of military conflict (like the World Wars), the adoption of an economically transformative social programme (like the welfare state) or systemically contagious financial risk-taking (like that which triggered the financial crisis discussed in Chapters 6 and 7), economic conditions can change very suddenly and very severely.

The ideal form of parliamentary control must be calibrated to those contextual facts of life in parliamentary constitutional systems. Because parliaments do not govern society or enforce law, they cannot hold total control of the formulation of financial proposals or absolute control over their execution and enforcement. Because economic conditions cannot invariably remain stable, there must also be some allowance for the financing needs of government in divergent economic conditions.

A framework of parliamentary control that secures financial self-rule and is calibrated to those facts of parliamentary life consists of two sets of 'conditions' of parliamentary control. The first set of conditions concerns the formal structure of legal norms governing public finance: the conditions of *legal control*. The second set of conditions concerns the effective realisation of parliamentary control in light of the political, administrative and economic realities of modern government: the conditions of *effective control*.

Legal Control

Four conditions must be met before it could be said that parliaments have legal control of public finance.

---

[17] At the level of strict legal form, judicial functions passed to the judiciary in Australia upon the enactment of the *Australian Constitution* (and its vesting of 'judicial power' in the 'federal judicature' (s 71)). In the UK, a judicial appendage of the House of Lords continued to exercise judicial functions until 2009 upon the entry into force of the relevant provisions of the *Constitutional Reform Act 2005* (UK).

First, parliaments would need to occupy a primary institutional position over public finance: holding the preponderance of authority over financial planning and the authorisation of lawful finance behaviour. Second, financial legislation would need to be sufficiently *formal* (*calculable* and *determinate*) to allow public officials and judges to assess compliance with its terms. Third, there would need to be some legislative recognition of the financial needs of economic emergencies. Fourth, there must be some effective mechanism for enforcing parliament's primary financial authority.

A sober evaluation of the design and operation of public finance law in Australia and the UK reveals that each of those four conditions of legal control are unmet.

Condition 1: Primary Financial Position

Parliaments must occupy the 'primary' institutional position over public finance: the *primary-position condition*. That condition has several aspects (*planning, legislative, temporal*), each of which recognises parliaments' primacy as financially self-governing institutions, while also recognising the reality that modern parliaments are not governing bodies.

The *planning* aspect requires that parliaments have the primary responsibility for formulating financial proposals. That role need not be exclusive, but it must extend far beyond simply rubber-stamping financial proposals formulated elsewhere. Without that responsibility, parliaments would not have any real impact on the economic outworking of public finance, and would lose any meaningful capacity to execute financial self-rule.

The *legislative* aspect requires that parliaments set the preponderance of the terms under which fiscal, debt and monetary activities are authorised through primary (rather than delegated) legislation. Requiring that parliaments exercise their legal authority through legislation recognises that modern parliaments exercise their institutional functions through enacting legislation. Requiring that the preponderance (but not totality) of financial activity be authorised by primary legislation recognises that parliaments may delegate authority to executives over a subordinate share of the conditions under which financial activity is legally authorised.

The *temporal* aspect requires that financial authority (provided by parliamentary legislation) must cease according to a pre-set timeframe so that a sustained stoppage of parliamentary financial processes (whether by non-convening parliament, or internal obstruction) halts the executive's lawful authority to use public money. Without that temporal aspect, once formally authorised by legislation, financial activity could continue in perpetuity and thereby sever the link between a given temporal parcel of representative authority and financial activity.

In both Australia and the UK, the primary-position condition is wholly unmet. The planning aspect is entirely defeated by the location of the financial initiative in executive governments, which deprives parliaments of any meaningful role in formulating financial proposals and originating financial legislation.

The legislative aspect is defeated by the delegation of significant levels of financial authority to treasury departments. The highest degree of delegation appears in relation to untethered standing appropriations, the accounting basis of government finances, sovereign borrowing and the absence of any meaningful legislative regulation of monetary finance. Lower (but still significant) delegations of financial authority occur in relation to the virement capacity of treasury departments and standing taxation. Although parliaments retain a degree of financial authority through tightly tethered standing appropriations and annual taxation, they are insufficient to retain the predominate share of primary legislative authority.

The temporal aspect of the primary-position condition is defeated by the combined extent of standing legislative authority over taxation, appropriations and debt financing. In each context, legislation authorises executives to undertake very large amounts of total public financing activity without any guaranteed future involvement by parliaments.

Condition 2: Formal Public Finance Legislation

The second condition of formal legal control concerns the design of financial legislation enacted by parliaments.

Financial legislation must be sufficiently formal *qua* calculable, predictable or determinate: the *formal law condition*.[18] Only formal law, so it is said, allows executive officials (*ex ante*) to behave in a way which complies with statutory stipulations and gives parliaments and judiciaries the capacity to assess (*ex post*) whether those officials have actually complied.[19] That understanding of formal, 'calculable' law was famously

---

[18] The descriptive and normative aspects of legal 'formality' are helpfully collected in Tamanaha (2004), *On the Rule of Law*, chapter 7.
[19] For a critique of the empirical accuracy of the guidance capacity of formal law, see Braithwaite (2002), 'Rules and Principles'.

propounded by Fuller and his 8 'standards' of 'legal excellence':[20] generality, publicity, prospectivity, intelligibility, consistency, practicability, stability and congruence with government behaviour. Each of those standards is formulated to optimise the extent to which individuals subject to law can predict the operation of, and comply with, law:[21] the 'guideposts by which [humans] coordinate their actions'.[22]

The formal law condition is necessary to ensure that parliamentary legislation provides a meaningful basis to restrain executive officials carrying out public financial activities. It recognises the reality that parliaments will delegate some measure of financial authority to those officials and that the capacity of public officials to obey law is bolstered by legislation which is which more, rather than less, formal.[23]

Again, in both the UK and Australia, the formal law condition is generally unmet because most public finance legislation is not designed in a way that provides strongly calculable limitations on financial authority. That feature of financial legislation is particularly evident in the nebulous terms of annual appropriation legislation (leaving ample room to *vire*), the plenary grants of debt financing power in sovereign borrowing legislation (leaving treasuries largely at liberty to borrow) and the paucity of legislation regulating monetary finance (failing to guide treasuries and central banks in providing exotic monetary finance).

Some financial legislation is, of course, more formal than others, particularly tightly bonded standing appropriation and tax legislation, both of which provide strongly calculable legal norms concerning fiscal activity. However, when viewed in the context of the totality of legislation concerning public financial activities, those more formal legislative practices fail to compensate for the preponderance of very informal public finance legislation.

Condition 3: Economic Emergencies

The third condition of formal control is a legislative accommodation of the financial consequences of economic emergencies: the *emergency condition*. The emergency condition simply recognises the reality that economic conditions are not invariably stable, and that parliament

---

[20] Fuller, *Morality of Law* (1969), 46–81 or 'desiderata', Rundle (2012), *Forms Liberate*, 69.
[21] Formal law *qua* calculable, individuated and generally applicable norms is critical to the understanding of 'good law' from a number of theoretical perspectives: Lovett (2016), *A Republic of Law*, 210–211 tracing it to Dicey, Hayek, Fuller, Rawls, Raz, Finnis.
[22] Rundle (2012), 136 quoting Fuller.
[23] Scheuerman (1994), 'The Rule of Law and the Welfare State'.

should have expressed a view on the manner in which financial authority should be exercised in the event of deteriorating social conditions which threaten or cause economic emergencies (or vice versa).

To be sure, some Australian and UK financial legislation does confers financial powers which can be deployed in emergencies, prominently the extremely broad powers conferred by standing appropriations and sovereign borrowing statutes. Importantly, however, those statutes fail to provide any coordinating role for the various public financial activities which are implicated by emergency conditions, leaving executive officials to formulate their own financial responses to economic emergencies.

Condition 4: Enforcing Financial Authority

The final condition of formal legal control is that there must be some institutional mechanism for enforcing parliament's financial authority: the *enforcement condition*. Although that enforcement mechanism need not be concentrated in a single institution, it must be capable of enforcing the totality of parliamentary authority over fiscal, debt and monetary activities. It must also be independent of the executive and vested with legal authority sufficient to determine whether the executive has exceeded the limits of parliamentary primary authority or self-established limits of its delegated authority.

Like the other conditions of formal legal control, the enforcement condition is not met. That is so despite the existence of judicial power and the audit responsibilities to Auditors-General. Audit legislation first confers wide authority on financial executives to determine the basis upon which public accounts will be kept, and then staples Auditors-General's audit functions to those public accounts.[24] Although Auditors-General can complain to parliaments about the accounting standards set by treasury departments, the vicissitudes of administering a complex bureaucracy materially limit the capacity of (both) Auditors-General and executive officials to identify irregularities in financial processes.[25] Additionally, Auditors-General have no formal legal power to intervene before a decision is made to spend public funds, reducing any oversight functions to *ex post* recommendation, rather than *ex ante* enforcement.[26]

---

[24] As explained in Chapters 2 and 6.
[25] As explained in Chapter 6 in relation to excess expenditure.
[26] The practical weakness of the capacity of Auditors-General to enforce public expenditure law is, again, revealed by the enormously large excess expenditure recorded by the UK's Treasury in 2008 discussed in Chapter 5. Despite recording a qualification of the Treasury's

Nor does the judiciary act as a systematic enforcement mechanism of parliamentary legislative authority over public finance. As Chapter 8 contended, judicial power does not meaningfully disturb the distribution of financial authority between parliaments and executive governments. Only the taxation side of fiscal activity is directly subject to judicial resolution, leaving the legality of public expenditure, sovereign borrowing and monetary finance outside judiciary's purview. Additionally, where judiciaries resolve disputes concerning tax legislation, they do so in a way which fails to provide a systematic enforcement mechanism for parliamentary authority over taxation.

Effective Control

In addition to those conditions of legal control, three conditions must be met before it could be said that parliaments have effective control of public finance.

First, the financial activities of government must be carried out in very particular institutional and economic conditions. Parliaments must be sufficiently well-resourced to formulate and scrutinise the financial plans of executive governments. Second, executive governments' financial activities must take place in an administrative context which permits compliance with the terms of parliamentary legislation. Third, those activities must occur in an economic context which permits parliamentary and enforcement processes sufficient time for deliberation on, and scrutiny of, financial proposals without economic catastrophe.

None of those conditions exist in the modern parliamentary governments studied in this work.

Condition 1: Parliamentary Resources

To exercise effective control over public finance, parliaments must have sufficient economic, temporal and intellectual resources to scrutinise the financial proposals and activities of executive governments: the *parliamentary resource condition*. Without those resources, parliaments' formal financial powers are devoid of meaningful content.

It is, however, a stark reality that parliaments have insufficient resources to scrutinise financial executives' financial proposals and use of economic resources. By (long ago) ceding the financial initiative to

---

accounts after the money was spent, no meaningful action followed from the existence of the UK's Auditor-General's review.

executive governments, parliaments deprived themselves of the expertise bank necessary effectively to develop and scrutinise financial plans. While some parliamentarians may be financially literate, individual knowledge cannot rival the vast institutional expertise possessed by treasury departments, the scale of which is evidenced by the complexity of the macroeconomic models used by treasuries.[27]

That intellectual expertise gap is widened by the temporal limitations on parliaments' practical capacity to absorb, scrutinise and formulate counter-positions to executives' financial proposals. The starkest illustration of those limitations appears in the processes surrounding review of estimates of expenditure. In principle, scrutiny of estimates is a vital mechanism for parliaments to exercise financial control, but practical limitations deprive that mechanism of most of its efficacy.

For FY2014/15, Australia's Treasury departments presented six annual appropriation Bills to Parliament, seeking the appropriation of ~$90 billion in funds for ~140 spending entities. The legal limits on expenditure contained in the Bills' schedules stretched over ~400 line items. Those line items were explained in more than 700 pages of explanatory material, presented by 18 departments. For the same fiscal year, the UK's Treasury presented two annual appropriation Bills to Parliament, seeking the appropriation of ~£571.4 billion across ~60 spending entities. The information explaining those Bills was contained in main and supplementary estimates (and supporting material) of around 1,500 pages in length. Nine days were set aside for public hearings concerning the Australian budgetary material, while only three days were set aside in the UK.

The gap between the volume of financial material presented to parliaments and the necessary time properly to scrutinise that material is patent. Assuming an average reading rate of ~1page/minute for 2hours/day,[28] an Australian parliamentarian will read the estimates (once, without stopping to perform any calculations) in ~58 days. On the same basis, a parliamentarian will read the UK's estimates in ~13 days.

Condition 2: Administrative Conditions

Effective parliamentary control also requires that executive governments are situated in an administrative context which permits compliance with

---

[27] The UK's macroeconomic model is publicly released, while only some parts of Australia's macroeconomic model are in the public domain.

[28] Taking the prevailing scientific view of 200–400 words/minute for 'college-educated adults who are considered good readers': Rayner et al (2016), 'So Much to Read, So Little Time; How Do We Read, and Can Speed Reading Help', 4.

legislative conditions on the use of public money and permits treasury departments effectively to oversee the wider bureaucracy's use of resources: the *administrative compliance condition*. Removed from that context, legislative commands governing financial activity cannot be followed, and any opportunity for meaningful judicial enforcement is significantly reduced.

Unfortunately, modern bureaucratic conditions make strict compliance with public finance law, particularly appropriations legislation, a practical impossibility.

Executive overspending arising from forecasting errors and actuarial adjustments illustrates that practical impossibility. As Chapter 6 recounted, in a single fiscal year the UK's NHS Pension Scheme overspent by ~£788 million from an overshoot of anticipated use of medical services and an undershoot of payments into the pension fund. Similarly, the UK's Ministry of Defence overspent ~£20.8 million by (literally) overshooting the forecasted number of planned Hellfire missiles in an active conflict zone and Australian social security departments overspends resulted from the provision of incorrect information by members of the public in connection with welfare state expenditure programmes.

Those overspends are significant because they demonstrate the practical obstacles in the way of executive governments seeking to comply strictly with legal limits contained in appropriation legislation. A complex of factors determines the extent of funding requirements of public welfare schemes and munitions usage which are far beyond the capacity of executive officials to forecast with iron-clad accuracy. Additionally, strictly complying with parliamentary legislation would have come at immense social cost: ceasing provision of welfare state services, stopping teachers' and doctors' pension payments and constraining operational military decisions.

Condition 3: Economic Cliff-Edges

Finally, effective parliamentary control would require that the financial activities of government occur in a social and economic context which permits parliamentary and enforcement processes sufficient time for deliberation on, and scrutiny of, those activities while remaining economically viable: the *economic viability condition*. If the consequence of a parliament refusing to enact or repealing financial legislation, or a judge voiding a central government's financial actions, is economic catastrophe, then neither parliament nor a judge is presented with a realistic option to exercise their formal authority.

Again, that requirement for effective parliamentary control is wholly unmet.

On the expenditure side of fiscal activity, a failure to pass annual appropriation legislation would have catastrophic economic consequences. In the UK and Australia, it would cause a failure to pay the salaries of most public sector employees, with the consequence of removing the spending capacity of a very large proportion of the total employed population, which would likely trigger a sizeable contraction in total economic output.[29] It would also cause the practical collapse of tax revenues on two grounds: the non-collection of tax by employees of revenue agencies; and the absence of income and consumption taxation by public sector employees. Finally, the non-payment of public servants would lead to the practical failure of many 'automatic stabilisers'[30] by removing the workforce behind the administrative arms of the welfare state. Each of those catastrophic economic and social consequences makes failure to pass an annual expenditure law a practical impossibility.

On the revenue side of fiscal activity, the failure to enact (or the repeal of) income and corporation tax legislation would also have catastrophic economic impacts for governments, by depriving them of the largest single revenue stream: around 50 per cent in Australia and 40 per cent in the UK between 2005 and 2016.

The economic impact of that financing hole can only be fully appreciated in a concrete context.

Take the expenditure requirements of the UK in Q1 2007, during rosy economic fortunes.[31] Income and company tax receipts stood at ~£131.5 billion. If those taxes had not been collected, there would have been a revenue shortfall of around 46 per cent of total receipts; 54 per cent of total expenditure and 147 per cent of total central government expenditure on goods and services, including public sector salaries for the quarter. Accordingly, only three months' non-collection of income and corporation tax would have led to an enormous compounding shortfall in vital public expenditure.

The extent of that shortfall can be seen in comparison with the contraction in tax receipts in a darker moment of the UK's economic life in Q2 2008. In that quarter, income and corporation tax receipts shrunk by

---

[29] It would also lead to the government being in standing breach of employment contracts for that proportion of the total employed population.
[30] Payments which keep the economy moving in times of economic contraction, like welfare benefits: Dolls, Fuest and Peichl (2010), 'Social Protection as an Automatic Stabiliser'.
[31] Figures for 2007 and 2008 UK public finances drawn from ONS PSF, PSA6A–PSA6E.

~£23 billion on Q1 2007: a 24 per cent contraction in financing contribution. That contraction resulted in an 11 per cent reduction of income and corporation taxes' contribution to total receipts, 22 per cent reduction in contribution to total expenditure and amounted to +50 per cent of spending on goods and services. The contraction of tax receipts contributed to the enormous increase in the UK's public sector borrowing requirement, which stood at £25.4 billion, representing a ~£32 billion increase on Q1 2007 net borrowing of −£7.4 billion.

In other words, removing the legal basis of income and corporation tax for a single financial quarter would create a funding emergency of immensely greater proportions than the funding shortfall caused by the financial crisis. Like the position with expenditure, the devastating consequences of a failure to pass, or a sudden repeal of, income or corporation tax legislation leaves a parliament with no real choice to take those actions.

The impossibility of submitting financial proposals and activities to parliamentary veto and judicial enforcement without causing economic catastrophe is also illustrated in the context of economic emergencies. Again, the UK's experiences during 2008–2009 provide the clearest example.

Between November 2008 and April 2009, the UK deliberately spent ~£24 billion without legal authority and borrowed ~£19.5 billion from the Bank of England.[32] Both were emergency financing measures in response to an extremely grave liquidity crisis and prudential regulatory failings. They were also significant diversions from regular financial practice, which would have, in a world of effective parliamentary control, been submitted to the Commons for debate or to the courts for enforcement. However, to go through those processes would have been impracticable and likely self-defeating, in the sense that a slow response time would likely have led to more banking collapses and the destruction of a core aspect of the UK economy. Economic conditions demanded a response from the financial executive which was economically effective, but deprived the UK's Parliament and judiciary of any meaningful opportunity to prevent those financing activities from occurring.

Nature and Extent of the Deficit of Parliamentary Control

Applied to the case-study analysis undertaken in Chapters 6–8, the important point to be drawn from that assessment of the conditions of

---

[32] As Chapters 6 and 7 explained.

parliamentary control is not one of *comparative ranking* (Australian's control deficit is higher/lower than the UK's), but one of *common descriptive failure*: parliamentary control fails to describe the distribution of financial authority in both jurisdictions.

Complexities of Comparison

While the exact size of the Australian and UK control deficit was not uniform over the years 2005–2016, assigning a definitive ranking to the two jurisdictions is fraught with difficulty.

Australia's heavy reliance on standing appropriations and standing taxation means that parliamentary financial processes could halt, but many state activities could continue. In comparison, the UK's maintenance of a (minority) proportion of annual taxation and a far smaller reliance on standing appropriation gives the UK's financial executive a far lower capacity to execute fiscal activities without annual parliamentary approval. On that measure, Australia has a wider legal control deficit than the UK.

When, however, debt and monetary finance are added to the picture, the variation in the legal control deficit narrows, as both Australian and UK sovereign borrowing legislation confer plenary power to assume debt finance and both systems share a similar distribution of monetary finance authority towards the financial executive, given the absence of a meaningful legal framework governing monetary finance in both jurisdictions. The variation between the two jurisdictions is also narrowed because neither jurisdiction's judiciary plays a totalising role in enforcing parliamentary legislation concerning public finance.

Nor is there any appreciable variation in the extent of the effective control deficit between the two jurisdictions. While the detailed institutional design of the parliaments and bureaucracies in each jurisdiction differs, the imbalance of power between the two sets of institutions is strikingly similar, as are the economic conditions in which public finance activities must be undertaken.

More complexities emerge when Australian and UK public finance law is analysed in a manner sensitive to the divergent economic conditions experienced between 2005 and 2016. Pre-2007, before the nadir of the financial crisis, public finance law operated in a constant manner in both jurisdictions, maintaining a stable (albeit uneven) distribution of financial authority between parliaments and executives. As economic output contracted during and immediately after the financial crisis, the control deficits in each jurisdiction expanded. The UK executive spent enormous volumes of money unlawfully and the Australian Parliament delegated plenary power to issue sovereign debt to the Treasury. In both jurisdictions, the proportional share of expenditure pursuant to standing appropriations, which were un-tethered to parliamentary conditions of payment, rose, further shifting the distribution of financial authority away from parliaments.

Given those complexities, the most satisfactory conclusion is that: the idea of parliamentary control fails to describe the distribution of financial authority in both jurisdictions between 2005 and 2016.

Variation across Constitutional Systems

Generalising that specific conclusion beyond Australia and the UK is not straightforward.

The historical analysis undertaken in Chapters 2–5 observed the striking similarities in the basic model of parliamentary public finance which was exported to many parliamentary constitutional systems. Combining that observation with the detailed analysis of Australia and the UK between 2005 and 2016 permits the identification of a prima facie position: *parliamentary constitutional* systems contain a deficit of parliamentary control of public finance. The ultimate applicability of that prima facie position can be tested by reference to the detailed design of public finance law in any particular jurisdiction and the way that such law operates in different economic conditions.

Performing that exercise will need to await future scholarly work, but tentative conclusions can be surmised by inference from the Australian and UK experience.

New Zealand's and Canada's executive governments hold the financial initiative and have extensive authority over the formulation and control of public accounts.[33] To that extent, a strong analogy may be drawn with Australia and the UK. The profile of other Canadian and New Zealand legal practices makes drawing analogies less straightforward. New Zealand (like the UK) has a low relative level of standing (permanent) appropriations,[34] but (like Australia), has no annual income taxation and (like both Australia and the UK) has sovereign borrowing legislation conferring plenary debt-finance authority and no meaningful legislative

---

[33] Standing Order 326 (NZ); *Public Finance Act 1989* (NZ), parts 3 and 4; *British North America Act 1867*, s 54; *Financial Administration Act* (1985 RSC), part II.
[34] Reported at ~15 per cent of total expenditure in FY2014/15: Harris et al (2017), *Parliamentary Practice in New Zealand*, 526.

treatment for monetary finance.[35] Canada (like Australia and unlike the UK) relies heavily on standing (statutory) appropriations and has no annual taxation.[36] Canada also has very broadly framed sovereign borrowing legislation (like both Australia and the UK),[37] and has legislation which specifically regulates monetary finance (unlike Australia, the UK and New Zealand).[38] From that superficial review, meaningful variations in the size of the legal control deficit in both Canada and New Zealand can be expected.

There is, however, no particular reason to doubt that the size of a deficit of effective parliamentary control in Canada and New Zealand would be meaningfully different to Australia and the UK. Assuming that Canadian and New Zealand parliaments are small and poorly resourced (compared to treasury departments), financial activities are undertaken in complex institutional contexts which prevent strict compliance with financial legislation and economic realities prevent large-scale diversions from existing patterns of financial authorisation (without economic catastrophe), it is safe to posit the existence of a large deficit of effective control.

Three propositions, requiring further contemplation, arise from that superficial extension of the lessons learned in Australia and the UK to other parliamentary constitutional systems. The first is that the existence and extent of a deficit of parliamentary control may not correlate with the existence of mostly written federal (Australia and Canada) or mostly unwritten unitary (New Zealand and the UK) constitutions. The second is that significant differences may arise in parliamentary constitutional systems with highly varied political, cultural and economic profiles, like the constitutional jurisdictions which were formed from the decolonisation of the British Empire.

The third proposition is that there may be a generalisable correlation between a contraction in economic output and a reduction of parliamentary control. The Australian and UK experiences between 2005 and 2016 indicated that the size of the control deficit appears to correlate inversely to economic contraction: during good economic times, the control deficit shrank; while in bad economic times, the deficit widened. Generalising that observation to other parliamentary constitutional systems is (of course) contingent on the particular design of the legal practices and the

---

[35] *Public Finance Act 1989* (NZ), Part 6.
[36] Calculated at ~60 per cent of total expenditure in FY2017/18: Treasury Board, *Tabled Expenditure Authorities* (2018).
[37] *Financial Administration Act* (1985 RSC), part IV.
[38] *Bank of Canada Act 1985* (1985 RSC), s 18(j).

institutional context in which they are located. But, assuming a largely similar distribution of financial authority, it could be surmised that the same correlation between economic contraction and a widening control deficit will hold.

Implications for Financial Self-Rule

The most important, and obvious, implication of identifying a deficit of parliamentary control is that the level of financial self-rule instantiated by the model of parliamentary public finance is relatively low. As parliaments lose control of public money, their position as an institutional mechanism to steer public financial and macroeconomic activity is proportionally weakened.

While other mechanisms may exist to support parliaments' financial self-ruling, such as ministerial and bureaucratic accountability, the loss of parliamentary control through the legal practices of public money remains a significant detraction from parliaments' potential as the financial self-ruling institution.

Of course, where executive governments are required to have the parliament's (usually the lower house's) confidence, it could be contended that the simple fact of maintaining parliamentary confidence is sufficient to supply democratic support for the executive's financial activities. Voting confidence in an executive government does provide a type of democratic legitimacy for a government's financial activities, but a general confidence vote provides a far lower level of representative democratic legitimacy than would flow if parliamentarians had legal and effective control, as those concepts have been explained, over public finance.

The normative implications of that loss are sketched in Chapter 10.

Parliamentary Ratification

Given the descriptive failure of parliamentary control, it is worth examining alternative ideas which more adeptly explain the lopsided distribution of financial authority in parliamentary constitutional systems.

Control by Financial Executive

Some writers have occasionally hinted at the idea that the 'executive', rather than the parliament, is in control of public money.[39] The most

---

[39] E.g., Turpin and Tomkins (2011), *British Government and the Constitution*, 644–647.

blatant hint was made by Bagehot in *The English Constitution* (1867), as an aspect of his broader critique of English constitutional conditions in the mid-nineteenth century.

Adopting a deeply sceptical attitude towards the English constitution, Bagehot depicted its customs and practices as an artifice of rules which channelled political power through 'dignified' and 'efficient' parts.[40] The dignified parts were those ceremonial and formal constitutional practices which 'excite and preserve the reverence of the population' by being 'very complicated and somewhat imposing, very old and rather venerable',[41] including the Queen,[42] the Lords[43] and the Commons.[44] Chief amongst the efficient parts was the 'efficient secret' of the 'close union, the nearly complete fusion of the executive and legislative powers [in] ... the cabinet'.[45] That understanding of the organisation of constitutional authority reflected Bagehot's broader intellectual approach: focusing less on legal formality and more on political and economic practicalities. It can be extended to any parliamentary system in which there is a significant gap between the ceremonial and practical operation of constitutional institutions.

Applying his approach to public finance, Bagehot quickly jettisoned the notion that parliament controlled public money. Setting aside the 'legal technicalities' of 'financial legislation', he concentrated on the impact of the financial initiative, concluding that:[46]

> the principal peculiarity of the House of Commons in financial affairs is nowadays not a special privilege but an exceptional disability. On common subjects any member can propose anything, but not on money – the minister only can propose to tax the people.

From that 'truth', Bagehot concluded that the Commons had no 'special function with regard to financial different from its functions with respect to other legislation'.[47]

For Bagehot, the Cabinet was in financial control. 'The ministry is (so to speak) the breadwinner of the political family and has to meet the cost of philanthropy [civil expenditure] and glory [military and imperial

---

[40] Bagehot (1867), *The English Constitution*, 5.
[41] Ibid., 5, 8.
[42] In whose absence 'English government would fail and pass away': ibid., 34.
[43] Particularly its 'reverence': ibid., 68–69.
[44] As 'very stately': ibid., 94.
[45] Ibid., 9.
[46] Ibid., 97.
[47] Ibid.

expenditure].' In that political reality, Bagehot saw another constitutional 'truth' that:[48]

> *when a cabinet is made the sole executive, it follows it must have the sole financial charge, for all action costs money, all policy depends on money, and it is in adjusting the relative goodness of action and policies that the executive is employed.*

In favour of Bagehot's position stands the executive government's exclusive responsibility for the formulation of financial legislation, the maintenance of public accounts and the breadth of its functions concerning sovereign borrowing. So too does parliament's tacit consent to the executive's deliberate non-compliance with appropriation legislation, its exercise of autonomous authority over monetary finance and the absence of any hard judicial check on significant parts of the executive's financial authority.

Other features of parliamentary public finance push against an idea of 'executive control'. Most prominently, parliaments retain a meaningful institutional position in setting the legal standards under which financial executives may execute their responsibilities over economic resources. That must be so, unless the entire body of financial legislation is an artifice: a position which is difficult to maintain in the face of retrospective appropriation of excesses which evidence the financial executive's commitment to treating the legal limitations on public expenditure imposed by parliament as something more than purely hortatory.

Further grinding against the idea that executives control public money is the enactment of (high economic impact) standing appropriation legislation that is closely tethered to legislative conditions of payment, like welfare benefit or tax credit legislation.[49] Once enacted, that legislation removes large swathes of the state's resources from the executive's economic planning discretion because the criteria for payment of welfare benefits and tax credits are legally pre-determined by parliament and practically dependent on the extent of demand in the general population (matters outside executive control).[50] The impact of that constraint will, of course, vary with the proportional significance of tightly tethered standing appropriations: the smaller the proportion relative to total

---

[48] Ibid., 98.
[49] Discussed in detail in Chapter 6.
[50] As Chapter 6 explained, the same reasoning does not apply to untethered standing appropriations, because the executive retains the capacity to determine the conditions under which spending will occur.

expenditure, the greater the executive's autonomy over the formulation of financial proposals, because there will be a larger corpus of funds authorised through annual or un-tethered standing appropriations.

Finally, the executive's financial control is limited by the independent authority of other public institutions. Where emergency monetary finance is required, financial executives must contend with the independent institutional authority of central banks, which influence the conditions under which the financial executive obtains monetary finance. The monetary finance that was obtained via the UK's QE Transfers occurred pursuant to a process of negotiation between the Treasury and the Bank of England, rather than the use of formal legal authority to command the Bank to behave in particular ways.[51]

Where the collection of taxation is required, the financial executive must contend with the judiciary, which may shift its attitudes towards executive claims to recover revenue through taxation. As Chapter 8 concluded, the judiciary may be supportive of tax authorities, but there is no guarantee that such an attitude will be adopted.

For that collection of reasons, 'control by financial executive' is not an entirely persuasive description of the distribution of financial authority in parliamentary government.

Financial Interdependence

Pulling back from Bagehot-esque absolutism, it has been proposed that parliaments and executives are 'interdependent' in financial affairs. Writing by exclusive reference to British government Daintith and Page have argued that in finance, as elsewhere, the relationship between parliament and executive is one of 'interdependence' rather than hierarchy.[52] Critical to that conclusion was Daintith and Page's use of 'systems theory' and the idea of 'structural coupling' of parliament and executive.[53]

---

[51] Exactly how such power could be exercised is unclear given that the UK Treasury has limited power to direct the Bank 'in the public interest ... in relation to monetary policy': *Bank of England Act 1946* (9 & 10 Geo 6, c 27), s 4.

[52] Daintith and Page (1999), *The Executive in the Constitution: Structure, Autonomy and Internal Control*, 7, 107, 142, 201. The idea of 'interdependence' is also present in their notion that the executive is an 'autonomous body which can manage its own resources save where Parliament ordains otherwise': Daintith and Page (1999), 39. The explanatory utility of interdependence and autonomy are recognised in Prosser (2014), 21.

[53] Daintith and Page (1998), 4–5 (citing Teubner (1992), 'Social Order from Legislative Noise?') and 105. Although seminal to Daintith and Page's approach, the influence of

Daintith and Page's idea of interdependence revolves around 'external' and 'internal' 'controls'. Legislation is a form of external control, as is the possibility of judiciary review of matters concerning public finance. Executive directions regarding the use of public resources (like value for money directives, procurement guides and internal financial manuals) are 'internal' controls. Their conclusion is that both of those controls operate in an interdependent manner because there 'is little or no difference between the interests of Parliament in financial control and those of the people within government entrusted with these tasks'.[54]

As a descriptive concept applied to the legal practices of public money, 'interdependence' makes significant progress on the idea of control by financial executive, but it is not without shortcomings.

In ordinary times, parliaments are dependent on executive governments to formulate financial proposals, to administer expenditure legislation, oversee the broader executive's use of resources and to cooperate with Auditors-General. Governments are dependent on parliaments to enact financial legislation (formalising their financial proposals), legally validate non-compliant behaviour (through retrospective authorisation of overspending) and provide legal legitimacy to their fiscal activities. In emergencies, however, the degree of inter-dependence in fiscal activities is markedly reduced. Executives spend as necessary to avoid economic catastrophe and turn only to parliaments when the emergency has abated.

There is a much lower degree of interdependence in relation to debt finance activities, and virtually none in relation to monetary finance.

The various designs of sovereign borrowing legislation, observed in Chapters 2, 5 and 7, evidence a diminishing degree of interdependence between parliaments and financial executives. Sovereign borrowing legislation enacted annually by parliament (as was the norm until the mid-twentieth century) does, of course, make the financial executive's debt financing decisions dependent on parliament.[55] Legislation with a deficit finance or a quantitative ceiling only makes financial executives dependent on parliaments to the extent that the operation of expenditure and fiscal revenue legislation contributes to fiscal or cash deficits or financing requirements exceed the pre-set quantitative limit.[56] Sovereign borrowing

---

systems theory on their project has been largely ignored by reviewers: McEldowney (2001) 'Review', Turpin (2000) 'Review', Himsworth (2001) 'Review'.
[54] Daintith and Page (1999), 105.
[55] As the UK did until 1968, Australia did until 2008.
[56] UK between 1968 and 1983, and Australia between 2008 and 2013.

legislation which contains no formal deficit finance or quantitative limitation leaves financial executives independent of parliaments in acquiring debt finance.[57]

Parliaments' position in relation to monetary finance fits even less comfortably within a concept of interdependence. The absence of any meaningful legislative framework governing monetary finance[58] leaves central banks essentially unguided by parliamentary directions in extending credit to central governments.[59] Although clearly coordinated with the Treasury, the Bank of England's monetary financing actions from 2008 were essentially independent of the UK Parliament.

Parliamentary Ratification

The best description of the distribution of financial authority in the studied jurisdictions is 'parliamentary ratification of public finance', wherein parliaments approve the executives' financial plans, provide a forum to ventilate uses of public money and to structure the executive's financial activities.

Approving Financial Proposals

Parliaments approve (rather than formulate) the financial proposals of the executive. *Ex ante* approval occurs when parliaments approve, by enactment, proposals for expenditure and taxation formulated by executive governments. Modelled in that way, the concept of *approval* recognises that executives, rather than parliaments, formulate the proposals upon which appropriation and taxation legislation is premised, and present them to parliaments as a financial fait accompli. While parliaments retain the formal capacity to refuse to approve those financial proposals, the practical spending needs of government limit their available choices to approving (and maintaining confidence in a government) or refusing (and leading to the downfall of a government).

Parliaments may have stronger and weaker roles in approving the executive's financial proposals. In approving the expenditure side of those proposals, that role is limited to the binary act of enacting or refusing to enact appropriation legislation. In relation to taxation, parliaments' approval role is more textured. Although executive governments

---

[57] UK post-1983, and Australia post-2013.
[58] Exceptional cases like Canada aside.
[59] Placing aside legislation concerning central bank dividend payments.

retain the capacity to formulate the taxation side of financial proposals, parliaments do have a meaningful capacity to alter the economic and legal content of taxation legislation once introduced.

Ventilating Financial Behaviour

In addition to approving executives' financial plans, parliaments are also a forum for the ventilation of the executive's use of economic resources.[60]

The limited idea of *ventilating* reflects the legal and practical limitations on parliaments' financial accountability functions. Auditors-General necessarily rely on accounting and internal control mechanisms of financial executives, and parliaments rely on Auditors-General to provide an independent check on the total bureaucracy's use of public resources. Thereby, the financial judgments of executive governments fundamentally frame the auditing and accountability processes. Focusing on ventilating also avoids the contortions of understanding parliament as enforcing the terms of financial authority. Given the limitations of the institutional and economic context in which public financial activity occurs, the best parliaments can hope for is the passive release of information regarding the executive's use of public resources.

Finally, parliamentary legislation permits the financial executive to 'structure' its financial activities by reference to legislative norms which provide a set of discernible standards within which the financial executive must comply if its financial activities are to be legally authorised.

Structuring Financial Activities

Parliamentary legislation helps to *structure* financial executives' activities in two senses. First, it establishes a set of conditions which limit the lawfully permissible actions of the executive itself, and thereby setting a baseline of legal legitimacy for the executive's own actions. Second, it provides a set of conditions which can be used by treasury departments to evaluate the financial activities of the broader executive.

As was noted above in analysing the formal law condition, the legislative practices of public money are designed in different ways, some of which are more formal than others, and the manner in which different legislative practices structure the executive's activities varies accordingly.

Legislation concerning taxation is the most formal of all financial legislation, being composed of precisely framed legislative norms concerning tax liability. Standing appropriation legislation which is tightly

---

[60] This usage is inspired by Daintith and Page (1999), 105.

tethered provides the next most formal set of legislative norms, where the legality of payment is determined by clearly expressed legislative conditions: such as eligibility to receive welfare benefits or tax credits.

Annual appropriation legislation is noticeably less formal than tax and tightly tethered standing appropriation legislation; however, it still provides a basis upon which executives may structure the expenditure side of their fiscal activities. While the legal limits of annual appropriation legislation are wide and flexible, they are the ultimate reference point against which the more detailed non-legal limits set by estimates operate. In that fashion, annual appropriation legislation provides a set of standards which permit treasury officials to structure their own internal rules for expenditure control and thereby control the broader executive's expenditure functions. That function of annual appropriation legislation is particularly prominent where overspending is retrospectively authorised. Viewed from the perspective of parliamentary ratification, excesses appear as a means for financial executives to bring order to the wider bureaucracy's use of resources, rather than providing a mechanism for parliaments to assert their authority regarding illegal behaviour.

Untethered standing appropriation and sovereign borrowing legislation is far more informal, in the sense that it contains few legally discernible limitations. In that sense, untethered standing appropriation and sovereign borrowing legislation provide a far weaker structuring basis for financial action. Some structuring function is still served by sovereign borrowing legislation, as it concentrates legal authority in treasury departments, preventing other parts of the executive from engaging in sovereign borrowing and limiting the public actors which may acquire debt finance.

The legal practices concerning monetary finance provide only a nominal structure of financial executives' actions. Because of the paucity of legal practices concerning monetary finance, financial executives are left largely autonomous in their decisions regarding the engagement with central banks' monetary powers as a public finance lever.

Ratification and Financial Self-Rule

A conclusion that parliamentary ratification is the best explanation for the distribution of financial authority has obvious implications for financial self-rule.

The approval aspect of parliamentary ratification secures a measure of representative accountability in the use of economic resources, but is limited by the location of the financial initiative in executives and the vast institutional imbalance of power between parliaments and executive governments.

The ventilation aspect also secures some measure of representative involvement, but is limited by executive officials' own legal authority to choose the conditions under which disclosure of financial information will occur and their comparatively superior institutional resources to scrutinise wider bureaucracies' uses of resources. The structuring aspect of parliamentary ratification could only secure financial self-rule if parliaments could determine the form and content of financial legislation. Given the location of the financial initiative in executives, the structuring aspect of parliamentary ratification is really a question of executives *self-binding*. In total, the degree of financial self-rule secured by the structuring aspect of parliamentary ratification of public finance is rather low.

Conclusion

This chapter closes the book's descriptive analysis of the way law (legislation and case law) distributes authority over public finance between different constitutional organs of government.

The historical analysis undertaken in Chapters 2–5 charted the development of legal and constitutional practices concerning public finance, first in the UK, then throughout the parliamentary constitutional world. Those chapters concluded by identifying a model of parliamentary public finance which gave the preponderance of financial authority to executive governments rather than parliaments, the contemporary analysis in Chapters 6–8 used two case studies (Australia and the UK) as vehicles to investigate the impact of varying economic conditions on the operation of the model of parliamentary public finance and the complex role of judiciaries in relation to the financial activities of central governments. Amongst other things, that analysis revealed that the financial authority of executive governments waxed as economic output waned and that judiciaries had a rather limited role in the administration of public finance.

The impact of those conclusions on prevailing constitutional doctrine, particularly the idea that parliaments 'control' public money, was the focus of this concluding chapter. After articulating a model of parliamentary control by reference to an idea of self-rule, the chapter concluded that neither the formal legal characteristics of parliamentary public finance, nor the administrative, economic or political context in which government is undertaken, secure anything which could sensibly be called 'parliamentary control'. Alternative constitutional descriptions of parliamentary public finance were then evaluated: concluding that 'parliamentary ratification' best described the distribution of power between parliaments, executive and judiciaries, and that such a model protected a relatively low level of financial self-rule.

In that sense, the chief task set by this book to analyse the distribution of financial power between the chief constitutional institutions is concluded. The following chapter explores the ramifications of that analysis for future thinking about the financial aspect of constitutional government.

10

Theory and Practice of Financial Self-Rule

Once parliamentary control is jettisoned as a meaningful description of the financial aspect of parliamentary government, the natural next inquiry concerns the future design of constitutional principles. That is an intrinsically normative inquiry which may be approached in different ways.

One normative approach is deeply practical and would focus on the design of concrete legal institutions. Should new kinds of appropriation legislation be enacted which explicitly accommodate virement and the inevitability of excess public expenditure? Should judiciaries adopt a public-revenue-protecting approach to taxation disputes? Should legal restrictions on central banks' public finance activities be tightened or loosened? Each of those questions raises technical and political issues deserving close attention by policy-makers and parliamentarians. Although tempting, no attempt is made here to present a smorgasbord of policy proposals.

The other kind of normative approach focuses on the constitutional thinking which influences legal and institutional analyses of public finance. Within that type of normative inquiry, several major topics arise for future work. How much financial power should be concentrated in representative assemblies? Does law govern the state if not enforced by the judiciary? Should an analytical wall be constructed between 'public' and 'private' finance in constitutional thinking?

This book concludes by reflecting on those topics.

Virtues of Financial Self-Rule

If this book's conclusions about the descriptive inadequacy of parliamentary control are accepted, constitutional jurists must broach the question whether a greater share of 'financial self-rule'[1] should be sought by vesting parliaments with a greater (or lesser) share of financial authority.

---

[1] In the sense that expression is explained in Chapter 9 above.

An intellectually credible answer to that question requires engaging with a set of empirical and normative questions at the periphery of most lawyers' comfort zones.[2]

One line of inquiry concerns the relative merits of assembly decision-making in financial contexts. It may be that assemblies of people are more likely, compared to individuals, to make rational decisions. Something like that idea can be extracted from the 'jury theorem' articulated by Condorcet and adopted by political scientists and economists:[3] a larger number of perfectly rational agents is more likely to arrive at a correct answer to certain problems than a smaller number of the same agents. Using that theory to argue that parliaments should hold a greater share of financial authority is risky without data concerning the financial information available to individuals in parliaments and treasury departments, their respective incentives and expertise, and the compromises between speed and accuracy of decision-making.

Consideration should also be given to empirical projects concerning legislative behaviour in formulating national budgets. A good starting point is Wehner's work, which has investigated the impact of 'institutional organisation' on 'fiscal discipline', in order to discover whether 'a pro-spending bias' increases with 'the number of decision makers' involved in the budget process.[4] Using a global set of 80 comparator jurisdictions,[5] Wehner concludes that '[i]nstitutional arrangements may constrain legislative choice without affecting fiscal outcomes, and it is even possible for such constraints to have adverse effects on fiscal discipline'.[6] Plainly put, there is no simple causal relationship between a particular institutional design (parliamentary or congressional systems) and a particular kind of fiscal discipline (balanced budgets).

Another line of inquiry would focus on the impact of greater parliamentary involvement on substantive political agendas particularly the viability of welfare state policies.[7]

---

[2] They may also be perceived as too complex or costly by parliamentarians themselves.
[3] This simplified rendering does not capture the complexities of the jury theorem: Condorcet (1785), 'Essay on the Application of Mathematics to the Theory of Decision-Making'; Landemore (2012), *Democratic Reason: Politics, Collective Intelligence and the Rule of the Many*; McLean and Hewitt (1994), *Condorcet: Foundations of Social Choice and Political Theory*.
[4] Wehner (2010a), *Legislatures and the Budget Process*, 13, 15.
[5] Ibid., 16, 89.
[6] Ibid., 15.
[7] Substantive political policies will, of course, also impact heavily on the viability of public sector financing.

It is an historical fact that the inception of strong parliamentary involvement in public finance reflected a political programme to reduce the potency of executive governments. As Chapter 2 explained, annual statutory appropriation grew from a perspective on government which sought to shrink the independent financial authority of the, then monarchical, executive government.

It is also an historical fact that a significant reduction in parliamentary involvement in public finance coincided with the growth of the welfare state. Chapter 5 observed that the legal basis of social insurance budgets was never fully integrated into annual parliamentary processes. As the complexity of twentieth-century public finance grew, the legal basis for sovereign borrowing was also detached from those processes. Thereby, the financial administration of the modern welfare state is legally supported by executive officials exercising statutory powers which are not presented for regular parliamentary scrutiny.

In light of those facts, it is worth seriously considering whether conferring vastly greater financial authority on parliaments would adversely impact the operation of welfare state policies. Sight should not be lost here of Dicey's influence and legendary hostility to the welfare state. In *The Relation of Law and Public Opinion in England*, Dicey described the combination of universal adult suffrage and old-aged pensions as 'evil' and spoke, in pointedly non-complimentary terms, of the UK's early welfare legislation as harmonising 'with the principle or the sentiment of collectivism'.[8] The precise relationship between Dicey's idea of parliamentary control and his aversion to socialism can be disputed, but avowed enemies of the twentieth-century welfare state, particularly Milton Freidman and Fredrick Hayek, enlisted Dicey as their jurist of choice.[9] That enlistment makes sense when account is taken of Dicey's hostility to any understanding of constitutional government which accorded significant authority or influence to the executive.

The critical point is that parliamentary government Dicey-style could never have accommodated the growth of the twentieth-century welfare state, which required the development of institutions which accorded relatively low priority to parliamentary participation in financial management. Given that welfare state expenditure is the largest single

---

[8] Dicey (1917), *Law and Public Opinion in England during the Nineteenth Century*, xxxv, xxxix.
[9] Friedman (2002), *Capitalism and Freedom*, 11, 194–195, 201; Hayek (2011), *The Constitution of Liberty*, 321, although Hayek's attitude towards Dicey was not unwaveringly supportive, cf Hayek (2011), chapter 13.

spending object of contemporary government (and has been for almost a century), a claim that parliaments should be given significantly greater financial authority has transformative potential.

Law without Judges

If, as Chapters 3 and 8 argued, disputes about the legality of decisions concerning appropriation, sovereign borrowing and monetary finance are non-justiciable, a serious question arises regarding the applicability of the 'rule of law' to central governments' financial behaviour: how does law 'rule' actions of government officials over which there is no judicial oversight?

If the rule of law is intrinsically connected to the exercise of judicial power, an absence of judicial control over most of the state's financial activities leaves a wide gap in the rule of law. As Chapters 3 and 4 pointed out, that gap is not new, but it widened as governments scaled up their fiscal activities throughout the nineteenth and twentieth centuries. It cannot be understood as immaterial. Public spending and sovereign borrowing are seminal to all functions of government and their ultimate legal foundation is parliamentary legislation. If disputes about that legislation are non-justiciable, then seminal functions of governments are not ruled by law.

From a perspective which might be labelled orthodox (or perhaps romantic), it could be contended that a current lack of judicial precedents does not foreclose future judicial involvement. Taking appropriation legislation as a high-point of historical non-justiciability, it could be argued that neither an historical void of judicial expertise, nor the severe social consequences which might flow from curial supervision of public spending supply a reason to prevent the deployment of judicial power. *Fiat justitia ruat caelum*: let justice be done though the heavens fall.

As knowledge of the actual operation of public finance increases, the attractiveness of that perspective diminishes. For over 150 years, the orthodox position in the common law has been that breaches of appropriation legislation are not curable by judicial order and the settled institutional relationship governing public expenditure reveals a strong preference for non-judicial treatment of those breaches. *A fortiori*, where the consequences of withholding public funds which are not authorised by an appropriation Act are extreme. Faced with those facts, the romantic perspective of the rule of law has limited attraction.

The position of the rule of law in public finance could also be saved from a perspective which does not locate judges at the centre of legality. To whit, if law can still rule without judicial enforcement, then non-justiciable legislation presents no threat to the rule of law. Support for that position can be identified in the work of scholars (and policy-makers) who see judicial enforcement as non-essential to legal effectiveness. A prominent example of that approach to law appears in some strains of regulation theory which do not assume that law must be enforced by judges to be effective.[10] Where public finance law is non-justiciable, self-regulatory ideas could act as fillers for the rule-of-law gap.

Alternatively, public finance could be understood as ruled by law if that concept referred to the existence of a 'settled ethical' commitment of public officials to follow the spirit and letter of written rules, rather than the enforcement of those rules by the judiciary.[11] On that view, law rules where government officers act with integrity in discharging their responsibilities. Loughlin attributes that understanding of the rule of law to Dicey, and it may provide another way to fill the rule-of-law gap in public finance.

Finally, the absence of judicial power in critical financing contexts carries interesting implications for broader critiques of liberal constitutionalism.

If judiciaries cannot impose legislative limits on much of the state's financial behaviour, parliaments have no institutional mechanism to enforce their will on executive governments. Absent such a mechanism, parliaments have no formal capacity to set the rules for public financial behaviour and a core type of democratic legitimacy for economic and social policy is lost. If the financial behaviour of executive governments is not limited by democratic will, then its liberal bona fides are questionable.

A similar critique of the efficacy of modern parliaments to constrain executive governments has been made by Scheuerman, in his contention that liberal constitutional institutions cannot function properly under modern technological, economic and social conditions.[12] Posner and Vermeuel applied Scheuerman's thought in their, occasionally polemical, argument that executive governments, not parliaments or judiciaries, must be understood as the central representative and adjudicative

---

[10] See e.g., Braithewaite, (2002) 'Rules and Principles', 69–82.
[11] Shklar (1987), 'Political Theory and the Rule of Law', 3.
[12] Scheuerman (2004), *Liberal Democracy and the Social Acceleration of Time*.

constitutional institutions.[13] Both approaches harken back to Schmitt's arguments regarding the subservience of judicial and parliamentary institutions to executive power on all vital matters of state.[14]

A distillation of those approaches produces a modified-Schmittean position: traditional democratic (parliamentary) and legal (judicial) institutions cannot govern executive governments' financial activities under the technological and administrative complexity of modern states. In favour of that modified-Schmittean position, are the obvious structural weaknesses in traditional parliamentary and judicial oversight. As Chapter 9 contended, a refusal to enact, or invalidation of, an appropriation or income tax Act would wreak such catastrophic consequences that no sane parliament or judge would choose to exercise their powers in that fashion.

Standing against the modified-Schmittean contention, however, is the long-standing nature of the gap in judicial and parliamentary power over public finance. If liberal constitutional institutions were fixed by the mid-nineteenth century, then executive predominance was built into parliamentary government from its modern inception. To be sure, Chapter 5 observed that military and welfare state developments did increase the degree of financial authority delegated to executive governments, but it also acknowledged that such an increase was a continuation of trends set in the preceding century, wherein the fiscal pressures of imperial and military expansion coincided with the bestowal of ever-greater financial flexibility for executive governments. Viewed through that historical lens, financial gaps in the liberal constitutional model are not the result of technological growth or social change: they are design features of liberal constitutionalism itself. Where such a conclusion leaves a Schmittean account of liberal constitutionalism and public finance is not entirely clear.

Public and Private Finance

The final topic for future thinking is the constitutional position of 'private' finance, in the sense of the behaviour of private financial market actors.[15]

---

[13] Posner and Vermeule (2011), *The Executive Unbound: Life after the Madison Republic*.
[14] Schmitt (1922), *Political Theology*.
[15] Rather than the UK's prominent public/private financing programme known as the 'Private Finance Initiative': Freedland (1994), 'Public Law and Private Finance – Placing the Private Finance Initiative in a Public Law Frame'.

In a trite sense, all economic behaviour is the product of 'public law' because it occurs within a framework of legal rules fashioned by public institutions. As Pistor has noted, judicial institutions, and their application of contract and property law norms, are the enforcement mechanisms for the commercial exchanges that typify modern economic behaviour.[16] Legislative frameworks also sit at the heart of modern economic behaviour, particularly the banking statutes, of vast scale and complexity, which provide the ultimate source of authority to engage in financial behaviour.

In a less trite sense, law and constitutional practice concerning public finance have played a decisive role in developing private financial markets. As Dickson explained in his seminal work on eighteenth-century British finance, the UK's modern stock markets grew from the markets which traded government debt securities.[17] The Bank of England grew to be the chief clearing house for the global financial system because of the statutory monopolies it held as the British Empire's debt manager and issuer of paper currency.[18] 'Parliamentary security' for UK sovereign debt was thereby integral to the Bank of England's position as the conductor of the gold standard 'orchestra' by the beginning of the twentieth century.[19] Thereby, foundational features of private finance (stock markets and central banks) grew from institutions designed to finance the growth of modern constitutional government.

Public institutions remained vitally important to private finance as the twentieth and twenty-first centuries unfolded. From the 1950s, monetary policy, and the survival of the private credit system, became evermore reliant on the trading of government bonds between commercial banks and central banks. Because those bonds represented claims on the issuing government's collected tax revenues, the private financial system's regulation became ultimately, although perhaps not proximately, linked to that government's public financial processes.

When the private financial system collapsed in 2007, the integration of public and private financial systems was starkly revealed. Ensuring the survival of private financial markets required the deployment of public

---

[16] Pistor (2019), *The Code of Capital*, chapter 1.
[17] Dickson (1967), *The Financial Revolution in England: A Study in the Development of Public Credit*.
[18] The Bank of England's historical development (from a private financer of government to a modern central bank) is canvassed in Chapters 2 and 4 above.
[19] Eichengreen (1987), 'Conducting the International Orchestra: Bank of England Leadership under the Classic Gold Standard'.

resources on an enormous scale. Short- and long-term fixes came in the shape of vast subsidies to insolvent financial institutions, fiscal stimulus and unconventional monetary policies, most prominently the central bank asset-purchase programmes called 'quantitative easing'.

The economic and political prudence of those actions will continue to be a topic of vibrant debate, which will only be enriched by reflecting on the position of private financial markets in constitutional government.

BIBLIOGRAPHY

This bibliography contains the references to all primary and secondary material cited in the book and select texts which were influential in its drafting. Those references are organised into four categories (i) secondary sources, (ii) cases, (iii) legislation and (iv) government publications. To permit easier cross-referencing with the book those categories are organised alphabetically, rather than subdivided jurisdictionally.

Secondary Sources

Association of Certified Chartered Accountants (2014), 'Whole of Government Accounts: Who Is Using Them': www.accaglobal.com/content/dam/acca/global/PDF-technical/public-sector/tech-tp-woga-whole-of-government.pdf.

Ahearne, Alan et al. (2002) 'Preventing Deflation: Lessons from Japan's Experience in the 1990s' (Board of Governors of the Federal Reserve System, International Finance Discussion Papers 729/2002).

Allan, TRS (1994), *Law, Liberty, and Justice: The Legal Foundations of British Constitutionalism* (Clarendon Press).

Allen, Robert (2016), 'Revising England's Social Tables Once Again' (Oxford Working Papers in Economic and Social History, No. 146): www.economics.ox.ac.uk/materials/papers/14550/paper-146-july-2016.pdf.

Allison, JWF (2007), *The English Historical Constitution: Continuity, Change and European Effects* (Cambridge University Press).

Allison, JWF (2013), *A.V. Dicey, The Law of the Constitution by AV Dicey* (Oxford University Press).

Allison, JWF (2013), 'History to Understand, and History to Reform, English Public Law', 72 *Cambridge Law Journal* 326.

Anson, William (1897), *The Law and Custom of the Constitution: Part 1 Parliament* (3rd ed., Clarendon Press).

Anson, William (1907), *The Law and Custom of the Constitution* (3rd ed., Clarendon Press).

Anson, William (1912), 'The Parliament Act and the British Constitution', 12 *Columbia Law Review* 673.

Appleby, Gabrielle and McDonald, Stephen (2011), 'The Ramifications of Pape v Federal Commissioner of Taxation for the Spending Power and Legislative Powers of the Commonwealth', 37 *Monash Law Review* 162.

Ashton, Robert (1957), 'Deficit Finance in the Reign of James I', 10 *Economic History Review* 15.
Ashton, Robert (1960), *Crown and Money Market* (Oxford University Press).
Bagehot, Walter (1867), *The English Constitution* (Cambridge University Press, 2001 reissue).
Baker, John (2017), *The Reinvention of Magna Carta, 1216-1616* (Cambridge University Press).
Baker, Ron and Rennie, Morina (2006), 'Forces Leading to the Adoption of Accrual Accounting by the Canadian Federal Government: An Institutional Perspective', 5 *Canadian Accounting Perspectives* 83.
Balding, Christopher (2012), *Sovereign Wealth Funds* (Oxford University Press).
Barber, NW (2018), *Principles of Constitutionalism* (Oxford University Press).
Bassan, Fabio (2011), *The Law of Sovereign Wealth Funds* (Oxford University Press).
Basu, Durga (1955), *Commentary on the Constitution of India (Vol 1)* (3rd ed., SC Sarkar & Sons).
Basu, Durga (1965), *Commentary on the Constitution of India (Vol 1)* (5th ed., SC Sarkar & Sons).
Bernanke, Ben (2012), 'The Great Moderation', in Koenig, Evan (ed.), *The Taylor Rule and the Transformation of Monetary Policy* (Hoover Institute Press).
Bindseil, Ulrich (2014), *Monetary Policy Operations and the Financial System* (Cambridge University Press).
Binney, JED (1958), *British Public Finance and Administration 1774-92* (Clarendon Press).
Birch, AH (1995), *Federalism, Finance and Social Legislation* (Clarendon Press).
Black, Julia (2010), 'The Credit Crunch and the Constitution', in Oliver, Dawn, Prosser, Tony and Rawlings, Richard (eds.), *The Regulatory State: Constitutional Implication* (Oxford University Press).
Blackburn, Robert (2014), *Halsbury's Laws of England, Volume 20* (LexisNexis).
Blackburn, Robert and Kennon, Andrew (2003), *Griffith & Ryle on Parliament: Functions, Practice and Procedures* (Thomson).
Blejer, Mario and Cheasty, Adrienne (1999), *How to Measure the Fiscal Deficit: Analytical and Methodological Issues* (IMF).
Blöchliger, Hansjörg and Charbit, Claire (2008), 'Fiscal Equalisation', 44 *OECD Economic Studies* 1.
Borio, Claudio and Disyatat, Piti (2009), 'Unconventional Monetary Policies: An Appraisal' (Bank of International Settlements Working Paper No. 292): www.bis.org/publ/work292.pdf.
Bosc and Gagnon (2017), *House of Commons Practice and Procedure* (Parliament of Canada).
Braddick, MJ (1996), *The Nerves of State: Taxation and Financing of the English State, 1558-1714* (Manchester University Press).

Braddick, MJ (2000), *State Formation in Early Modern England, c. 1550–1700* (Cambridge University Press).
Bradshaw, Kenneth and Pring, David, *Parliament and Congress* (Quartet Books, 1973).
Braithwaite, John (2002), 'Rules and Principles: A Theory of Legal Certainty', 27 *Australian Journal of Legal Philosophy* 47.
Brewer, John (1989), *The Sinews of Power: War and the English State 1688–1783* (Unwin Hyman).
Brindle, Michael and Cox, Raymond (2018), *Law of Bank Payments* (5th ed., Sweet & Maxwell).
Broadway, Robin W and Watts, Ronald L (2004), 'Fiscal Federalism in Canada, the USA and Germany' (Queens University Working Paper no. 6/2004): www.queensu.ca/iigr/sites/webpublish.queensu.ca.iigrwww/files/files/WorkingPapers/Archive/2004/2004-6Boadway_Watts2004.pdf.
Brooks, Colin (1984), 'The Country Persuasion and Political Responsibility in England in the 1690s', 4 *Parliaments, Estates and Representation* 135.
Burnet, Gilbert (1753), *Bishop Burnet's History of His Own Time* (A Millar).
Campbell, Todd (2004), 'Sound Finance: Gladstone and British Government Finance, 1880-1895' (PhD Dissertation, LSE): http://etheses.lse.ac.uk/2403/.
Cane, Peter (2016), *Controlling Administrative Power* (Cambridge University Press).
Capie, Forrest, Goodhart, Charles and Schnadt, Norbert (1994), 'The Development of Central Banking' in Fischer, Stanley, Goodhart, Charles and Schnadt, Norbert (eds.), *The Future of Central Banking: The Tercentenary Symposium of the Bank of England* (Cambridge University Press).
Carlin, Tyrone (2005), 'Debating the Impact of Accrual Accounting and Reporting in the Public Sector', 21 *Financial Accountability and Management* 309.
Carpenter, S and Demiralp, S (2012), 'Money, Reserves, and the Transmission of Monetary Policy: Does the Money Multiplier Exist?', 34(1) *Journal of Macroeconomics* 59.
Chalmers, George (1814), *Opinions of Eminent Lawyers on Various Points of English Jurisprudence, Chiefly Concerning the Colonies, Fisheries, and Commerce of Great Britain, Collected and Digested, from the Originals in the Board of trade and other Depositories* (Reed and Hunter).
Chester, Norman (1981), *The English Administrative System, 1780–1870* (Clarendon Press).
Chitty, Joseph (1820), *A Treatise on the Law of the Prerogatives of the Crown and the Relative Duties of the Rights of the Subject* (Joseph Butterworth and Sons).
Choudhry, Moorad (2001), *The Bond and Money Markets* (Butterworth).
Clark, Gregory (2009), 'The Macroeconomic Aggregates for England 1209–2008' (UC Davis, Economics Working Paper 19/2009): http://faculty.econ.ucdavis.edu/faculty/gclark/papers/Macroagg2009.pdf.

Clark, Tom and Dilnot, Andrew (2002), 'Long Term Trends in British Taxation and Spending' (The Institute for Fiscal Studies, Briefing Note No. 25).

Clode, Walter (1887), *The Law and Practice of Petitions of Right* (William Clowes and Sons Ltd).

Condorcet, Nicolas de (1785), 'Essay on the Application of Mathematics to the Theory of Decision-Making', in Baker, Keith (ed.), *Condorcet: Selected Writings* (Macmillan).

Connolly, C and Hyndman, N (2006), 'The Actual Implementation of Accruals Accounting: Caveats from a Case within the UK Public Sector', 19 *Accounting, Auditing and Accountability Journal* 272–290.

Cooray, Joseph (1973), *Constitutional and Administrative Law of Sri Lanka (Ceylon)* (Hansa Publishers).

Corbacho, A and Schwartz, G (2007), 'Fiscal Responsibility Laws', in Kumar, MS and Te-Minassian, T (eds.), *Promoting Fiscal Discipline* (IMF).

Cottarelli, Carlo (1993), *Limiting Central Bank Credit to Government* (IMF).

Cross, Michael, Fisher, Paul and Weeken, Olaf (2010), 'The Bank's Balance Sheet during the Crisis' (Bank of England, Quarterly Bulletin 1).

Daunton, Martin (2007), *Trusting Leviathan: The Politics of Taxation in Britain, 1799–1914* (Cambridge University Press).

Day, Ron (2009), 'Implementation of Whole-of-Government Reports in Australia', 29 *Public Money and Management* 229.

De Bellescize, Ramu (2019), *Le Système Budgétaire du Royaume-Uni* (LDGJ).

Desan, Christine (2015), *Making Money: Coin, Currency, and the Coming of Capitalism* (Oxford University Press).

Dewar, David and Funnell, Warwick (2016), *A History of British National Audit* (Oxford University Press).

Di Matteo, Livio (2017), *A Federal Fiscal History* (Fraser Institute).

Dicey (1885), 'Introduction to the Study of the Law of the Constitution', in Allison (2013), *AV Dicey, The Law of the Constitution* (Oxford University Press).

Dicey, AV (1917), *Law and Public Opinion in England during the Nineteenth Century* (1967 re-issue, Macmillan & Co).

Dicey, AV (1939), *Introduction to the Study of the Law of the Constitution* (9th ed., Macmillan & Co).

Dick, Caroline (2014), 'Taxation in Australia up until 1914: The Warp and Welt of Protectionism', 12 *eJournal of Tax Research* 104.

Dickson, PGM (1967), *The Financial Revolution in England: A Study in the Development of Public Credit, 1688–1756* (1997 re-issue).

Dolls, Mathias, Fuest, Clemens and Peichl, Andreas (2010), 'Social Protection as an Automatic Stabiliser' (Institute for the Study of Labour, Policy Paper no. 18): http://ftp.iza.org/pp18.pdf.

Dornbusch, Rudiger and Draghi, Mario (1990), *Public Debt Management* (Cambridge University Press).

Dowell, Stephen (1884), *A History of Taxation and Taxes in England from the Earliest Times to the Present Day: Volumes 1 and 2* (1965 re-print, Frank Cass).
Durell, AJV (1917), *The Principles and Practice of the System of Control over Parliamentary Grants* (Gieves Publishing Company).
Dworkin, Ronald (1998), *Law's Empire* (Hart Publishing).
Eichengreen, Barry (1987), 'Conducting the International Orchestra: Bank of England Leadership under the Classic Gold Standard', 6 *Journal of International Money and Finance* 5.
Eichengreen, Barry and Garber, Peter (1991), 'Before the Accord: US Monetary–Financial Policy', in Glenn Hubbard (ed.), *Financial Markets and Financial Crises* (University of Chicago Press).
Einzig, Paul (1959), *The Control of the Purse: Progress and Decline of Parliament's Financial Control* (Secker & Warburg).
Elias, TO (1962), *The British Commonwealth: The Development of Its Laws and Constitutions (Vol 10, Ghana and Sierra Leone)* (Stevens).
Elias, TO (1967), *The British Commonwealth: The Development of Its Laws and Constitutions (Vol 14, Nigeria)* (Stevens & Sons).
Elliott, Mark and Thomas, Robert (2017), *Public Law* (Oxford University Press).
Epstein, David and O'Halloran, Sharyn (1999), *Delegating Powers: A Transaction Cost Politics Approach to Policy Making under Separate Powers* (Cambridge University Press).
European Union (2014), *European Union Public Finance* (Publications Office of the European Union).
Farmer, Roger and Zabczyk, Pawel (2016), 'The Theory of Unconventional Monetary Policy' (NBER Working Paper No. 22135): DOI:10.3386/w22135.
Fenno, Richard (1966), *The Power of the Purse: Appropriation Politics in Congress* (Little, Brown & Company).
Ferlie, Ewan, Lynn, Laurenace and Pollitt, Christopher (2005), *The Oxford Handbook of Public Management* (Oxford University Press).
Fernandes, David (2016), 'A Principled Framework for Assessing General Anti-Avoidance Regimes', 2 *British Tax Review* 172.
Finn, Paul (1987), *Law and Government in Colonial Australia* (Oxford University Press).
Fisher (1979), 'The Authorisation–Appropriation Process in Congress: Formal Rules and Informal Practices', 29 *Catholic University Law Review* 51.
Fuller, Lon (1969), *The Morality of Law* (Yale University Press).
Fuller, Lon (1978), 'The Forms and Limits of Adjudication', 92 *Harvard Law Review* 353.
Germov, John (2005), 'Managerialism in the Australian Public Health Sector', 6 *Sociology of Health and Illness* 738.
Gleeson, Murray (2009), 'The Meaning of Legislation: Context, Purpose and Respect for Fundamental Rights', 20 *Public Law Review* 26.

Glynn, J (1985), 'Value for Money Auditing: An International Review and Comparison', 1 *Financial Accountability and Management* 113.
Goldsworthy, Jeffrey (2001), *The Sovereignty of Parliament: History and Philosophy* (Oxford University Press).
Goodhart, Charles (1989), 'The Conduct of Monetary Policy', 99 *The Economic Journal* 293.
Goodhart, Charles (2003), 'The Constitutional Position of the Central Bank' in Friedman, Milton and Goodhart, Charles, *Money, Inflation and the Constitutional Position of the Central Bank* (Institute for Economic Affairs).
Goodhart, Charles (2010), 'The Changing Role of Central Banks' (Bank of International Settlements, Working Paper, 326/2010): www.bis.org/publ/work326.pdf.
Harding, Andrew (1996), *Law, Government and the Constitution in Malaysia* (Malayan Law Journal).
Harris, Mary, and Wilson, David. (2017), *Parliamentary Practice in New Zealand* (Parliament of New Zealand).
Harris, Peter (2006), *Income Tax in Common Law Jurisdictions* (Cambridge University Press).
Hart, HLA (1997), *The Concept of Law* (2nd ed., Oxford University Press).
Hatsell, John (1818), *Precedents of Proceedings of the House of Commons* (Luke Hansard and Sons).
Hawke, Lewis and Wanna, John (2010), 'Australia after Budgetary Reform', 69 in Wanna, John, Lessen, Lotte and de Vries, Jouke (eds.), *The Reality of OECD Budgetary Reform in OECD Nations* (Elgar).
Hayton, David (1984), 'The "Country" Interest and the Party System, 1689–c1720', in Jones, Clyve (ed.), *Party and Management in Parliament, 1660–1784* (Leicester University Press).
Hearn, William Edward (1886), *The Government of England: Its Structure and Its Development* (George Robertson and Co).
Heinemann, Friedrich, Osterloh Steffen and Kalbb, Alexander (2014), 'Sovereign Risk Premia: The Link between Fiscal Rules and Stability Culture', 41 *Journal of International Money and Finance* 110.
Hemming (2013), 'The Macroeconomic Framework for Managing Public Finance', in Allen, Hemming and Potter (eds.), *The International Handbook of Public Financial Management* (Palgrave Macmillan).
Hoffmann, Leonard (2005), 'Tax Avoidance', 2 *British Tax Review* 197.
Hogg, Peter (2000), *Liability of the Crown* (3rd ed., Carswell).
Hood, Christopher (1995), 'A Public Management for All Seasons?', 69(1) *Public Administration* 3.
Hood, Christopher (1995), 'The "New Public Management" in the 1980s: Variations on a Theme', 20(2) *Accounting, Organizations and Society* 93.

Horne, Alexander and Le Sueur, Andrew (2016), *Parliament: Legislation and Accountability* (Hart).
Horsefield, Keith (1982), 'The "Stop of the Exchequer" Revisited', 35 *Economic History Review* 511.
Huber, John and Shipan, Charles (2002), *Deliberate Discretion? The Institutional Foundations of Bureaucratic Autonomy* (Cambridge University Press).
Jack, Malcolm, et al. (2011) *Erskine May's Treatise on the Law, Privileges, Proceedings and Usage of Parliament* (25th ed., LexisNexis).
Jácome, Luis et al. (2012), 'Central Bank Credit to the Government: What Can We Learn from International Practices?' (IMF WP/12/16): http://dx.doi.org/10.5089/9781463931216.001.
Jaconelli, Joseph (1991), 'The Parliament Bill 1910–1911: The Mechanics of Constitutional Protection', 10 *Parliamentary History* 277.
Jaconelli, Joseph (2010), 'The "Bowles Act": Cornerstone of the Fiscal Constitution', 69 *Cambridge Law Journal* 582.
Jennings, Ivor (1939), *Parliament* (Cambridge University Press).
Jennings, Ivor (1959), *Cabinet Government* (3rd ed., Cambridge University Press).
Joppke, Christian (1987), 'The Crisis of the Welfare State, Collective Consumption, and the Rise of New Social Actors', 32 *Berkley Journal of Sociology* 237.
Jowell, Jeffrey (2003), 'Judicial Deference and Human Rights: A Question of Competence' in Craig, Paul and Rawlings, Richard (eds.), *Law and Administration in Europe* (Oxford University Press).
Joyce, Michael, Tong, Matthew and Woods, Robert, (2011), 'The United Kingdom's Quantitative Easing Policy: Design, Operation and Impact', *Bank of England Quarterly Bulletin: Q3* 200.
Kantorowicz, Ernst (1997), *The King's Two Bodies: A Study in Mediaeval Political Theology* (2nd ed., Princeton University Press).
Kavanagh, Aileen (2008), 'Deference or Defiance? The Limits of the Judicial Role in Constitutional Adjudication' in Huscroft Grant (ed.), *Expounding the Constitution: Essays in Constitutional Theory* (Oxford University Press).
Keith, Arthur Berriedale (1928), *Responsible Government in the Dominions* (2nd ed., Clarendon Press).
Keith, Arthur Berriedale (1930), *Constitutional History of the First British Empire* (Clarendon Press).
Kennedy, WPM (1922), *The Constitution of Canada: An Introduction to Its Development and Law* (Oxford University Press).
Keynes, John Maynard (1936), *The General Theory of Employment, Interest and Money* (2013 re-issue, Cambridge University Press).
Kier David (1955), *The Constitutional History of Britain* (5th ed., A and C Black).
Kier, David (1936), 'The Case of Ship Money', 52 *Law Quarterly Review* 546.
King, Jeff (2012), *Judging Social Rights* (Cambridge University Press).

King, Jeff (2007), 'The Justiciability of Resource Allocation', 70(2) *Modern Law Review* 197.
King, Jeff (2008a), 'Institutional Approaches to Judicial Restraint', 28 *Oxford Journal of Legal Studies* 409.
King, Jeff (2008b), 'The Pervasiveness of Polycentricity', *Public Law* 101.
Knight (2009), 'Bi-Polar Sovereignty Restated', 68 *Cambridge Law Journal* 361.
Kumarasingham, Harshan (2015), *Constitution-Maker: Selected Writings of Sir Ivor Jennings* (Cambridge University Press).
La Nauze, JA (1972), *The Making of the Australian Constitution* (Melbourne University Press).
Landemore, Hélène (2012), *Democratic Reason: Politics, Collective Intelligence and the Rule of the Many* (Princeton University Press).
Lapsley, I, Riccardo, M and Paulsson G (2009), 'On the Adoption of Accrual Accounting in the Public Sector: A Self-Evident and Problematic Reform', 18 *European Accounting Review* 719–723.
Lapsley, Irvine, Mussari, Riccardo and Paulsson, Gert (2009), 'On the Adoption of Accrual Accounting in the Public Sector', 18 *European Accounting Review* 719.
Lenza, Michele, Pill, Huw and Reichlin, Lucrezia (2010), 'Monetary Policy in Exceptional Times' (European Central Bank, Working Paper 1253/2010): www.ecb.europa.eu/pub/pdf/scpwps/ecbwp1253.pdf.
Lewis, Clive (2014), *Judicial Remedies in Public Law* (Sweet and Maxwell).
Likierman, A (2003), 'Planning and Controlling UK Public Expenditure on a Resource Basis', 23 *Public Money & Management* 45–50.
Littlewood (2016), 'In the Beginning: Taxation in Early Colonial New Zealand' (available at SSRN: https://ssrn.com/abstract=2762003).
Loughlin, Martin (1992), *Public Law and Political Theory* (Clarendon Press).
Loughlin, Martin (2003), *The Idea of Public Law* (Oxford University Press).
Loughlin, Martin (2010), *Foundations of Public Law* (Oxford University Press).
Lovett, Adan (2016), *A Republic of Law* (Cambridge University Press).
Lyon, Bryce (1980), *A Constitutional and Legal History of Medieval England* (2nd ed., Harper & Row).
Maitland, FW (1901), 'The Crown as Corporation', 17 *Law Quarterly Review* 131.
Maitland, FW (1908), *The Constitutional History of England* (Cambridge University Press).
Manin (1997), *The Principles of Representative Government* (Cambridge University Press).
Mashaw, Jerry (2005), 'Between Facts and Norms: Agency Statutory Interpretation as an Autonomous Enterprise', 55 *University of Toronto Law Journal* 497.
Maxwell, Peter (1875), *On the Interpretation of Statutes* (William Maxwell and Sons).
May, Erskine (1844), *A Practical Treatise on the Law, Privileges, Procedures and Usage of Parliament* (1st ed., Butterworths).

May, Erskine (1851), *A Practical Treatise on the Law, Privileges, Procedures and Usage of Parliament* (2nd ed., Butterworths).
McEldowney, John (1988), 'The Contingencies Fund and the Parliamentary Scrutiny of Finance', *Public Law* 232.
McEldowney, John (2001), 'Review', 64 *Modern Law Review* 135.
McEldowney, John (2016), *Public Law* (Sweet & Maxwell).
McEldowny, John (2015), 'Public Expenditure and the Control of Public Finance', in Jowell, Jeffrey, and Oliver, Dawn (eds.), *The Changing Constitution* (8th ed., OUP).
McKay, William and Johnson, Charles (2010), *Parliament and Congress* (Oxford University Press).
McLean, Iain and Hewitt, Fiona (1994), *Condorcet: Foundations of Social Choice and Political Theory* (Edward Elgar).
McLean, Iain and McMillan, Alistair (2003), 'The Distribution of Public Expenditure across UK Regions', 24 *Fiscal Studies* 45.
McLean, Ian (2009), *What's Wrong with the British Constitution* (Oxford University Press).
McLean, Janet (2012), *Searching for the State in British Legal Thought: Competing Conceptions of the Public Sphere* (Cambridge University Press).
McLeay, Michael, Radia, Amar and Thomas, Ryland (2014), 'Money Creation in the Modern Economy' (Bank of England Quarterly Bulletin, Q1 2014).
McLeod, Henry (1875), *Theory and Practice of Banking* (Longmans, Green, Reader, & Dyer).
Melbourne, ACV (1963), *Early Constitutional Development in Australia: New South Wales 1788–1856, Queensland 1859–1922* (2nd ed., University of Queensland Press).
Mendel, Michael (1989), 'The Ship Money Case, *The Case of Shipmoney*, and the Development of Henry Parker's Parliamentary Absolutism', 32 *The Historical Journal* 413.
Micklethwait, Robert (1976), *The National Insurance Commissioners* (Steven & Sons).
Mishkin, Fredrick (2013), *The Economics of Money, Banking and Financial Markets* (Pearson).
Mitchell, Brian (1988), *British Historical Statistics* (Cambridge University Press).
Mitchell, Charles (2010), 'Recovery of Ultra Vires Payments by Public Bodies', *Public Law* 747.
Nicol, Dany (2010), *The Constitutional Protection of Capitalism* (Bloomsbury).
O'Faircheallaigh, Ciaran and Wanna, John (1999), *Public Sector Management in Australia* (Macmillan).
O'Brien, Patrick (2005) 'Fiscal and Financial Preconditions for the Rise of British Naval Hegemony 1485-1815' (LSE Department of Economic History Working Paper 91/2005): http://eprints.lse.ac.uk/22326/.

O'Connell, DP and Riordan, Ann (1971), *Opinions on Imperial Constitutional Law* (Law Book Company).
Obrien, Derek (2014), *The Constitutional Systems of the Commonwealth Caribbean* (Hart).
OECD (2013), *Sovereign Borrowing Outlook* (OECD): https://doi.org/10.1787/sov_b_outlk-2013-en.
Oliver, Adam (ed.) (2014), *Behavioral Public Policy* (Cambridge University Press).
Palgrave, Reginald and Bonham-Carter, Alfred (1893), *Erskine May's Treatise on the Law, Privileges, Proceedings and Usage of Parliament* (10th ed., William Clowes and Sons Ltd).
Pearce, John (2009), 'The Role of Central Government in Determining Liability to Income Tax in England and Wales', in Tiley, John (ed.), *Studies in the History of Tax Law – Volume 4* (Hart Publishing).
Phillips, Fred (1985), *West Indian Constitutions: Post-Independence Reform* (Oceana Publishing).
Pistor, Katharina (2019), *The Code of Capital* (Princeton University Press).
Pollitt, Christopher and Bouckaert, Geet (2004), *Public Management Reform: A Comparative Analysis* (Oxford University Press).
Poole, Thomas (2015), *Reason of State: Law Prerogative and Empire* (Oxford University Press).
Posner, Eric and Vermeule, Adrian (2011), *The Executive Unbound: Life after the Madison Republic* (Oxford University Press).
Price, George (1830), *A Treatise on the Law of the Exchequer* (Saunders and Benning).
Prosser, Tony (2011), '"An opportunity to take a more fundamental look at the role of government in society": The Spending Review as Regulation', *Public Law* 596.
Prosser, Tony (2014), *The Economic Constitution* (Oxford University Press).
Prosser, Tony (2010), *The Regulatory Enterprise* (Oxford University Press).
Radin, Max (1980), 'Statutory Interpretation', 43 *Harvard Law Review* 863.
Rayner, Keith et al. (2016), 'So Much to Read, So Little Time: How Do We Read, and Can Speed Reading Help', 17 *Psychological Science in the Public Interest* 4.
Redlich, Josef and Ilbert, Courtenay (1903), *The Procedure of the House of Commons: A Study of Its History and Present Form: Volume 3* (Archibald Constable & Co Ltd).
Reid, Gordon (1966), *The Politics of Financial Control* (Hutchinson).
Reitan, EA (1966), 'The Civil List in Eighteenth-Century British Politics: Parliamentary Supremacy versus the Independence of the Crown', 9 *Historical Journal* 318.
Richardson, Henry (2002), *Democratic Autonomy: Public Reasoning about the Ends of Policy* (Oxford University Press).
Roseveare, Henry (1969), *The Treasury: The Evolution of a British Institution* (Allen Lane).

Roseveare, Henry (1973), *The Treasury 1660–1870. The Foundations of Control* (Barnes and Noble).
Rubin, Ed (2005), *Beyond Camelot: Rethinking Law and Politics for the Modern State* (Princeton University Press).
Rundle, Kristen (2012), *Forms Liberate: Reclaiming the Jurisprudence of Lon Fuller* (Hart).
Samuel, Geoffrey (2009), 'Interdisciplinarity and the Authority Paradigm: Should Law be Taken Seriously by Scientists and Social Scientists', 36 *Journal of Law and Society* 431.
Sayles, GO (1988), *The Functions of the Medieval Parliaments of England* (Hambledon Press).
Scheuerman, Bill (1994), 'The Rule of Law and the Welfare State: Towards a New Synthesis', 22 *Politics and Society* 195.
Scheuerman, William (2004), *Liberal Democracy and the Social Acceleration of Time* (Johns Hopkins University Press).
Schmitt, Carl (1922), *Political Theology* (1985, Schwab, trans, University of Chicago Press).
Shklar, Judith (1987), 'Political Theory and the Rule of Law' in Hutchinson, Allan and Monahan, Patrick (eds.), *The Rule of Law: Ideal or Ideology* (Carswell).
Singleton, John (2011), *Central Banking in the Twentieth Century* (Cambridge University Press).
Smailes, David (2017), *Tolley's Income Tax 2017–2018* (LexisNexis).
South, Jim (2014), 'Are Legislative Intentions Real?', 40 *Monash Law Review* 853.
Stebbings, Chantal (2009), 'Consent and Constitutionality in Nineteenth-Century Taxation', in Tiley, John (ed.), *Studies in the History of Tax Law – Volume 3* (Hart Publishing).
Story, Joseph (1833), *Commentaries on the Constitution of the United States* (1st ed., Hillard, Gray and Company).
Stubbs, William (1906), *The Constitutional History of England: In Its Origin and Development* (Clarendon Press).
Sugarman, David (1986), 'Legal Theory, the Common Law Mind and the Making of the Textbook Tradition' in Twining, William (ed.), *Legal Theory and Common Law* (Basil Blackwell Press).
Sweetman, Edward (1925), *Australian Constitutional Development* (Macmillan & Co. Limited and Melbourne University Press).
Taggart, Michael (2008), '"Australian Exceptionalism" in Judicial Review', 36 *Federal Law Review* 1.
Talisse, Robert (2012), 'Deliberation', in Estlund David (ed.), *The Oxford Handbook of Political Philosophy* (Oxford University Press).
Tamanaha, Brian (2004), *On the Rule of Law* (Cambridge University Press).

Tan, Kevin (1999), 'A Short Legal and Constitutional History of Singapore', in Tan, Kevin (ed.), *The Singapore Legal System* (2nd ed., Singapore University Press).

Tanzi, Vito and Schuknecht, Ludger (2000), *Public Spending in the 20th Century* (Cambridge University Press).

Tapping, Thomas (1853), *The Law and Practice of the High Prerogative Writ of Mandamus* (T & JW Johnson).

Teubner, Gunther (1992), 'Social Order from Legislative Noise', in Teubner, Gunther and Febbrajo, Alberto (eds.), *European Yearbook in the Sociology of Law: State, Law and Economy as Autopoetic Systems* (Guiffre).

Thain, Wright and Thain, Colin (1995), *The Treasury and Whitehall: The Planning and Control of Public Expenditure, 1976–1993* (Oxford University Press).

Thomas, PDG (1971), *The House of Commons in the Eighteenth Century* (Clarendon Press).

Thornton, John (2009), 'Do Fiscal Responsibility Laws Matter? Evidence from Emerging Market Economies Suggests Not', 12 *Journal of Economic Reform* 127.

Todd, Alphaeus (1884), *Parliamentary Government in the British Colonies* (Longmans, Green and Co).

Todd, Alphaeus (1887), *Parliamentary Government in England: Its Origins, Development and Practical Operation* (2nd ed., Longmans, Green and Co).

Tooze, Adam (2018), *Crashed: How a Decade of Financial Crises Changed the World* (Viking).

Turner, Adair (2015), 'The Case for Monetary Finance: An Essentially Political Issue', 16th Jacques Polak Annual Research Conference: www.imf.org/external/np/res/seminars/2015/arc/pdf/adair.pdf.

Turpin, Colin and Tomkins, Adam (2011), *British Government and the Constitution* (Cambridge University Press).

Twomey, Anne (2004), *The Constitution of New South Wales* (Federation Press).

Twomey, Anne (2010), 'Pushing the Boundaries of Executive Power: Pape, the Prerogative and Nationhood Powers', 34 *Melbourne University Law Review* 313.

Vermeule, Adrian (2013), *The Constitution of Risk* (Cambridge University Press).

Vick, Douglas (2004), 'Interdisciplinarity and the Discipline of Law', 31 *Journal of Law and Society* 163.

Vohrah, Koh and Ling, Peter (2004), *The Constitution of Malaysia* (5th ed., Malayan Law Journal).

Wade, ECD and Phillips, Godfrey (1931) (1946), *Constitutional Law* (1st and 4th eds., Longmans, Green and Co).

Waldron, Jeremy (2012), 'Democracy' and Talisse, 'Deliberation', in Estlund David (ed.), *The Oxford Handbook of Political Philosophy* (Oxford University Press).

Webber, David (2004), 'Managing the Public's Money: From Outputs to Outcomes – and Beyond', 4 *OECD Journal on Budgeting* 101.
Wehner, Joachim (2003), 'Principles and Patterns of Financial Scrutiny: Public Accounts Committees in the Commonwealth', 41(3) *Commonwealth and Comparative Politics* 21.
Wehner, Joachim (2006), 'Assessing the Power of the Purse: An Index of Legislative Budget Institutions', 54 *Political Studies* 767.
Wehner, Joachim (2010a), *Legislatures and the Budget Process: The Myth of Fiscal Control* (Palgrave Macmillan).
Wehner, Joachim (2010b), 'Cabinet Structure and Fiscal Policy Outcomes', 49 *European Journal of Political Research* 631.
White, Fidelma and Hollingsworth, Kathryn (1999), *Audit, Accountability and Government* (Oxford University Press).
White, Fidelma and Hollingsworth, Kathryn (2001), 'Public Finance Reform: The Government Resources and Accounts Act 2000', *Public Law* 50.
Williams, John (2005), *The Australian Constitution: A Documentary History* (Melbourne University Press).
Williams, Mike (2013), 'Debt and Cash Management', in Allen, Richard, Hemming, Richard and Potter Barry (eds.), *The International Handbook of Public Financial Management* (Palgrave Macmillan).
Wormell, Jeremy (1999), *National Debt in Britain 1850–1930, Volumes 1–9* (Rutledge).
Wray, Randall (1998), 'Modern Money' (Levy Economics Institute Working Paper No. 252): www.levyinstitute.org/publications/modern-money.
Wright, BC and Fowler, PE (2012), *House of Representatives Practice* (Parliament of Australia).

Cases

A v. *Secretary of State for the Home Department* [2005] 2 AC 68.
Abe v. *Minister of Finance* [1994] 2 LRC 10.
Alcock v. *Fergie* (1867) 4 W W & A'B (L) 285.
Anderson v. *Commissioner of Taxes (Vict)* (1937) 57 CLR 233.
Anisminic Ltd v. *Foreign Compensation Commission* [1968] 2 AC 14.
Attorney-General (Vic); Ex rel Dale v. *Commonwealth* (1945) 71 CLR 237.
Attorney-General v. *Great Southern and Western Railway Co* (1925) 41 TLR 576.
Attorney-General v. *Wilts United Dairies Ltd* (1922) 91 LJKB 897.
Auckland Harbour Board v. *The King* [1919] *Gazette Law Reports* (NZ) 352.
Auckland Harbour Board v. *The King* [1924] AC 318.
Bahad v. *Union of India* [1970] SC 530.
Bakewell v. *McPherson* (1992) BC9200236 (Supreme Court of South Australia).
Balaji v. *Government of Tamil Nadu* [2013] INSC 658.

Barclays Mercantile Business Finance Ltd v. *Mawson (Inspector of Taxes)* [2005] 1 AC 684.
Bate's Case (1606) 2 ST 371.
Baxter v. *Commissioners of Taxation (NSW)* (1907) 4 CLR 1087.
Bowles v. *Bank of England* [1913] 1 Ch 57.
Buckley & Young Ltd v. *Commissioner of Inland Revenue* [1978] 2 NZLR 485.
Campbell v. *Hall* (1774) 1 Cowp 204 [98 ER 1045].
Canada Trustco Mortgage Co v. *Canada* [2005] 2 SCR 601.
Commissioners of Inland Revenue v. *Duke of Westminster* [1936] AC 1.
Commonwealth v. *Colonial Ammunition Co Ltd* (1924) 34 CLR 198.
Confederation des syndicats nationaux v. *Canada (Attorney General)*, [2008] 3 SCR 511.
Council of Civil Service Unions v. *Minister for the Civil Service* [1985] AC 374.
Covert v. *Minister of Finance of Nova Scotia* [1980] 2 SCR 774.
Craven (Inspector of Taxes) Appellant v. *White* [1989] AC 398.
D'Emden v. *Pedder* (1904) 1 CLR 91.
Davis v. *The Commonwealth* (1988) 166 CLR 79.
Davis v. *The Governor and Company of the Bank of England* (1824) 2 Bingham 393 [130 ER 357].
De la Chaumette v. *The Bank of England* (1831) 2 Barnewall and Adolphus 385 [109 ER 1186]; (1829) 9 Barnewall and Cresswell 208 [109 ER 78].
Ex parte The Bank of England, in the Matter of Richard Stephens, a Bankrupt (1818) 1 Swanston 10 [36 ER 277].
Five Knights Case (1627) 3 How ST 1.
Fortier v. *Lambe* (1895) 25 SCR 422.
Foster v. *The Governor and Company of the Bank of England* (1846) 8 Queen's Bench Reports 689 [115 ER 1032].
Franklin v. *The Bank of England* (1826) 1 Russell 575 [38 ER 221].
Furniss (Inspector of Taxes) v. *Dawson* [1984] AC 474.
Gauweiler v. *Deutscher Bundestag* (c-62/14).
Governor and Company of the Bank of England v. *Davis* (1826) 5 Barnewall and Cresswell 185 [108 ER 69].
Governor and Company of the Bank of England v. *Newman* (1703) 12 Modern 241 [88 ER 1290].
Haward v. *the Bank of England* (1722) 1 Strange 550 [93 ER 693].
In re McFarland [2004] 1 WLR 1289.
In re S (Minors) (Care Order: Implementation of Care Plan) [2002] 2 AC 291.
Inland Revenue Commissioners v. *Burmah Oil Co Ltd* [1982] STC 30.
Inland Revenue Commissioners v. *McGuckian* [1997] 1 WLR 991.
Inland Revenue Commissioners v. *National Federation of Self-Employed and Small Businesses Ltd* [1982] AC 617.
Inland Revenue Commissioners v. *Sheffield and South Yorkshire Navigation Company* [1916] 1 KB 882.

Ipatas v. *Balakau* [1996] PNGLR 248.
John v. *Federal Commissioner of Taxation* (1989) 166 CLR 417.
Kariapper v. *Wijesinha* (1966) 68 NLR 529.
MacNiven v. *Westmoreland Investments Ltd* [2003] 1 AC 311.
Mohammed (Serdar) v. *Ministry of Defence* [2017] 2 WLR 2879.
Mullens v. *Federal Commissioner of Taxation* (1976) 135 CLR 290.
New South Wales v. *Bardolph* (1934) 52 CLR 455.
New South Wales v. *Commonwealth* (1908) 7 CLR 179.
Pape v. *Federal Commissioner of Taxation* (2009) 238 CLR 1.
Partington v. *Attorney General* (1869–70) LR 4 (HL) 100.
Partridge v. *The Governor and Company of the Bank of England* (1846) 9 Queen's Bench Reports 396 [115 ER 1324].
Permanent Secretary of the Department of Education of the Government of the Eastern Cape Province v. *Ed-U-College* 2001 (2) SA 1.
Pioneer Laundry & Dry Cleaners Ltd v. *The Minister of National Revenue* [1939] SCR 1.
Plaintiff S157/2002 v. *Commonwealth* (2003) 211 CLR 476.
Prebble v. *Television New Zealand Ltd* [1995] 1 AC 321.
Pryce v. *The Directors and Company of the Monmouthshire Canal and Rail Way Companies* (1879) 4 App Cas 197.
R (Bancoult) v. *Secretary of State for Foreign and Commonwealth Affairs (No. 2)* [2009] AC 453.
R (Hooper) v. *Secretary of State for Work and Pensions* [2005] 1 WLR 1681.
R (Lord Carlile of Berriew) v. *Secretary of State for the Home Department* [2015] 1 AC 945.
R (Miller) v. *Secretary of State for Exiting the European Union* [2017] UKSC 5.
R (Public Law Project) v. *Lord Chancellor* [2016] AC 1531.
R v. *Inland Revenue Commissioners* (1884) 12 QBD 461.
R v. *Inland Revenue Commissioners, ex parte National Federation of Self-Employed and Small Businesses Ltd* [1982] AC 617.
R v. *Lords Commissioners of the Treasury* (1836) 4 Ad & E 976 [111 ER 1050].
R v. *Secretary of State for Foreign Affairs ex parte World Development Movement Ltd* [1995] 1 All ER 611.
R. v. *The Lords Commissioners of the Treasury; in re Hand* (1836) 4 Ad & El 984 [111 ER 1053].
Rattenbury v. *Land Settlement Board* [1929] SCR 52.
Re Baron de Bode (1845) 8 QB 208 [115 ER 854].
Re Euring Estate [1998] 2 SCR 565.
Reference by Executive Council of the Enga Provincial Government [1990] PNGLR 532.
Regina v. *Secretary of State for the Environment, Transport and the Regions* [2001] 2 AC 349.

Sherdley v. *Sherdley* [1986] 1 WLR 732.
Sherdley v. *Sherdley* [1988] AC 213.
Shergill v. *Khaira* [2015] AC 359.
Sloman v. *Bank of England* (1845) 1 Holt Equity Reports 1, 9 [71 ER 649].
Steele Ford & Newton Respondents v. *Crown Prosecution Service (No. 2)* [1994] 1 AC 22.
Sutton, Bart v. *The Governor and Company of the Bank of England* (1824) Ryan & Moody 52 [171 ER 940].
The Case of Mines (1568) 1 Plowden 310 [75 ER 472].
The King v. *Lords Commissioners of the Treasury; in re Hand* (1836) 4 Ad & E 984 [111 ER 1053].
The King v. *Lords Commissioners of the Treasury; in re Smyth* (1835) 4 Ad& E 286 [11 ER 794].
The King v. *The Governor and Company of the Bank of England* (1819) 2 Barnewall and Alderson 620 [106 ER 492].
The King, on the Prosecution of Parbury and Another, Executors of Dawes v. *The Governor and Company of the Bank of England* (1780) 2 Douglas 524 [99 ER 334].
The Queen v. *Lords Commissioners of the Treasury* (1872) 7 QB 387.
The Queen v. *The Secretary of State for War* [1891] 2 QB 326.
Victoria v. *The Commonwealth* (1975) 134 CLR 338.
Williams v. *Commonwealth (No. 1)* (2012) 248 CLR 156.
Williams v. *Commonwealth (No. 2)* (2014) (2012) 252 CLR 416.
Windsor & Annapolis Railway Co v. *The Queen and the Western Counties Railway Co* (1885) 10 SCR 335.
Woolwich Equitable Building Society v. *IRC* [1993] AC 70.
WT Ramsay Ltd v. *Inland Revenue Commissioners* [1982] AC 300.
X (Minors) v. *Bedfordshire County Council* [1995] 2 AC 633.

Legislation (Including Delegated Legislation and Constitutions)

A New Tax System (Commonwealth-State Financial Arrangements) Act 1999 (Cth).
A New Tax System (Goods and Services Tax) Act 1999 (Cth).
Act of 1665 (7 Ch II) c 1.
Act of 1692 (4 W & M) c 3.
Act of 1697 (8 & 9 Will III) c 20.
Act of 1701 (12 & 13 Will III) c 12.
Act of 1709 (8 Ann) c 1.
Act of 1713 (12 Ann) c 11.
Act of 1714 (1 Geo I) c 12.
Act of 1716 (3 Geo I) c 8.
Act of 1717 (3 Geo I) c 9.

Act of 1729 (2 Geo II) c 18.
Act of 1742 (16 Geo II) c 13.
Act of 1760 (1 Geo III) c 1.
Act of 1782 (22 Geo III) c 82.
Act of 1783 (23 Geo III) c 82.
Act of 1785 (25 Geo III) c 52.
Act of 1787 (27 Geo III) c 13.
Act of 1793 (33 Geo III) c 32.
Act of 1822 (3 Geo IV) c 113.
Act of 1826 (7 Geo IV) c 64.
Act of 1833 (3 & 4 Will IV) c 98.
Act of 1845 (8 & 9 Vict) c 4.
Act of 1848 (11 & 12 Vict) c 8.
Act of 1851 (14 & 15 Vict) c 12.
Act of 1852 (15 & 16 Vict) c 20.
Act of 1853 (16 & 17 Vict) c 34.
Act of 1854 (17 Vict) c 23.
Act of 1860 (23 Vict) c 14.
Act of 1861 (24 Vict) c 20.
Act of Union 1840 (3 & 4 Vict) c 35.
Acts Interpretation Amendment Act 1976 (Cth).
Acts of 1728 (2 Geo II) cc 1, 3 and 4.
Aged Care Act 1997 (Cth).
Alcohol Liquor Duties Act 1979 (UK) c 4.
Appropriation Act (No. 1) 2005–2006 (Cth).
Appropriation Act (No. 2) 2006 (UK) c 24.
Appropriation Act (No. 2) 2011–2012 (Cth).
Appropriation Act (No. 2) 2012–2013 (Cth).
Appropriation Act 1815 (55 Geo III) c 187.
Appropriation Act 1833 (3 & 4 Will IV) c 96.
Appropriation Act 1846 (9 & 10 Vict) c 116.
Appropriation Act 1862 (25 & 26 Vict) c 71.
Appropriation Act 1873 (36 & 37 Vict) c 79.
Appropriation Act 1895 (NZ).
Appropriation Act 1901 (1 Edw VII) c 21.
Appropriation Act of 1834 (4 & 5 Wil IV) c 84.
Appropriation Act, No. 5 2014–15 (Can).
Appropriation (Confirmation and Validation) Act 2014 (NZ).
Audit Act 1858 (NZ).
Audit Act 1870 (NSW).
Audit Act 1878 (Can).
Audit Amendment Act 1979 (Cth).

Auditor-General Act 1977 (can).
Australian Constitutions Act 1850 (13 & 14 Vict) c 59.
Australian Courts Act 1828 (9 Geo IV) c 83.
Australian Education Act 2013 (Cth).
Bank Charter Act 1844 (7 & 8 Vict) c 32.
Bank of Canada Act 1934 (Can).
Bank of Canada Act 1934 (Can).
Bank of England Act 1694 (5 & 6 W & M) c 20.
Bank of England Act 1819 (59 Geo III) c 76.
Bank of England Act 1946 (9 & 10 Geo 6) c 27.
Bank of England Act 1998 (UK) c 11.
Bank of England and Financial Services Act 2016 (UK) c 14.
Banking Act 2009 (UK) c 1.
Bill of Rights 1688 (1 & 2 W & M) c 2.
Borrowing Authority Act 1996–1997 (Can).
British North America Act 1867 (30 & 31 Vict) c 3.
Budget Responsibility and National Audit Act 2011 (UK) c 4.
Charter of Budget Honesty Act 1998 (Cth).
Civil Contingencies Fund Act 1919 (9 & 10 Geor V) c 6.
Civil List Act 1837 (1 & 2 Vict) c 2.
Coinage Act 1971 (Cth).
Commissioners for Customs and Revenue Act 2005 (UK) c 11.
Commonwealth Bank Act 1911 (Cth).
Commonwealth Inscribed Stock Act 1911 (Cth).
Commonwealth Inscribed Stock Amendment Act 2009 (Cth).
Commonwealth Inscribed Stock Amendment Act 2013 (Cth).
Commonwealth of Australia Constitution Act 1901 (63 & 64 Vict) c 12.
Confirmatio Cartarum 1297.
Consolidated Fund (Appropriation) Act 1874 (37 & 38 Vict) c 56.
Consolidated Fund Act (No. 1) (1901) (1 Edw VII) c 1.
Consolidated Fund Act 1838 (1 Vict) c 21.
Consolidated Fund Act 1848 (11 Vict) c 3.
Consolidated Fund Act 1872 (35 Vict) c 1.
Consolidated Fund Act 1872 (35 Vict) c 11.
Consolidated Revenue and Audit Act 1931 (Can).
Constitution of Barbados 1966.
Constitution of India 1950.
Constitution of Kenya 2010.
Constitution of Kiribati 1979.
Constitution of Lesotho 1966.
Constitution of Malawi 1966.
Constitution of Malaysia 1963.

Constitution of Malta 1964.
Constitution of Mauritius 1968.
Constitution of Nigeria 1963.
Constitution of Pakistan 1973.
Constitution of Sierra Leone 1978.
Constitution of the Independent State of Papua New Guinea 1975.
Constitution of the Kingdom of Swaziland Act 2005.
Constitution of the Republic of the Seychelles 1993.
Constitution of Uganda 1995.
Constitutional Reform Act 2005 (UK) c 4.
Contingencies Fund Act 1970 (UK) c 56.
Contingencies Fund Act 1974 (UK) c 18.
Crown Proceedings Act 1947 (10 & 11 Geo VI) c 44.
Crown Suits Act 1881 (NZ).
Currency Act 1965 (Cth).
Currency Act 1982 (UK) c 3.
Currency Act 1983 (UK) c 9.
Currency and Bank Notes Act 1954 (2&3 Eliz II) c 12.
Currency and Bank Notes Act 1928 (18 & 19 Geo V) c 13.
Customs Act 1901 (Cth).
Customs Tariff Act 1995 (Cth).
European Communities Act 1972 (UK) c 68.
Exchange Equalisation Account Act 1979 (UK) c 30.
Exchequer and Audit Departments Act 1866 (29 & 30 Vict) c 39.
Exchequer Bills Act 1838 (1 Vict) c 12.
Excise Act 1901 (Cth).
Excise Tariff Act 1921 (Cth).
Federal Financial Relations Act 2009 (Cth).
Finance Act 1921 (11 & 12 Geo V) c 32.
Finance Act 1954 (2 & 3 Eliz II) c 44.
Finance Act 1965 (UK) c 25.
Finance Act 1982 (UK) c 39.
Finance Act 1986 (UK) c 41.
Finance Act 1998 (UK) c 36.
Finance Act 2003 (UK) c 14.
Finance Act 2012 (UK) c 14.
Finance Act 2013 (UK) c 29.
Finance Act 2013 (UK) c 29.
Finance Act 2014 (UK) c 26.
Financial Framework (Supplementary Powers) Act 1997(Cth).
Financial Management and Accountability Act 1997 (Cth).
Financial Management and Accountability Regulations 1997 (Cth).

Fiscal Responsibility Act 1994 (NZ).
Fiscal Responsibility Act 2010 (UK) c 3.
Government Resources and Accounts Act 2000 (UK) c 20.
Health Care (Appropriation) Act 1998 (Cth).
Health Insurance (Diagnostic Imaging Services Table) Regulation 2016 (Cth).
Health Insurance (General Medical Services Table) Regulation 2016 (Cth)
Health Insurance Act 1973 (Cth).
Higher Education Support Act 2003 (Cth).
Hydrocarbon Oil Duties Act 1979 (UK) c 5.
Income and Corporations Taxes Act 1988 (UK).
Income Tax Act (Sing).
Income Tax Act 1803 (41 Geo III) c 122.
Income Tax Act 1842 (5 & 6 Vict) c 35.
Income Tax Act 1915 (Cth).
Income Tax Act 1962 (South Africa).
Income Tax Act 1967 (Malaysia).
Income Tax Act 1986 (Cth).
Income Tax Assessment Act 1936 (Cth).
Income War Tax Act 1917 (Can).
Inheritance Tax Act 1984 (UK) c 51.
Inland Revenue Ordinance (HK).
Invalid and Old-Age Pensions Act 1943 (Cth).
Land and Income Tax Act 1954 (NZ).
Land Bank Act 1696 (7 & 8 Wm III) c 31.
Loan (Temporary Revenue Deficits) Act 1953 (Cth).
Loan Act 1888 (Can).
Loan Act 1901 (UK) (1 Edw VII) c 12.
Loan Act 1942 (Can).
Loans Securities Act 1919 (Cth).
Local Government Finance Act 1988 (UK) c 41.
Local Government Finance Act 1992 (UK) c 14.
Magna Carta 1215.
Maternity Allowance Act 1943 (Cth).
Miscellaneous Financial Provisions Act 1946 (9 & 10 Geo VI) c 40.
Miscellaneous Financial Provisions Act 1955 (4 & 5 Eliz II) c 6.
National Assistance Act 1948 (11 & 12 Geo VI) c 29.
National Audit Act 1983 (UK) c 44.
National Debt Act 1972 (UK) c 65.
National Debt Reduction Act 1786 (26 Geo III) c 31.
National Health Act 1946 (9 & 10 Geo VI) c 81.
National Health Act 1953 (Cth).
National Health Contributions Act 1957 (UK) c 54.

National Health Service Contributions Act 1965 (5 & 6 Eliz II) c 34.
National Insurance Act 1911 (1 & 2 Geo V) c 55.
National Insurance Act 1946 (9 & 10 Geo VI) c 67.
National Insurance Act 1965 (UK) c 51.
National Loans Act 1939 (2&3 Geo VI) c 117.
National Loans Act 1941 (4 & 5 Geo VI) c 18.
National Loans Act 1968 (UK) c 13.
National Savings Bank Act 1971 (UK) c 29.
National Welfare Fund Act 1943 (Cth)
National Welfare Fund Repeal Act 1985 (Cth).
New South Wales Act 1823 (4 Geo IV) c 96.
New South Wales Constitution Act 1842 (5 & 6 Vict) c 76.
New South Wales Constitution Act 1855 (18 & 19 Vict) c 54.
New Zealand Constitution Act 1852 (15 & 16 Vict) c 72).
New Zealand Loans Act 1904 (NZ).
New Zealand Loans Act 1953 (NZ).
Old-Age Pensions Appropriation Act 1908 (Cth).
Parliament Acts 1911 and 1949 (1 & 2 Geo V) c 13 and (12, 13 & 14 Geo VI) c 103.
Pensions Act 2014 (UK) c 19.
Petitions of Right Act 1860 (23 & 24 Vict) c 34.
Pharmaceutical Benefits Act 1944 (Cth).
Private Health Insurance Act 2007 (Cth).
Provisional Collection of Taxes Act 1968 (UK) c 2.
Public Finance Act 1977 (NZ).
Public Finance Act 1989 (NZ).
Public Governance, Performance and Accountability Act 2013 (Cth).
Public Revenues and Consolidated Fund Act 1854 (17 & 18 Vict) c 94.
Public Works Loan Act 1884 (NSW).
Reserve Bank Act 1959 (Cth).
Reserve Bank of Canada Act 1985 (Can).
Reserve Bank of New Zealand Act 1933 (NZ).
Social Security (Administration) Act 1999 (Cth).
Social Security Act 1938 (NZ).
Social Security Act 1964 (NZ).
Social Security Act 1991(Cth).
Social Security Administration Act 1992 (UK) c 5.
Social Security Contributions and Benefits Act 1992 (UK) c 4.
Social Services Consolidation Act 1947 (Cth).
Superannuation Act 1990 (Cth).
Supply Act 1873 (36 & 37 Vict) c 26.
Supply Act 1873 (36 & 37 Vict) c 3.
Surplus Revenue Act 1908 (Cth).

Tax and Superannuation Laws Amendment (2014 Measures Act No. 5) 2015 (Cth).
Tax Bonus for Working Australians Act (No. 2) 2009 (Cth).
Taxation Administration Act 1953 (Cth).
Taxation of Chargeable Gains Act 1992 (UK) c 12.
Tobacco Products Duty Act 1979 (UK) c 7.
Treasury Bills Act 1877 (40 & 41 Vict) c 2.
Treasury Bills Act 1914 (Cth).
Treaty on the Functioning of the European Union C-326 (26/10/2012).
Value Added Tax Act 1994 (UK) c 23.
War Loan Act 1914 (4&5 Geo 5) c 60.
War Loan Act 1914 (Cth).
War Loan Act 1914 (Cth).
War Loan Act 1915 (5 & 6 Geo V) c 55.
War Purposes Loan Act 1917 (NZ).

Government Publications

Auditor-General, of Australia *Financial Statement Audits* (2005–2017).
Australian Bureau of Statistics, *Australian System of Government Finance Statistics: Concepts, Sources and Methods* (2005).
Australian Office of Financial Management, *Annual Reports and Accounts* (2005–2016).
Australian Office of Financial Management, *Information Memorandum Treasury Bonds* (2014).
Australian Taxation Office, *Addressing the Gap* (2017).
Australian Taxation Office, *Annual Reports and Accounts* (2005–2017).
Bank of England and Debt Management Office, *Statement on Gilt Lending* (6 August 2009).
Bank of England Asset Purchase Facility Fund Limited, *Annual Reports and Accounts* (2010–2017).
Bank of England Asset Purchase Facility Fund Limited, *Certificate of Association* (30 January 09).
Bank of England Asset Purchase Facility Fund Limited, *Memorandum of Association* (30 January 09).
Bank of England Asset Purchase Facility Fund Limited, *Memorandum of Association* (10 February 2009).
Bank of England, *Annual Reports and Accounts* (2005–2016).
Bank of England, *The Bank's Forecasting Platform* (Working Paper No. 47, 2013).
Beveridge, William 'Social Insurance and Allied Services' (1942).
Commissioner of Audit, *13th Report of the Commissioners appointed to Examine, Take, and State the Public Accounts of the Kingdom* (1875).

Commons Journal (1705, 1706, 1728, 1870).
Commons Library, 'National Insurance Contributions (NICs)' (2017, Briefing Paper 4517).
Commonwealth of Australia, *Budget Papers* (2005–2017).
Debt Management Office and Debt Management Account, *Reports and Accounts 2005*–2015.
Department for Culture, Media and Sport, *National Lottery Distribution Fund Accounts 2005*–2015.
Department of Finance, *Commonwealth Entities Financial Statements Guide* (2012–2018).
Department of Finance, *Consolidated Financial Statements* (2005–2015).
Department of Finance, *Is Less More? Towards Better Commonwealth Performance* (2012).
Department of Health, *Annual Reports and Accounts* (2005–2015).
Durham, Lord, *Report on the Affairs of British North America* (1839).
Federal-Provincial-Territorial Directors of Income Support: *Social Assistance Statistical Report* (2016).
HC Deb, 7 August 1833.
HC Deb 11 August 1848.
HC Deb 08 June 1875.
HC Deb, 07 April 1913.
HC Deb 14 March 1934.
HC Deb 24 March 1958.
HC Deb 11 December 1967.
HC Deb 12 July 1982.
HC Deb 12 July 1982.
HC Deb 25 October 1999.
HC Deb, 22 November 2017.
HC Deb, 28 November 2017.
HM Treasury, *Alignment ('Clear Line of Sight') Project* (November 2008).
HM Treasury, *Alignment (Clear Line of Sight) Project* (March, 2009).
HM Treasury, *Annual Reports and Accounts* (2005–2015).
HM Treasury, *Annual Report and Accounts (2008–2009)*.
HM Treasury, *Changes to Cash Management Operations* (Press Release, 9 November 2012).
HM Treasury, *Consolidated Fund Account and National Loans Fund Account* 2005.
HM Treasury, *Consolidated Fund Accounts* (2006–2016).
HM Treasury, *Contingencies Fund Accounts* (2005–2016).
HM Treasury, *Contingencies Fund Accounts* (2005–2016).
HM Treasury, *Dear Accounting Officer Letters (2005–2016)*.
HM Treasury, *Exchange Equalization Fund Accounts* (2005–2015).
HM Treasury, *Government Finance Reporting Manual* (2004–2016).

HM Treasury, *Financial Reporting Manual (2017/18)*.
HM Treasury, *Main Supply Estimates* (2005–2016).
HM Treasury, *National Loans Fund Accounts* (2005–2016).
HM Treasury, *Offering Circular* (2014).
HM Treasury, *Public Expenditure Statistical Analysis* (2010–2017).
HM Treasury, *Statements of Excesses* (2005–2015).
HM Treasury, *Supplementary Estimates* (2005–2016).
HM Treasury, *The Future of UK Government Debt and Cash Management (1997)*.
HM Treasury, *Votes on Account* (2005–2016).
HMEC, *Annual Reports and Accounts* (2005–2015).
HMRC, *Annual Reports and Accounts* (2006–2015).
HMRC, *National Insurance Fund Accounts (Great Britain)* (2005–2016).
HMRC, *National Insurance Fund Accounts (Northern Ireland)* (2005–2016)
House of Commons Paper No. 56/2015–16.
House of Commons, 'Financial Scrutiny: Parliamentary Control over Government Budgets' (2009, HC804).
House of Lords: Select Committee on the Constitution, *The Pre-emption of Parliament* (2013).
Joint Committee of Public Accounts, *Advance to the Minister for Finance* (Report No. 289, 1988).
Malaya Constitutional Commission, *Report of the Federation of Malaya Constitutional Commission* (1957).
Ministry of Defence, *Excess votes 2007–08 – 2012–13* (2014, Hc 1075).
National Audit Office, *Evaluating the Government's Balance Sheet* (2017, HC526).
National Audit Office, *The Asset Protection Scheme* (2010).
National Audit Office, *Understanding Central Governments Accounts* (2014).
New Zealand Treasury, *A Guide to the Public Finance Act* (2005).
OECD, *Real GDP Forecast Indicator* (2017).
Office of Budget Responsibility, *The Macroeconomic Model* (Briefing Paper No. 5, 2013).
Osborne, George to King, Mervyn, 'Transfer of Excess Cash from the Asset Purchase Facility to HM Treasury' (9 November 2012).
Parliament of Commonwealth of Australia, *Bills Digest No. 129* (2007–2008).
Report of the Commissioners appointed to Examine, Take, and State the Public Accounts of the Kingdom (1785).
Reserve Bank of Australia, *Annual Reports* (2005–2016).
Second Reading Speech, *Commonwealth Securities and Investment Legislation Amendment Bill 2008* (4 June 2008).
Secretary of State for Justice and Lord Chancellor, *Green Paper: 'The Governance of Britain'* (2007, Cm7170).
Treasury Board of Canada, *Guide on Grants, Contributions and Other Transfer Payments* (2002).

Treasury Select Committee, *Government's Cash and Debt Management* (22 May 2000).

United States Government Accountability Office, Office of the General Counsel, *Principles of Federal Appropriations Law* (2014) (3rd ed., USGAO).

USGAO, *Opinion on Commodity Futures Trading Commission–Liabilities Outside of the Government's Control* (B-328450, 2018).

Votes and Proceedings of the Legislative Council of New South Wales (1851 and 1852).

Official Statistics

Australian Bureau of Statistics, *Australian System of National Accounts: Time Series Workbook 55120DO002)* (27 October 2017).

Australian Bureau of Statistics, *DO001_2016–17 Employment and Earnings, Public Sector, Australia, 2016–17* (9 November 2017).

Australian Bureau of Statistics, *Government Finance Statistics DO002_201617* (26 April 2018).

Australian Bureau of Statistics, *Labour Force, Australia* (2018).

Bank of England, *B72A Ways and Means Advance: Weekly and Quarterly Outstanding figures: 2006–2017* (6 December 2017).

Bank of England, *BEAPFF Gilt Purchase Operational Results* (9 January 2018).

Debt Management Office, *Gilt Market: Gross and Net Issuance History* (27 September 2017).

Debt Management Office, *Money Markets: Issuance of Treasury Bills and Treasury Bill Stock* (6 Jan 2018).

HM Treasury, *Public Expenditure Statistical Analysis, Tables 1–10* (2010–2017).

HM Treasury, *Public Expenditure Statistical Analyses: Tables and Datasets* (2013–2017).

Office of National Statistics, *Public and Private Sector Employment; Headcount* (1 May 2018).

Office of National Statistics, *Public Sector Finances* (20 October 2017).

Office of National Statistics, *United Kingdom National Accounts* (31 October 2017).

Treasury Board, *Tabled Expenditure Authorities* (2018).

Statistics Canada, *Table 385–0033: Canadian Government Finance Statistics (CGFS), Statement of Operations and Balance Sheet for the Federal Government* (21 November 2017).

Statistics Canada, *Table 385–0042: Canadian Government Finance Statistics (CGFS), Statement of Operations and Balance Sheet for the* Consolidated Governments (21 November 2017).

StatsNZ, *Government Finance Statistics (General Government): Year ended June 2016* (16 December 2016).

StatsNZ, *Local Authority Statistics: June 2017 Quarter* (6 September 2017).

Freedom of Information Requests

HM Treasury, Response to FOI Request (FOI2017/20111, 11/12/17).

INDEX

appropriation legislation
  annual and standing, 136
  historical balance, 61
  modern balance 91,
  contemporary judicial review, 180
  historical judicial review, 67
  history, 31
  justiciability, 177
  parliamentary processes, 29
  relationship to estimates, 32
  retrospective, history, 36
  standing, appropriations
  modern use, 131
  history, 38
  Supply Acts distinguished from, 31
Auckland Harbour Board
  v. *The King*, 72
audit
  Comptroller and Auditor-General,
    history, 58
  historical development, 56
  reliance on treasury, 57, 147
Australia
  colonial history, 84
  Commonwealth of Australia
    Constitution Act, 87
  modern public finance law
    appropriation legislation, 130
    audit, 148
    financial crisis, 125, 152, 162
    monetary finance, 164
    sovereign borrowing, 159
    taxation, 133

Bagehot
  executive financial control, 218
Bank of England
  during financial crisis, 156
  history, 46
  history of judicial review, 76
  quantitative easing, 156, 166
  sovereign debt manager, 46,
    74, 113
  Ways and Means Advance, see,
    monetary finance
Bankers' Case, 74
Bowles v. *Bank of England*, 66
British Empire
  history of public finance and, 81

Canada
  British North America Act, 87
  colonial history, 83
  modern public finance law, 215
central banks
  financial crisis, 156, 166
  historical development, 111
  independence, 113
  monetary finance, 12, 115, 155, 164
  monetary policy, 12, 113
  sovereign debt management, 113
Commonwealth of Nations
  history, 89
consolidated fund
  history, 49
  colonies, 84
  Commonwealth constitutions, 90
  dominions, 87
  relationship to National Loans Fund

Dicey
  judiciary and public expenditure,
    4, 71
  parliamentary control, 3
  welfare state, hostility towards, 229

economic conditions
  impact on debt finance, 162

262   INDEX

economic conditions (cont.)
　　impact on fiscal authority, 136
　　impact on monetary finance, 156, 166
excess expenditure
　　administrative errors, 142
　　deliberate, 144
　　demand-driven, 141
　　history, 36, 60
　　impact on parliamentary
　　　　control, 145

financial crisis
　　excess expenditure, 144
　　impact on Australia and UK, 125
　　impact on Australian sovereign
　　　　borrowing, 162
　　impact on standing
　　　　appropriations, 136
　　monetary finance, 156
financial initiative
　　contemporary use, 145
　　export throughout British Empire,
　　　　84, 85, 87, 90
　　history, 51
　　impact on parliamentary
　　　　control, 211
fiscal responsibility laws, 78, 118

Gladstone, 57

India, 91

judiciary
　　historical tax jurisdiction, 63
　　impact on tax agencies, 189
　　impact on parliamentary
　　　　control, 209
　　in Commonwealth of Nations, 93
　　justiciability, 117, 172
　　polycentricity, 174
　　review of public expenditure, 179
　　tax evasion, 64, 108, 192

MacNiven v. Westmoreland
　　Investments Ltd, 192
Malaysia, 92
monetary finance
　　central bank dividends, 165

central bank overdrafts, 165
contemporary use, 155
direct cash transfers, 166
impact on parliamentary control, 207
financial function, 12
justiciability, 178
legislative history, 115
quantitative easing, 156, 166
use in post-War UK, 99
Ways and Means Advance, 99, 115,
　　156, 166

Nepal, 91
New Public Management
　　impact on public finance, 116
New Zealand
　　colonial history, 86
　　modern public finance law, 215
　　Nigeria, 93

sovereign borrowing
　　modern use, 152
　　history, 43
　　impact on parliamentary
　　　　control, 164
　　impact of World Wars, 101
　　justiciability, 178
　　legal structure, 157

taxation
　　annual and standing, modern, 133
　　annual and standing, history, 39
　　evasion, judiciary and, 64, 108, 192
　　general anti-avoidance rule, 110
　　hypothecated, 49
　　parliamentary processes, 29
Treasury
　　development of treasury control, 54
　　historical judicial review, 67
　　history, 51
　　history as audit institution, 57
　　relationship with Auditor-General, 59
　　sovereign borrowing, history, 45

United States
　　comparison with parliamentary
　　　　government, 16
　　historical divergence from Britain, 82

virement
  history, 34
  during financial crisis, 145

welfare state
  authorising expenditure, 105
  impact on public finance, 98

parliamentary control, 228
Williams v. *Commonwealth*, 185
World Wars
  impact on public finance, 96
WT Ramsay Ltd v. *Inland Revenue Commissioners*, 108

Lightning Source UK Ltd.
Milton Keynes UK
UKHW022045160822
407413UK00008B/89